Institutionalization of UX

Second Edition

Institutionalization of UX

A Step-by-Step Guide to a User Experience Practice

Second Edition

Eric Schaffer
Apala Lahiri

♠♠ Addison-Wesley

Upper Saddle River, NJ • Boston • Indianapolis • San Francisco
New York • Toronto • Montreal • London • Munich • Paris • Madrid
Capetown • Sydney • Tokyo • Singapore • Mexico City

Library of Congress Cataloging-in-Publication Data

Schaffer, Eric.

[Institutionalization of usability.]

Institutionalization of UX : a step-by-step guide to a user experience practice / Eric Schaffer, Apala Lahiri. -- Second edition.

  pages cm

Includes bibliographical references and index.

ISBN 978-0-321-88481-7 (pbk. : alk. paper)

1. User interfaces (Computer systems) 2. Computer software--Development. I. Lahiri, Apala. II. Title.

QA76.9.U83S36 2013

005.4'37--dc23   2013039144

Text printed in the United States on recycled paper at RR Donnelley in Crawfordsville, Indiana.
First printing, December 2013

Contents

Preface

More than ten years ago, I wrote *The Institutionalization of Usability*. Now, so much has changed in the field that a very new edition is needed. For one thing, the name of the field has changed. We now call ourselves "user experience (UX) designers." With that change in title comes new responsibilities. We no longer can focus on simple tasks and human–computer interaction. Systems are embedded everywhere, and we must design for complex *ecosystems*. That means using ethnographically inspired methods and advanced tools for knowledge management. It is no longer enough to make a site or application easy to use. Usability is now a hygiene factor—to be competitive, most organizations must understand how to engineer persuasion into their digital systems. In turn, we need a whole new set of methods and insights that let us systematically design for engagement, psychological influence, and customer commitment.

The field has also reached up the value chain within organizations. A UX team that deals with only the details of radio buttons and check boxes is committing a disservice to its organization. Today UX groups must deal with strategy. We must help define how executive intent can be turned into successful designs and the desired business results. So the executive wants to transition customers into low-cost, digital channels—why will the customer want to make that transition? The UX team must design the cross-channel integration and optimization so that customers will understand which channel to use and will experience a common but appropriate interaction on the Web, mobile device, tablet, or other device.

Finally, the UX team is a key component of the organization's innovation process.

When I wrote *Institutionalization of Usability*, the idea of a mature, industrial-strength practice seemed remote to most people. I debated this topic with the great usability pioneer Jared Spool in a session that was billed as "The Celebrity Death Match." His argument was that usability could be practiced only as craftsmanship—that it could not be institutionalized. Yet I was already institutionalizing it within my own company, Human Factors International, Inc. (HFI), and starting to help my corporate clients build their own practice. Today, most organizations of any size and sophistication are building UX teams, and there is widespread recognition that customer-centered design is the best practice for system development. In the process of helping to mature our clients' UX teams, we have learned quite a lot.

The challenges of institutionalization have clearly changed. In the past, the major issue was securing executive championship. Today, however, most high-level executives understand that customer experience is a key business goal. They have read about the user experience economy, seen Apple Computer thrive, and read innumerable executive briefings on customer experience. Unfortunately, these executives often have no idea how to bring about UX, and they take a fairly predictable set of wrong paths to try to make it happen. In addition, there are still challenges in culture change and governance—cultural and organizational design issues are pivotal today. Staffing also poses serious challenges. It is common for organizations to get perhaps 2% of the UX staff they need and then drop the initiative when they find that their designs have not substantially improved, and their UX team seems demoralized. Yet the pool of qualified UX specialists remains small. HFI is by now quite experienced in hiring practices, internal training, and the use of offshore resources.

Setting up a UX infrastructure today is relatively easy. Training and certification are available. Methods and standards simply need to be customized to fit an organization's needs, and plenty of new UX tools can be readily accessed. These foundational components should no longer be an impediment to creating a UX capability.

The best practice of UX work has been a bit of a surprise. My initial thought was that institutionalized UX work would be like what it was in the 1990s, except that there would be more of it. I thought implementing UX would involve more craftspeople and apprentices. They would have methods and standards, of course, but, I thought, the experience would essentially be more of the same. Instead, it turns out that pivoting to a serious UX practice entails fundamental changes in the way the work gets done. We have even seen the dawn of object-oriented UX work, which optimizes reuse.

Finally, in this book I would like to introduce Apala Lahiri, CEO of HFI's Global Customer Experience Institute and an expert in cross-cultural design. The Institute has one objective: to answer the question, "How does one best operate a UX practice that must design for users worldwide?" Do we need to have a UX team in each of our 115 target countries? Clearly not. Yet Apala's motto is "think globally and lose locally." A design created for "the world" will rarely compete with a design created with sharp focus on a given culture and context. Based on my experiences, and with Apala's contributions, we will share the current best practices for a global UX operation in this edition.

—Eric Schaffer

Acknowledgments

This book was drafted from my personal experience with thousands of individuals who, over the last thirty-five years, have struggled to instill usability engineering capabilities within their companies. While I cannot possibly name them all, I am sure they will see themselves within these pages, sharing their insights and knowledge through my eyes. This book is theirs more than mine.

I would like to thank Dr. Robert Bailey, Dr. Darryl Yoblick, and Gary Griggs, who were my mentors when I first joined the field. Without them, I don't know if I ever would have figured out how to do this work right. I would also like to thank the pioneers of institutionalization who created effective usability departments. Among these, special thanks go to Dr. Arnie Lund, Dr. Ed Israelski, and Dr. Tom Tullis, from whom I learned much.

I would like to thank the staff at Human Factors International, Inc. (HFI). Our president, Jay More, has been at my side for nearly twenty-five years, helping me to see usability from a business perspective. I am indebted to Dr. Phil Goddard, Dr. Susan Weinschenk, and Dr. Kath Straub for their technical contributions and review of this book. Indeed, my entire staff at HFI has contributed in many ways to this book, developing methods, sharing ideas, and working directly on the book itself.

I would like to thank the pioneering clients I have been able to work with in applying institutionalization strategies. In particular, thanks go to Abdul Notcha, Amanda Seboli, Reynard Uys, and the other leaders at Standard Bank who have been so supportive of advanced work toward industrial-strength customer-centricity. And a note of thanks to my editor at Addison-Wesley, Peter Gordon, who has supported both editions and provided invaluable counsel and support. Thanks go also to Douglas Gorney, who helped refine the manuscript, making your reading experience far better.

xviii   A<small>CKNOWLEDGMENTS</small>

Finally, I would like to thank Apala Lahiri, who has been a great innovator in the transition of the field to process-oriented work, not to mention her contribution to the internal design strategies that she shares in this book.

—Eric Schaffer

Read This First!

Cultural Transformation

➤ This is a journey to create a user-centered organization.

➤ Change your organization's focus from building lots of functions to meeting user needs.

➤ Change your organization's focus from developing cool and impressive technology to creating software that is simple, practical, and useful.

➤ Help executives and project managers focus on the value of user experience design.

➤ Customize and follow a systematic and complete process for institutionalizing user experience design.

You are embarking on a program to institutionalize user experience design in your organization. What is the long-term view? You may find that your company already has some of the organization or groundwork in place, and you may be well on your way to establishing a user-centered process. This book can help you get all the way there—that is, to a full, mature practice. If you are starting from scratch, you can expect it to take about two years before the full implementation is in place and user experience design has become routine. Significant benefits and progress will occur before then, however, and you'll recognize and appreciate gains as you work toward full implementation.

Of course, some setbacks may occur along the way. These almost always come in the areas of mindset, relationships, and communication. Remember that we are changing the way people think about design. We may move control of the design process to a new set of user-centered staff, and those changes can be contentious. Even so, these setbacks will illuminate the deep issues that you must work on continuously. These issues are explored in the first chapter of this book and are **not** fully covered in the following chapters, which explore infrastructure components, staffing requirements, and other activities. We will talk about cultural change here because it transcends the surface level and permeates the whole initiative. Addressing these issues involves shifting the core belief system of your organization, and that is why they are so important to consider early in the process.

For decades, a major thrust of the user experience field was to train developers to create better interfaces. Today, however, there is a clear global understanding that user experience design is best done by specialists in the field. The user experience design field is quite complex, skill intensive, and always growing. For these reasons, it generally does not make sense to have these responsibilities be the part-time job of a developer or business analyst. In addition, the characteristics of a good user experience designer are generally very different from those of a developer. It is a bit like asking the engineer who specializes in the tensile strength of steel to design the architecture of a building, decorate the entrance, and arrange the flowers on the side table. In our case, the business analysts and technical staff need to accept the user experience design staff and work with them effectively.

Unless the internal environment is changed through training and repeated showcase projects, there is a large natural disconnect between the viewpoint of the user experience design staff and that of the technical development team. It's not unusual to experience some conflict and misunderstanding. If developers or business analysts have been doing the interface design, they will be attached to their designs, so criticism will likely create hard feelings. People also tend to be attached to their design decisions (like the use of tree-view menus as a solution to all navigation). People see the world in terms of their own context, and it can be difficult to get them to see the user's viewpoint. What is even harder is taking control of the user experience design from staff who have previously had control over these decisions (even if their skills, processes, and tools did not allow for a successful outcome). Certainly, it is possible to train, and have some user experience design tasks be done by technical staff or business analysts. Nevertheless, the control of the user experience design effort must always be placed within a central user experience design group.

Once you realize the value of user experience design engineering, it is difficult to be patient with those who haven't made this leap in understanding. But ignoring the hard work of shifting others' perspectives makes it likely that all your accomplishments will do little. Good standards and facilities will sit idle if these deeper shifts fail to happen. The following section explores the deep changes that the real institutionalization of user experience design requires.

Changing the Feature Mindset

A deep philosophical change must take place in the shift to user-centered development. Most companies build applications intent on meeting a given time frame and providing a specific level of functionality. There is a whole flow of feature ideas, but this flow is not really user centered; rather, it is usually a combination of executive inspiration and customer comments. So how can a selection of features based partly on customer comments and requests not be considered user centered? Certainly, customer comments need to be considered (mostly as a way to discover bugs). But listening to customer comments merely gives the illusion of listening to the user. In many situations, these "customer" requests come from executives, marketing departments, or sales staff. They are not in any way representative. The real user is not studied or fully understood by most of these well-meaning "user representatives." In other situations, comments do flow from actual users. The users may share ideas, but typically only very happy or very angry customers send feedback. Also, these comments tend to focus on features, rather than the overall design, error handling, page layout, or other user experience design issues. The result is the design of features that may not represent the needs of the majority of end users and may not address the application as a whole.

It isn't enough to just apply standard user experience design techniques such as user experience design testing, because just applying techniques does not address the underlying issue. There is still a need to change the focus away from functionality. Software developers often build applications that have unneeded functions. They focus on completing a checklist of features for each product. Unfortunately, a clutter of irrelevant features makes the product harder to use. The whole focus of the development team is on creating all these functions on time, but if those functions are not needed or cannot be used, is timeliness so important?

It will take some work to get your organization to understand that the function race was one of the roads to success in the 1990s, but is no longer critical. Certainly, users want features. Some users focus on obtaining the maximum set of features and actually thrive on the challenge of learning their operation, but they typically comprise a small group of early adopters. In this new millennium, software and website developers must deliver adequate features that are simple and useful. Most users want information appliances to be as easy to operate as a toaster—practical, useful, usable, and satisfying solutions. Achieving this feat requires a broader change to the mindset of design and development.

Changing the Technology Mindset

Most people who work in information technology (IT) love the technology. They are in the field because technology is fun, challenging, and impressive. The developer's job is to understand the technology and use it. Therefore, developers naturally focus on learning about the technology, and they feel excited about using the latest, most powerful facility. To a degree, this bias creates development groups that are more focused on creating something impressive and cool instead of practical and useful.

Knowledge of the scientific principles, together with working with user experience design engineers, helps create a major shift in the way that IT professionals see technology. Technology is a tool that lets you meet user needs. Much like a professional carpenter who picks the tool that best meets the need and does not anxiously seek an excuse to use the latest hammer, developers need to focus on creating the design that customers need, rather than just exercising the software technology that will make them feel proud.

The people who have to use the things we design may not be using a product because it is new and fun. Although there are always early adopters, most technology users want to use your design to get something done—get information from a website, pay their bills online, or look up directions, for example. Most users are not looking for technology that is challenging and interesting; instead, they want the **result** to be useful and interesting. In fact, many users expect the technology to be not challenging but actually transparent. Professional developers are often intrigued by the technology and its quirks. Users often find the same quirks annoying.

Changing the Process Mindset

In organizations that are dominated by business analysts, the focus can be on defining and optimizing efficient processes. This approach might sound like it would be a good one from a user experience design viewpoint. In fact, there is a very big difference between efficient processes and customer-centered design. You might create a generic account origination process that covers all the functions necessary in a very efficient way. There might even be efficiencies put into place, such as the concatenation of multiple account origination requirements so that the user will never have to enter the same data twice. But would this be optimized from the user experience design viewpoint? It might not. The user might need to think about each account separately. It might make more sense to customers to configure each account as a unit, because they think about each account separately. In contrast, a logical functional model might have the beneficiaries set up all at once and then the alerts established all at once. The functional analysis would also probably include the customer's data (e.g., name, addresses) first in the flow, as this is more logical. But user experience design experts know better than to implement this model: You want to first configure the accounts so that the customers feel ownership and have an investment in their acquisitions. Only then should the application ask for the boring registration details. In this way, customers become invested in the accounts and are unlikely to abandon the application.

Business analysts with a functional viewpoint can be wonderful supporters of a user experience design effort. With training, they can really contribute to the design workload. Nevertheless, an organization that is focused on process efficiency needs to be brought around to see that success requires much more than a functional viewpoint.

Changing the Graphics Mindset

Good-quality visual design is often an important part of a successful user-centered design. It generally increases trust. Moreover, visual designs that are developed around focused persuasion engineering strategies are very powerful. But visual design is only a small part of what it takes to be successful in user experience design. In fact, interesting counter-examples can be cited. A target population such as "youth," for example, would seem like a natural fit for exciting graphic treatments. Yet Facebook is wildly successful with youth, even though its graphics are limited and unimpressive. Why? Because Facebook fulfills a set of fundamental needs for youth.

Some organizations equate user experience design with rich and polished graphics. When this is done without exploring the underlying strategic and structural design, it is like putting lipstick on a bulldog. The results are not pretty. Executives are often focused on the appearance of the design, but this is a common mistake.

Some executives seem really wedded to the graphic issue. In a way, this emphasis might simply reflect the fun of doing uncontrolled graphic work, much in the same way that people love to select colors for their house or clothing. In classic visual design work, the graphics team often focuses on creating a design that pleases the executive. Their criterion for success is that the executive likes it. In such a case, the graphics team creates one good design and two bad designs, and then they hope the executive picks the good design from the lineup. There is no real measurement of success, so the process of graphics development can be free, easy, and entertaining. In contrast, in serious graphic development, the design needs to be informed and validated. The criteria for success, in turn, are based on observed user behavior.

Graphic designers can be trained and can learn to do the more analytic and interpersonal work of the user experience design practitioner. Even the most sophisticated creative directors, however, do not have training in the user experience design field.

Executives

Today, it is hard to find an executive who does not care about customer experience. As executives around the world play the chess game of business strategy, most of them are having the same realization: Every organization can get hardware that works (usually better than really matters), and every organization can get software to run and not crash and hold tons of data. Thus, there is now one primary differentiator among companies in the digital space: customer experience. Today, the organization with the best customer experience wins.

Top executives are usually determined to optimize their organization's customer experience, but they usually try things that don't work well. They give passionate speeches that address caring about customers, with sweet stories describing how their kids were treated in Disneyland. In reality, the problem with digital customer experiences is not a problem with staff motivation. Being motivated does not make for good designs. Being motivated without the training, and certification, and methods, and standards, and tools of the user experience design field just makes for dispirited staff—and shouting at them until they panic just makes things worse.

Some executives get frustrated, rip off their ties, roll up their sleeves, and start designing interfaces themselves. Of course, most executives have no human–computer interface design skills. What they create makes sense to them (because they know what it's supposed to do), but it rarely makes sense to the users.

Some executives think that "customer-led design" means design work that is "led by customers." As a result, they arrange for real customers to be a part of the design process. Unfortunately, users are not designers, so they don't know what the designs should be. Also, the users allocated to the design committee are really never representative (you tend to get either users who are experts in the software or users who are below average and therefore expendable). In addition, the users quickly become less representative as they learn the organization's viewpoint and language, so they quickly stop being even a good source of insight into "how things are" (subject-matter expertise).

Exhausted by the effort, senior executives finally turn to other key areas such as security and advertising. They decide that user experience design is a mystical thing and hope that a miracle occurs. With luck, the scattered user experience design people in the organization will climb up the organizational structure and share a clear understanding of what it takes to make an industrial-strength practice in user experience design. Otherwise, the whole initiative dissipates—perhaps to be reinvigorated later by a startling loss in market share, wasted design efforts, or a change in leadership.

When presented with an understanding of the requirements for the development of a mature practice, many top executives become very excited and want to get started right away. It is a challenge to persuade them to carefully plan the overall institutionalization process.

In many cases, they may demand to start something tangible, at which point they typically kick off a user interface standards program. Even worse, they may insist on persona definitions (at the end of which, no one will be sure why you spent so much money). This "Ready, fire, aim!" approach results in an inefficient, uncoordinated, and unreliable path to a mature practice—so please insist on a strategy before serious investments start.

Changing Middle Management Values

While the development community makes the move away from fixation on features and new technologies, middle management must also change. Management is used to asking whether milestones are met and budgets are under control and establishing compensation schemes that reinforce the need to produce functions on schedule. This approach has worked well in the past, but it won't work well in the future. Things that were thought of as secondary intangibles and "nice-to-haves" must be quantified and managed, because those "soft" design capabilities are now the key to the organization's future.

Management must understand that the company is building not just systems that will function, but also systems that will work in the context of a given range of users, doing a given set of tasks, in a given environment. Success is measured as the real business value of the application. Achieving success takes much more than just delivering the website or application on time. The deliverable must be usable and satisfying to operate. In many cases, the emotional engagement and resulting conversion of customers is the real target. And it is not enough to simply make designs that are easy to operate. The target outcome of the design will depend on the organization and may include increased sales or enrollment, more leads, increased willingness to pay fees, larger sets of items per purchase, and so on. These are the results that user experience design buys you. Few organizations will not directly benefit from good user experience engineering.

Once organizations realize that user experience design is a key area in ensuring their success, they sometimes will charge executives with making improvements, which is great. Unfortunately, they often compensate those executives based on moving the results on a customer satisfaction survey up a fraction of a point. This is not quite right, as customer satisfaction ratings don't really equate to user experience design quality. Instead, they are more like a rough indication of whether the customer's expectations are met. You can probably lower a customer's expectations and get a nice jump in satisfaction.

Advice for Those Considering an Investment in User Experience Design

Harley Manning, Research Director, Forrester Research

The single biggest gap in knowledge we see at Forrester is a lack of understanding of *what* and *why*. *What* makes for a great user experience, and *why* you should care—tied to numbers. That's the great barrier. People must understand that there are objective methods of improving user experience and that user experience moves business metrics.

The second biggest gap is a lack of the right skills. We see a hierarchy of skills, process, and organization, where skills are the most important. Whether you try to do this kind of development internally (which is a trend we see) or hire out, you still need somebody on the inside with a deep clue. Otherwise, you're not going to follow the right processes, even if you have them in place, and you're not going to hire the right vendors or manage them effectively.

Regarding processes, there are many good processes out there—just pick one and use it consistently. I was talking with the Web development team at Michelin Tire, and I said, "You guys don't wake up in the morning and say, how should we manufacture tires today, do you?" And they said, "Of course not, but we never thought of a website that way." They're smart—as soon as I said this, they got it.

Business schools have always taught about marketing issues and brand management, but now they must go further. Marketing can point out a potential market niche; user experience engineering can help build a product that will reliably succeed in that niche. The implications of poor user experience design can be catastrophic for a company. It therefore makes sense that executives and senior management attend to this critical success factor. Project and business line managers are interested in identifiable metrics. As user experience design matures within an organization, it is not enough to occasionally review the latest "customer satisfaction rating" or "net promoter score." Depending on the type of website or application, managers must be concerned about task speed, task failure rates, drop-off rates, competitive metrics, return on investment (ROI), retention rates, and other factors. Executives must be aware of and support a user-centered process. Perhaps most importantly, middle managers must care about user experience and performance levels as an essential success factor.

Changing the Process for Interface Design

Many companies expect developers to sit down and just draft the interface design without doing expert reviews, data gathering, or any testing. If your organization currently uses this approach, you must be willing to learn and use a different approach. User interface design must be an iterative process. You sketch and prototype an interface, then change it, then get feedback from users, then change it, again and again. There are two reasons why effective interface design must be iterative:

1. Design is a process of deciding among many sets of alternatives. Getting them all correct the first time is impossible.
2. As users see what an interface is actually like, they change their conceptions and expectations—so the requirements change.

User interface design, by its very nature, is too complex for anyone to accomplish successfully without feedback. Even user experience

User Experience Design within Government

Janice Nall, Managing Director, Atlanta, Danya International, Inc.
Former Chief, Communication Technologies Branch,
National Cancer Institute

There are probably three or four core things we have done to institutionalize user experience design. Number one is involving the leadership—through presentations and participating in testing or showing them results of a usable site versus an unusable site.

Number two is using the language from leaders driving the new trend to e-government. Because the National Cancer Institute is part of the government, it helps to be able to tell our leadership that user experience design and user-centered design are supported, from the president of the United States to the Office of Management and Budget to the Department of Health and Human Services (HHS). Using their own words, language, and documents has been very powerful.

Number three is training, which has been hugely successful—a way to institutionalize user experience design across HHS and the federal government. We believe in teaching people to fish rather than feeding them the fish. We also use tools and resources, like the Research-Based Web Design and User Experience Design Guidelines, to teach them.

Number four is our list of about 500 federal people who receive our online publication *U-Group* (shorthand for *user experience design group*) via the U-group listserv. Through this listserv, we are trying to get current information out, and we're saying, "Let's share information; let's collaborate"—encouraging people to share lessons learned.

design professionals with decades of experience don't expect to sit down to design a screen and get it right the first time.

Everyone developing software and websites needs to remember that both development and design are iterative processes. Being brilliant does help, but the willingness to get feedback and apply it selectively is more important. Designers must be willing to learn and create better designs each time, and organizations need to have a culture that supports such iterations without blame.

The Step-by-Step Process for Institutionalizing User Experience Design

The final deep challenge is the tendency to address user experience design in a piecemeal fashion. Many companies that see the value of user experience design still attempt to address it with a series of uncoordinated projects. Instead, there must be a managed user experience design effort. This section outlines the process covered in this book. It is gleaned from experiences of working with hundreds of companies across thirty years within the field of user experience design at Human Factors International, Inc. (HFI).

Figure 0-1 illustrates the typical flow of activities for institutionalizing user experience design in an organization. You need to make sure these activities fit with your corporate culture and circumstances. In fact, you cannot hope to be successful if you treat this process as you would treat steps within a simple kit. To succeed, you must proceed consciously and creatively. Since 1981, HFI has worked with many companies and organizations that have not institutionalized user experience design yet and many others that have made this transition. Based on thousands of projects and experiences with hundreds of clients, HFI has distilled, tested, and refined the key elements that lead to success. Hundreds of companies, large and small, have followed this process and experienced more efficient user experience design methods and processes, as well as more effective products and applications.

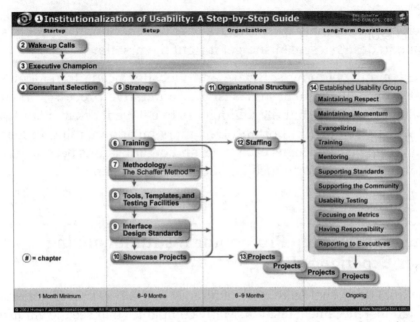

Figure 0-1: *Overview of the institutionalization of user experience design*

The following sections briefly describe each of these phases—Startup, Setup, Organization, and Long-Term Operations. Later chapters discuss each step in detail.

The Startup Phase

In the 2004, in *Institutionalization of Usability,* there was a whole section on how a company needed to experience a horrid disaster to provide a wake-up call. Only then would the organization really move forward. Today that is no longer true—user experience design is becoming a recognized global best practice in development. Nasty wake-up calls are no longer needed. Instead, enlightened executives can often understand the need based on their past experience and education as managers. Even so, the key to success with such a venture remains the identification of an **executive champion**. This person provides the leadership, resources, and coordination for going forward. This person takes the wake-up call to heart and moves institutionalization forward within the organization. The executive champion must be at a high enough level in the organization to motivate coordination across the siloed groups that affect customers. That person must also be able to influence the total development budget.

It is challenging to start a user experience design institutionalization program from scratch without help from a user experience design **consultant** who has experience, training, tools, intellectual property, and an established team. To establish this program, you must have or create an internal user experience design manager and an internal team—but you will need help from a consultant to set up a serious practice. Selecting a consultant is important because you need to find a person or company that has the skills and infrastructure to help your organization move ahead quickly. The consulting organization will often have to meet immediate tactical needs, complete showcase design projects, and concurrently set up your internal capabilities.

The Setup Phase

We always tell organizations that "Well begun is half done." When you set up a hospital, there are lots of interdependent systems that need coordination (e.g., walls, pipes, elevators, cables, operating manuals, and organizational designs). It is much the same with a user experience design practice. First, you need a **strategy** that fits your organization. The strategy should be specific about what will be done. It should include the timing, sequence, validation, and funding that will be necessary for your user experience design program to be successful. You may prefer to start with a short-term strategy that establishes the basics and then let the strategy evolve over time, or (ideally) you may develop an all-encompassing, multiple-year project plan.

Every company has a **methodology** for system development. It may be home-grown or purchased, but in either case the existing methodology is unlikely to do a good job of supporting user-centered design. It is important to have a user-centered design method in place—one that is integrated with current methods and accepted by management and staff. Otherwise, there is no common road map that will pull user experience design engineering into the design process.

Interface design standards are usually a high priority in the institutionalization process. Standards are easy to justify because they help both the developers and the user experience design staff. Even if you have several user experience design staff members on a project, you will likely have poor results if standards are lacking. The experts may independently design good interfaces, but their designs will be inconsistent and incompatible. Moreover, if the standards are not developed quickly, there will be an ever-growing installed base of inconsistent designs.

Without a central standardized set of **user profiles and ecosystem models,** you will find yourself paying to repeat research. And what is worse, the research you do will probably be underfunded (because it is justified by just one single project) and, therefore, will provide a weak set of insights about customers. It is far faster, cheaper, and better to have a central model of your customers and staff. Research can then be carried out and added to this model. In turn, the model gets richer and richer instead of accumulating a daunting stack of reports.

There is a whole toolkit of **tools, templates, and testing facilities** that you need to be able to work with effectively as part of user experience design. This toolkit should include a venue for testing, templates for questionnaires and deliverables, and user experience design testing equipment.

Of course, it makes no sense to have methods, standards, and tools if the skills to use them properly are lacking. The initial strategy for institutionalization of user experience design should include **training and certification** for in-house staff. You can provide general training for the development community and more extensive training and perhaps certification for those individuals who will be interface development professionals. Out of this training, staff who are talented and interested in the user experience design field will probably emerge.

During the Setup phase, it usually makes sense to have one or more **showcase projects**. Conducting these projects provides an opportunity for the infrastructure, training, and standards to come together, be shaken out, and be proven. Such projects also offer a chance to share the value of user experience design with the whole development community.

The Organization Phase

With successful completion of the Setup phase, you have a solid and proven infrastructure for user experience design work, methods, tools, and standards, as well as a process that works. At this point, you need to ensure that the practice can operate effectively within the organization. The main issue to pay attention to is **governance**. Will the user experience design practice be brought into your design programs? Will the recommendations and designs from the team actually be used? Will there be metrics that ensure that everyone focuses on user experience as a key area? Each of these questions springs from serious challenges faced by organizations worldwide. If a set of appropriate measures is not taken, the problem of governance will likely derail the entire effort.

It remains important to follow the **organizational design** principle of spreading user experience design throughout your company or agency. User experience design should not reside within a single group or team; instead, to succeed, user experience design must permeate the entire organization and become part of the system. In all cases, you need a small, centralized, internal group to support your user experience design initiatives. For medium- and large-sized companies, user experience design practitioners need to report to specific project teams. The executive champion needs to establish the right placement and reporting for the group and the practitioners.

The Organization phase is the appropriate time to start **staffing** the organization. Now the full process of user-centered design is working within your organization, and you can see the best way to put a team into the framework. The steps you went through in the Setup phase provide a clear understanding of the types of people needed. Remember that about 10% of your development headcount should be user experience design professionals.

When establishing a central user experience group, it is best to pull together a critical mass of your strongest practitioners. In the prior training process, there is a good chance that several people will have stood out. This is part of the reason that the internal organization is generally established after the initial training—it provides an opportunity for the best internal staff to join the team. It is usually important to hire some additional highly qualified user experience design staff. In this way, the organization benefits from both insiders who know the corporate culture and outsiders who are more knowledgeable about user experience design technology. A manager of the central user experience design group should be the main "go to" person for the user experience design staff.

With the user experience design staff in place, it is time to apply user experience design methods to a whole wave of **projects**. Doing so delivers immediate results and value. It will soon be possible to have every project completed with appropriate user-centered design methods, but in the immediate future you are likely to need to manage a shortage of user experience design staff. To remedy this problem and to cost-effectively manage large volumes of user experience design work, offshore user experience design teams can be a worthwhile addition to the overall staffing strategy.

The Long-Term Operations Phase

The established **central group** now has an ongoing role in supporting the user experience design engineering process. This role includes the maintenance of the user experience design infrastructure and skill sets within the organization. User experience design practitioners should now be involved in all development work, following the user-centered methodology and applying the resources established in the Setup phase and continually updated by the central user experience design team.

As the user experience design institutionalization effort matures, the relatively informal executive champion may give way (or be promoted) to the chief user experience officer (CXO). This is *not* a chief user experience design officer, but rather a broader role. The CXO is responsible for the overall quality of customer experience. Being a CXO requires expertise in user experience design, as well as a thorough understanding of many other disciplines, including aspects of branding, marketing, graphics, and content development. The CXO must be able to reach across lines of business to ensure compatibility of presentation and messaging. If the role of CXO is not established, the central user experience design team should be placed under some executive organization, such as marketing, and the company must ensure that the team members receive good executive stewardship.

Summary

In choosing to set an institutionalization process into motion at your organization, you are choosing to change the feature mindset, technology mindset, management values, and process for interface design that previously governed your operations. This bold move requires the commitment of staff and resources. Organizing your activities to align with the step-by-step process outlined in this book will help ensure visible progress. While this book presents a step-by-step approach, clearly this sequence may vary at specific organizations. Most organizations must face the problem of "changing the wings while the plane is in flight." At HFI, we must often use our own staff to meet our client organization's immediate needs, while we concurrently develop internal capabilities. This is not all bad, as we can use the immediate programs as a training opportunity for internal staff and as a proving ground for methods and standards.

Chapter 1 outlines some of the more typical wake-up calls to user experience design that companies experience. An exploration of some of the more common reactions to these experiences is valuable for capitalizing on initial momentum.

About the Authors

Dr. Eric Schaffer, founder and CEO of Human Factors International, Inc. (HFI), has gained a reputation as a visionary for recognizing that usability would be the driving force behind the "Third Wave of the Information Age," following both hardware and software as the previous key differentiators. Much as Gordon Moore realized that processor power would double every eighteen months, Dr. Schaffer foresaw that the most profound impact on corporate computing would be a positive online user experience—the ability for a user to get the job done efficiently, easily, and without frustration.

Dr. Schaffer has completed projects for more than 100 *Fortune 500* clients, providing user experience, design consulting, and training. He has extensive experience in the financial, insurance, manufacturing, government, healthcare, and telecommunications industries. Dr. Schaffer codeveloped The HFI Framework, an ISO-certifiable process for user-centered design, built on principles from human–computer interaction, ergonomics, psychology, computer science, and marketing. In addition, Dr. Schaffer has brought an array of certification programs to the user experience field, including the Certified Usability Analyst (CUA) and the advanced Certified User Experience Analyst (CXA) designations for user experience practitioners, and the Certified Practice in Usability (CPU) and Certified Usable Design (CUD) programs for organizations.

Apala Lahiri, global chief of technical staff at Human Factors International, Inc. (HFI), and CEO, Institute of Customer Experience, is one of the world's top experts in cross-cultural design and contextual innovation. Her innovative and pioneering techniques have benefited global giants such as HP Labs, Adidas, Nokia, Sony Ericsson, NCR, and Intel, among others.

Ms. Lahiri's vast array of data-gathering techniques—such as the Bollywood Method, Bizarre Bazaar, and Funky Facilitator—help companies understand user experience in diverse cultural and economic environments. The "Ecosystem Chart," developed by her team, organizes vast amounts of ethnographic data into a coherent model.

Serving with HFI since 1999 as managing director, HFI India, and as vice president, HFI Asia, Ms. Lahiri creates user experience strategies for organizations seeking a breakthrough user experience for their customers and other stakeholders. Her writing and classes on contextual innovation, ecosystem research, internationalization, and designing for emerging markets have won her acclaim in the United States, Canada, Europe, India, and China.

In addition to her usability certifications (CUA and CXA), Ms. Lahiri holds an M.Sc. with distinction in User Interface Design from London Guildhall University. She is also an award-winning designer (recipient of the Audi International Design Award) and a TedX speaker (http://www.youtube.com/watch?v=MiwjplU6kAc).

Ms. Lahiri coedited *Innovative Solutions: What Designers Need to Know for Today's Emerging Markets* (CRC Press, Taylor and Francis Group, 2010).

Part I

Startup

The Startup phase is about bringing attention to the issue of user experience (UX) design and aligning the mandatory executive attention and consultative support to start an initiative toward a more mature practice. You may have internal staff with appropriate degrees, training, and certification. Still, a strong executive hand and the specialized experience of a consultant will be critical.

Among those experienced in the UX field, there seems to be total agreement about the criticality of an executive champion. This champion should not be a lone evangelist in the trenches; rather, the champion should be someone high enough in the executive suite to have a real impact on the corporate focus as well as the ability to bring a strategic level of resources to bear on the problem. Without this executive, there is little hope of meaningful long-term success in establishing an effective user experience practice.

While the executive champion provides direction, resources, focus and accountability, the consultancy provides executive advisory—advice and benchmarks from a trusted expert outside the organization's politics and culture. The consultancy will guide you. Additionally, you should have an experienced and integrated team along with a full set of methods, tools, templates, and standards to help you build your infrastructure.

Chapter 1

The Executive Champion

> ➤ We don't need a train wreck—most executives are interested.
> ➤ The value of classic usability.
> ➤ The value of advanced user experience design.
> ➤ The CEO wants a great customer experience now—don't fall for usability fads or half-measures.
> ➤ Who can be a champion?
> ➤ The role of the executive champion.

Today, thankfully, few organizations need a disaster before they can get serious about usability. Most executives understand that customer experience is a key foundation for business success and a key differentiator. Many understand that the user experience of internal staff is also critical, and they will talk about ensuring that the organization is a "great place to work." For most of us, then, there is little convincing about the value of usability needed at the senior level of organizations. We don't need to wait for a "wake-up call" in the form of a decline in market share, rejected offerings, or rage in the social media space. For the most part, executives know that user experience design is important (even if they don't really understand what it is or what it takes to make it happen).

However, initiating or even discussing a serious user experience design practice often entails describing its exact benefits. The setup of a serious practice will usually cost $800,000 to $1.4 million, with an ongoing operation amounting to about 10% of the overall design expenditures. Those are numbers that require more justification than just a gut-level desire and some encouraging press.

The fact that you are reading this book suggests that you know that there is an ironclad case for user experience engineering. Nevertheless, this chapter will review the arguments for the value and criticality of this work so that you have the information readily available when you need to convince others that usability is worthwhile. Keep in mind that it is very rare to find an organization that decides to do serious usability work based solely on numeric calculations (such as ROI). Most organizations seem to need more—they need to see the work pay off in their own environment.

The Value of Usability

The need for basic usability is very real. It is really a hygiene factor, a basic requirement in most industries. Both consumers and technology companies have accepted that if a product is easy to use, more units are sold and the product requires less maintenance. There was a time when you needed to argue that point—but no longer. Usability specialists ensure that software is practical and useful. Primarily, though, usability work focuses on user experience and performance. These elements can be measured and quantified in terms of characteristics of the user:

- Speed
- Accuracy
- Training requirements (or self-evidency)
- Satisfaction
- Safety

By applying usability engineering methods, you can build a site or an application that is practical, useful, usable, and satisfying.

Experiencing the Wake-up Call and Beginning a Usability Process

Pat Malecek, AVP, CUA, User Experience Manager,
A.G. Edwards & Sons, Inc.

In 1999, we began a process to greatly and ambitiously reengineer our public and client-facing Web presence. An army of us just plunged right in and started marching right along. In the eleventh hour, we solicited an expert review from an external source. That expert review said that one of the critical applications, or critical pieces of our new Web presence, was unusable. And by the way, you need some usability people.

If I look back, I'm pretty sure that was the impetus for the creation of what has become my team and a recognition of usability issues. Almost immediately thereafter—within months—we had brought in training and crystallized the efforts.

I remember reading Eric's white paper, "The Institutionalization of Usability" [Schaffer 2001], and thinking, "This really sets the course for what we're up against." That paper says that going through the institutionalization process takes about two years. From the hard lessons I mentioned before up to today, it has been about two years.

Which steps have we taken? Well, we obviously hired people who had the skills or at least closely matched the skills we needed. Then we brought in multiple training opportunities to our campus. We've also sent people out for training. We have endeavored to incorporate my team and usability practices into the development methodology. We have representation on various committees that steer development, and we're also represented on essentially all Web-based projects. Our usability team is located within the Internet Services Department (ISD). ISD basically owns the Internet channel—anything that's delivered via the Internet or our intranet. We are involved as much as possible in everything that channel delivers.

In a *Dilbert* comic strip, Scott Adams had Dilbert present his manager with a tough choice: either spend a million dollars to fix the incomprehensible interface, or close your eyes and wish real hard the users won't care. The manager is left with eyes closed, wishing intensely, and thereby saving all that money.

Usability does require an investment. It costs money to provide staff, training, standards, tools, and a user-centered process. It takes time to establish the infrastructure. You may need to hire consultants and new staff.

Is it worth spending this money and time setting up a usability effort? Harley Manning, Vice President & Research Director of Customer Experience Practice at Forrester Research, posted on one of the studies that have shown a correlation between capability in user experience design and stock price [Manning, 2011]. While many factors affect share price, companies that are customer experience leaders clearly do better than customer experience laggards, even in a bear market. It really seems like investors have understood the criticality of customer experience. When HFI awarded ROLTA a certification for its usability practice, an article in *Yahoo Finance* ("ROLTA India Accelerates on Receiving an HFI Level V Certification") cited a 5.33% increase in share price. It is actually not a very surprising result when you look at the more detailed numbers.

It is common for a usable website to sell 100% or more than an unusable one [Nielsen and Gilutz 2003], and for site traffic, productivity, and function usage to more than double. Unfortunately, it is also common to see developers build applications that users reject because of lack of usability. For example, clients who have come to HFI recently include a major service provider whose new sign-up process had a 97% drop-off rate and bank with a voice response system that achieved only a 3% usage level. There is no question that usability work can prevent these types of multimillion-dollar disasters.

If you follow a user-centered design process, you can expect to spend about 10% of the overall project budget on usability work [Nielsen and Gilutz 2003]. This includes everything—from evaluation of previous and competitive designs to data gathering with users, to the design of the structure, standards, and detailed screens. It also includes usability testing.

There is a lot of work to do, and 10% is a big fraction of the budget. The good news is that the overall money and time required to create an acceptable site or application are unlikely to increase. In fact, the cost is likely to go down for several reasons, some of which are discussed in the following subsections.

Reducing Design Cycles

Today, it is still common to have projects that require major rework because the application does not meet user needs or is unintelligible to users. Implementing good usability practices greatly reduces the chances of having to rework the design. The cost of retrofitting a user interface is always staggering. The cost can be substantial if the detailed design must be improved. Nevertheless, these changes in wording, layout, control selection, color, and graphics are minor compared with the creation of a new interface structure.

When people use a site, Web application, software, camera, or remote control, the part of the product that the human interacts with is the **interface**. The interface, therefore, is the part of the product that gets the most usability attention. The **interface structure** determines the interface design—it defines the paths and navigation that the user of the product will take to find information or perform a task. If usability engineering is not applied at the beginning of interface design, the interface structure is where serious usability problems emerge. Because 80% of the usability of an interface is a function of its structure, a retrofit often amounts to a redevelopment of the entire presentation layer. That is why the best solution is to design the interface right the first time.

Avoiding Building Unnecessary Functions

Often, users evaluate software against a checklist of features, and companies feel compelled to include these features to be competitive. In fact, users may not need or want certain functions. Discovering this earlier—*before* the product is fully designed or coded—makes the user interface better because there are fewer functions to manage and the interface can become cleaner. There is also a huge savings in development and maintenance costs. Unnecessary functions need not be designed, coded, tested, and maintained.

Expediting Decision Making

There is a great deal of research on how best to design interfaces. For example, it is well known that using all capital letters slows reading speed by 14–20% [Tinker 1965, 1963], that using three nouns in a row confuses people [Waite 1982], and that users expect to find the home button at the top left corner of webpages [Bernard 2002]. This means the development team need not spend hours second-guessing design decisions of this sort. Familiarity with these and other usability research principles saves development and testing time and contributes to development of a more usable product.

Increasing Sales

If you are developing a product for sale, a usable product will sell more units. If you are developing a website to sell a product or service, a usable site will sell more products and services. Usable products mean more sales. For example, an insurance company has a site that is currently feeding 10 leads per day to its insurance agents. The company could be feeding them 15 leads per day, but it is losing 5 leads per day because of usability problems. Visitors are dropping out because they can't figure out how to contact an agent or finish using the "insurance quote application" on the site. If usability became routine in this organization and those usability problems were fixed or prevented, how much would the company be able to increase its sales? The answer can be determined with a few simple calculations.

1. The company estimates it is losing at least 5 leads per day from usability problems, which is 1825 leads per year.
2. The company assumes that for every 5 leads received, it can get 1 customer. This means the company is losing 365 customers per year.

3. Each customer provides an average of $600 in income from premiums per year. This means the company could increase sales in the first year by $219,000 if did not lose the 5 leads per day.

4. Using an average customer retention time of 12 years, fixing the current usability problems could increase the company's sales during those 12 years by $2,628,000.

Avoiding "Reinventing the Wheel"

Good usability engineering, much like other engineering processes, means designing with reusable templates. There is no need to reinvent conventions for the design of menus, forms, wizards, and so on. This saves design time. Moreover, because it is easy to create reusable code around these templates, they save development and testing time as well.

Avoiding Disasters

Users are highly adaptable. Even when an interface is poorly designed, some users have enough motivation to keep trying to use the product, even if the application is remarkably complex and awkward. But sometimes a design is completely rejected. The people who are supposed to use the product may refuse to stick with it; they go back to their old ways of getting the task done, buy elsewhere, or just give up. These are usability and product disasters. It's best to get it right the first time.

For all these reasons, the 10% of the budget you should be spending on usability work is easily saved on every project, in addition to the benefit provided by the improved value of the end design. Even if you take into account only the typical savings from working with reusable templates, usability work pays for itself—it is really *free*. However, the decision to begin institutionalizing usability requires more than a simple calculation of benefits. The organization—and particularly the executives in the organization—need to understand how implementing usability means changing the way their business is done. For this realization to occur, a strong wake-up call is often required.

Usability within the Medical Industry

Dr. Ed Israelski, Program Manager, Human Factors, Abbott Laboratories

Usability or "human factors" are important to Abbott in two ways. First, the competitive landscape is such that more and more of our main competitors are putting an emphasis on their safe products by noting that they are also easy to use and learn. The second way involves the FDA and the safety regulations that Abbott must follow. If it were just the regulations, people could find loopholes; combine the regulatory requirements with the business case supporting human factors, however, and it's a good one–two punch.

Also, there are standards, such as the medical device standards, out there. An important organization called Association for the Advancement of Medical Instrumentation (AAMI, www.aami .org) develops standards and training courses for the medical device industry. One of the standards it has developed is a human factors standard. This process standard, which came out last year, is called "ANSI/AAMI HE 74:2001 Human Factors Design Process for Medical Devices." Now I can refer to the standard's human factors step and build it into the budget and product development schedule because it's a standard and the FDA will be looking for it. Then we can also show that it makes good business sense as well. We can show financial benefits because it saves money on training, produces fewer recalls, reduces liability exposure, and increases customers' satisfaction so they come back to buy more—all of which are important things.

If you institutionalize usability, you give people tools and methods and resources, including internal and external personnel. Then it's easy for people to do this—it's the path of least resistance. They don't feel they have to question it and make a business case each time they decide to put human factors process steps in the development project. So, if you institutionalize it, the decision-making process becomes more efficient.

Beyond Classic Usability

Around 2006, the usability field changed its name to the *user experience* field. The transition happened gradually, with groans from many of us. Our cards already read "Engineering Psychologist," "Human Performance Engineer," "Human Factors Specialist," "Software Ergonomist," "Human–Computer Interface Designer," and "Usability Specialist," to recount just a few titles. Printing another new set of cards sounded tedious. But the name change did, in fact, herald a new set of requirements and some new skills. We do not yet have much research on the value of these enhancements, but we are confident that they are of even greater value than the contribution made by the classic usability work.

Ecosystem Viewpoint

The foundation of classic usability work was a model of a person, interacting with a device, in a specific environment. That model was often simply a person in an office using a computer to do various tasks. We built a whole industry around optimizing that human–computer interaction. As early as the 1990s, however, that model started to fall apart. With graphical interfaces, interactions became so complex that we could not analyze all the tasks. Instead, we had to analyze a sample of tasks (which the industry has termed a *scenario* or, if involving only online activities, a *use case*). Since then, this model has also unraveled.

Today we have ubiquitous computing. Numerous devices (mobile devices, tablets, laptops, and desktops) are being used by many different people acting out various roles. These devices operate in diverse environments and employ a blizzard of artifacts. The field has been forced to adopt a set of methods modeled on the work of various ethnographers to handle this complexity. The ecosystem could be "everything that happens with a mobile device," "everything that happens in an x-ray room," or "everything involved in making a buying decision." We will see later in this chapter how this complex array of users, channels, and contexts plays out and pays off.

When we talk about user experience design, we are assuming an *ecosystem viewpoint* that allows us to consider movement through physical stores, mobile confirmations, and group decision making. With this perspective, the contribution of user experience design is far wider than it has ever been.

Strategy

If we don't have a good UX strategy, we are likely to build a *usable wrong thing*. Each siloed team builds a great offering. When all the features and points of entry are taken together, however, they are ineffective and confusing. Figure 1-1 is an example from a bank: imagine, as a customer, trying to work out whether you need to use telephone banking, speech-activated banking, mobile banking, or .mobi!

A good UX strategy will dictate the plan for how users will be motivated in the online environment. For example, if you are "the Asian

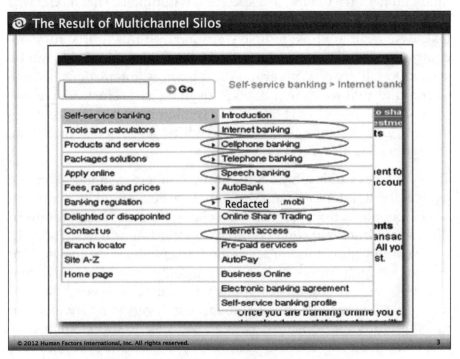

Figure 1-1: *The result of multichannel silos.*

Bank," what does that really mean in terms of your online designs? It is nice to say, "We are the Asian Bank"—but what do you do differently? In this situation, you will find that different parts of Asia need different designs. For example, Japanese people have a very low tolerance for ambiguity and risk, so the design needs to have lots of explanations, FAQs, help, and confirmations. Or suppose your organization wants to migrate mobile customers to digital self-service. It is a great idea, but just building a usable online facility probably won't make that shift happen. You need a scheme to pull people into a digital relationship. You might start with a small step, such as sending an alert for a low balance via SMS. Then you can gradually increase the online interaction (a method called compliance laddering). You might also appeal to a specific motivational theme as you move people into a digital relationship. Perhaps that theme could be the status of an account geared to the digital lifestyle. Perhaps it might be saving paper and being eco-friendly. Perhaps it might be the physical safety of paying bills online from the customer's home. In any case, we can never just hope that people will convert to the new system exactly the way we want them to; we have to plan a motivational strategy that compels them to migrate the new system.

Once you have a motivational plan, then you need to look at the way that the various channels fit together to meet your objectives in a coordinated way. This is the beginning of a journey toward cross-channel integration. The idea that "the user can do everything, everywhere, at any time" is very attractive, mostly because it is simple and has a certain rhythm. In reality, it is rarely the right answer. The ATM is not a great place to pay bills. Sure, you can do it. But people feel anxious at an ATM. Also, there is rarely enough room to lay out your bills, and the keyboard is not likely to be designed for bill payment tasks. Each channel has its own characteristics.

We need a simple story. If you can't tell the user where to go for which activities in a single breath, then you have a problem.

Once the overall design of the set of channels is in place (possibly with multiple Web properties and various mobile facilities), then it becomes possible to design the right facilities with proper alignment. There is still a lot to do, of course. We need to use the same information architecture in all the channels ("pervasive information architecture"). That means we keep task sequences and content organization the same. We need standards to maintain interface design conventions. We might even try to avoid forcing customers to remember a half-dozen different passwords.

Innovation

New product and business ideas are often developed by technology groups or business experts. There is no question that each of these groups adds a valuable perspective, but their ideas often fail because of a missing "human element." Part of being a user experience designer is participating in a systematic, industrial-scale innovation process. There is an enormous difference between implementing a professional innovation process and asking people to be innovative. Certainly, you can ask people to be aware of opportunities that they see. You can mobilize staff and customers to contribute ideas. Nevertheless, even "crowdsourcing," while popular, is unlikely to provide truly innovative origination.

When user experience design staff get involved with innovation work, they don't just sit around trying to be creative or evaluating other people's ideas. Instead, they do research to build an ecosystem model that then serves as the foundation of the creative work. For example, when we worked for Intel developing the Classmate PC, we first studied the educational ecosystems of several emerging markets. We understood the roles of students, parents, teachers, and tutors. We modeled their environments and their activities. I think the product was so successful because the innovation and design work continuously referenced research on those ecosystems.

Innovation projects are generally large-scale operations. They take months and require a strong and specialized team. There is a flow of foundational research, ideation, concept selection, concept elaboration, assessment, and economic/feasibility analysis. While the user experience design team is critical to success, it is always best to have participants who specialize in both business and technology.

Persuasion Engineering

In 2003, Dr. Don Norman published the brilliant book *Emotional Design: Why We Love (or Hate) Everyday Things*. This book marked a real transition in the usability field. Certainly, many of us had been interested in the motivational aspect of software for years (c.f., E. Schaffer, "Predictors of Successful Arcade Machines," *Proceedings of the Human Factors Society*, 1981). The focus of the usability field was on making it possible for people to use their computers, however (Figure 1-2). When you run usability tests and find that perhaps 6% of customers are able to check out, you are not concerned about making the checkout procedure fun—you just want it to work. But Don got the timing right. By the turn of the millennium, we were, fairly routinely, able to create software that people were able to use. It then became possible to turn to issues beyond basic

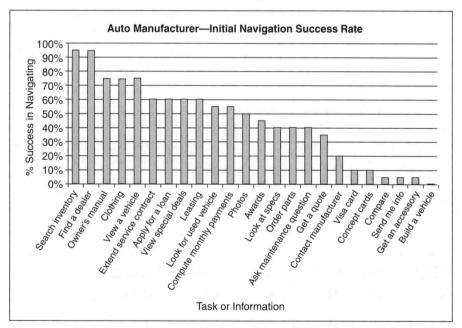

Figure 1-2: *Chart of findings from a car manufacturer's website. Only one-third of the users could get a quote.*[1]

---

1. Data taken from an HFI usability test of a major auto manufacturer's website, completed in 2002.

usability. That is why I say that basic usability ("I can do") is a hygiene factor. You pretty much have to get that right to even be in business.

In *Emotional Design*, Don talked about designing things that people love to use. This is a fascinating area that is certainly among the capabilities of a user experience designer. But it is generally not his or her main focus. The real question is, "Will people convert?" For most organizations, it is a plus if people love their designs, but it is making the sale that makes the company executives happy.

Conversion is partly about making things that people like, but it goes far beyond that. There is a whole world of *persuasion engineering* that determines whether people will buy the product, use the software, ask their doctor, vote for a candidate, tell their friends, migrate to a digital self-service channel, or otherwise do what the organization wants them to do. To reach this point, we have to go beyond "Can do" to "Will do." "Can do" is a hygiene factor—you really have to make it usable. But persuasion engineering is the key differentiator. Only advanced user experience design practitioners are good at it. Persuasion engineering is not magic: *PET* ("persuasion, emotion, and trust"), as we call this field at HFI, is based just as much on a scientific approach as human–computer interface design work. Research-based models on how to motivate customers have been developed, and there are so many ways to influence customers that I've felt the need for HFI to restrict the kinds of companies we work for. The methods of influence are just that powerful.

CEO Wants a Great Customer Experience: Now Don't Fall for UX Fads or Half-measures

The first edition of this book included a long section on how train wrecks were needed to alert executives to the need for good user experience design. I tossed it out. Today's executives are very much aware of the need for good customer experiences. Indeed, they often get very excited about it. But then what do they do? They usually go through a somewhat predictable set of attempts to move their organization toward effective user experience design. Let's go through some of the more common pitfalls.

Relying on Good Intentions

Many top executives start with this approach because it is attractive, not to mention cheap. It seems logical to think you can tell staff members to "Put the customer first" or "Be customer-centered," and then expect them to just be able to do it. The problem is that they can't "just do it."

Creating usable designs takes far more than good intentions. Today, everyone in the development field wants good usability, but usability is hard to achieve. The proof for this statement is painfully apparent in the awful designs that are so commonplace. Even highly motivated professionals often create usability disasters.

Simply motivating people won't result in good user experience design. In some cases, a manager taking this path needs to see a whole project built under his or her well-intentioned motivation, only to find that UX has not been greatly improved.

While the manager reviewing the designs may immediately see that the designs are unintelligible, it takes a serious application of usability engineering technology and methods to ensure that an organization's program will be successful.

Relying on Testing

Sometimes companies get the idea that all they need to create a good user experience is usability testing. It is good to be able to test, but testing alone is not enough. Testing pinpoints problems in the design and its usability that can be fixed. But to be successful and to institutionalize user experience design, companies need a complete methodology including concept development, data gathering, structural design, design standards, and so on. While testing is important, by itself it's not a long-term solution.

Relying on Training

It makes sense. You have smart people who know the domain and technology, so you think you can just give them some training in

Being an Advocate for the Process

Dana Griffith, CUA, Web Consultant—Interactive Media,
American Electric Power

One of the principles I have gained from usability training is that you should never become the advocate for the user. I thought that was really interesting because at the time I was sitting there during the session and thinking, "Of course I'm supposed to be the advocate for the user." But the idea presented was that, once you become the advocate for the user, people try to go around you. They just really don't want to stop what they are doing and change things. But if you simply become an advocate for the *technology* or the *process* and let people decide what they're going to do with that, you will have better success.

Becoming an advocate for the process can have very practical applications. Perhaps we're looking at a very simple application on a website (a form, for example), and someone wants to know whether one area should be populated already or whether it should drop down with selections. In this type of scenario, I can say to the people involved in that project, "I can test that for you tomorrow and find out."

usability, and things will be fine. If you pick a good program, training will help, and the staff will learn a good set of basic skills.

The key word here is *basic*. You will probably give people 3 to 10 days of training. In this time frame, they are not about to become doctors of user interface design. Instead, they will be paramedics. The trained staff members will see the problems clearly. As a result, they will create better designs, but they will still feel frustrated. The corporate culture won't have changed enough to value UX, and there will be no plan for user experience design in the corporate system development life cycle. There will be no design standards. Organizational channels won't be provided for testing with users. There will be no one to call with questions and no repository of examples and templates. The staff members will know when something isn't quite right, but they probably won't know how to fix it.

Relying on Repair Jobs

Repair jobs try to fix user experience design problems at the last minute. This is inefficient and creates only limited potential for improvement. Ideally, UX work should start when requirements are defined. If you bring UX engineering into the process late, you can improve small pieces of the design, such as the wording, layout, color, graphics, and control selection, but there will be no time for more profound changes such as standardizing user interface elements, the flow of logic, or other major elements.

Relying on Projects by Ad Agencies

Another common response to addressing UX concerns is to bring in the advertising agency with which the organization already works. Unfortunately, ad agencies currently have few real UX specialists on their staffs. While the agency will be able to help with branding and perception issues, advertising is a different skill set than user experience design work. There is some overlap, in that both advertising and UX staff members are focused on the customer, but the goals of the ad agency and the goals of the UX team are not always the same. The methods and processes each group uses to complete its work are also very different. Moreover, bringing in an ad agency will not spread user experience design throughout the organization, and it may not delve deeply enough into navigation structures to improve task usability on even a single project. Usability focuses on whether users can perform certain tasks with the technology product. Advertising concentrates on capturing and focusing attention, communicating brand information, and influencing behavior. Advertising and usability efforts should work hand in hand, but they are not the same.

Hiring UX Consultants

A common response to a wake-up call is to hire a consultant to review a site or application. This might be a good starting point and will probably help with a particular project, but it won't address the problems of the next application or website. That is, bringing in a consultant on one project will not disseminate usability engineering throughout the organization.

These consultants can be expected to do a good job and can be cost-effective. However, hiring consultants still leaves the client company without internal capabilities. The company may see the value of the good design work, but it will have to call the UX team back for each new project.

Some user experience design consultants try to transfer knowledge to the client organization. Following this practice does help company staff see that good UX practice makes a difference. Realistically, though, without training, standards, and tools, this approach leaves little behind that is useful over the long term.

Hiring New UX Staff

With a clear understanding of the competitive value of user experience design work, managers sometimes make the substantial commitment of hiring UX staff. This is laudable but, unfortunately, it often fails. The manager may not be able to find or screen for experienced UX specialists. Some people looking for work in usability believe that experience on one project that involved UX qualifies them to be a user experience design specialist. In reality, becoming an effective UX practitioner takes an educational foundation (e.g., cognitive psychology), specific training in usability work (e.g., expert review, structural design), and a period of mentoring by a seasoned expert. After attaining a master's degree in the field, it generally takes three to five years of mentored experience before totally independent work is advisable.

It is all too easy to hire people who need a lot more experience, training, and mentoring before they will be effective. Hiring one such staff member is time-consuming enough—you don't want to end up with an entire usability group whose members are immature or inexperienced.

Typically, a manager hires one or two people to start. Even if the new hires are experienced, having only one or two people often means that the "group" is quickly besieged and rendered ineffective. The team members may soon be so busy that they can't get design standards in place and may not have enough resources to provide training.

In these types of situations, it is best to have many of the initial activities completed by outside consultants who have an established team that has specialized skills in training and standards development and can work quickly and successfully. The consultants will be seen as outsiders, and employees may be more willing to have an outsider dissect the flaws in their designs. Outsiders can say things that an insider has left unsaid. The consultants will be there to get the internal UX staff headed in the right direction and can hand over their knowledge and expertise to help the internal staff become established and ready to take on projects on their own.

If you install a user experience design team, your efforts should include more than simply hiring the people to staff it. Making the team members effective means putting them in a position to be an integral and harmonious part of the organization, establishing clear roles and authority, and addressing the integration of the usability team with the other parts of the workforce.

Seeing the Real Numbers Creates a Call to Action, Too
Harley Manning, Research Director, Forrester Research

Let's say you do care about usability—the organizations we surveyed don't have a formal process for evaluating the usability of the packaged applications when they come in. They're rarely looking at the cost of ownership with regard to usability—and even if they do care about it, they don't know how to evaluate it.

Knowing that in theory it costs me money to have poor usability and being able to actually evaluate how poor the usability is and put a number on it—that's the huge gap. Once you do that and start looking at what the real numbers are, then you say, "I must do something about this!" But that's what the organizations we surveyed haven't done yet.

Who Can Be a Champion?

In discussions of executive championship, there is often an eager volunteer. This person will meet the criterion of being passionate about user experience design. This person will want the job. But this person is likely to be a great candidate for the position of UX Director. The executive champion must truly be a senior executive in the organization.

One criterion that seems to work is that the champion must influence the entire budget across the target design areas. Looking at the need for user experience design across an organization can be a bit overwhelming. There are needs on the public website(s). The call center has issues. Software products have issues. The intranet and back-office operations have issues. User experience design seems to be needed everywhere. If the champion is going to be really effective, he or she needs to have an overarching role across everything. This might seem to be a clear call for championship by the CEO. In fact, while CEO support is very useful, CEOs usually don't make great champions. The CEO will not have sufficient time and attention to spend on the job of executive champion. Instead, this role should usually be filled by someone just a bit lower in the organization. It is a real challenge to find a champion who will have time to really do the job well and at the same time covers a large enough area of the organization.

In the evolution of institutionalization, it is often the case that we start in one area of the business and then expand to the full organization. Certainly, there will eventually be a need for a single, central organization that supports the user experience design effort—otherwise, things will become fragmented and ineffective. But it is better to have a serious executive champion in a key area and focus on that area than to be spread thin and have spotty support.

The Role of the Executive Champion

The executive champion might be the most challenging role in the entire institutionalization effort. There will probably be no formal position and authority, and the organization may not have even begun the process of sensitization and assimilation. Yet the executive champion must gather resources, create a strategy, and keep the process moving. He or she must manage points of contention and chart the course to full acceptance.

Without a champion, the usability staff often has a hard time being included as part of a cohesive strategic effort. The presence of an effective executive champion is the best predictor of success for a UX institutionalization effort. Without a usability champion, the usability group does not have access to key players in the organization, and it is nearly impossible for them to effect change within the organization. With an executive champion, however, the group has a chance to create change and attain the visibility needed to succeed.

The executive champion doesn't need a background in usability engineering or software development, but he or she does need to understand the value of user experience design, its proper applications, and the importance of an implementation strategy. It is possible to get a sufficient foundation in usability engineering from a short course and some reading. First and foremost, though, the champion must have a clear understanding of the business imperatives of the organization and must see how UX work supports these objectives. He or she must understand the core value of user experience design in the organization and repeatedly reinforce this focus, with examples showing how UX design will reduce call time or increase sales.

The champion keeps the whole effort focused on the business goal. This guidance is the differentiator between an effective executive champion and an ineffective one. Ineffective champions say, "We need user experience design." That is nice, but the reality is that *no business ever needs UX for the sake of UX*. Effective executive champions say, "We need to sell more, get fewer returns, and reduce support costs." They know the specific things their business needs. They say this over and over, thousands of times. The business focus of the usability effort is their mantra—and it works.

The executive champion needs to be able to effectively influence the key people in the organization's power structure. This means arranging for project funding as well as convincing key people in an organization whose approval and support are necessary for the institutionalization program to succeed. The executive champion needs to employ the approach that works best with each person— understanding individuals' hot buttons and learning styles.

The executive champion must guide the UX staff through the project approval and selling process. The champion needs to check for acceptance and detect areas of resistance at all levels of the organization. The executive champion is the key agent of change and, therefore, must be able to network with key people in the company, detect areas of resistance before resistance emerges, remove organizational obstacles as they arise, and work continuously to promote acceptance. These skills are essential.

The executive champion must be responsible for the institutionalization strategy, no matter whether the practice is new or seasoned. There must always be a written strategy that directs how that operation will be maintained and enhanced. This means ensuring that the capability-building activities are aligned and that they progress. It also means identifying how the required usability work is to be staged and ensuring the proper allocation of responsibilities and resources. A good strategy is critically important (see Chapter 5), but beyond the content of the strategy, the champion must monitor progress and demand results. Progress takes place when an executive regularly asks for updates and checks milestones, keeping staff members on task. The executive champion cannot create a strategy and forget it. He or she must firmly ensure that the team carries out the strategy.

Keep Moving on the Strategy, Keep Expanding and Innovating

To be successful, executive champions cannot just avert problems and maintain the user experience design operation. Instead, they must find new methods, create new ways of working, and make new markets and business models. If they do not engage in innovation, they are caretakers, rather than executives.

Why Support from Senior Management Is Crucial

Harley Manning, Research Director, Forrester Research

The person at the top of the organization must believe that user experience is important and must require people to follow good practices. Unless that person is committed to this idea, good usability is not going to happen.

The companies that really get it tend to have C-level people who care deeply, like Charles Schwab. Charles Schwab himself, the guy who runs the company, uses the site every day. The woman who headed up the site design came to a workshop I ran a few years ago. She said that Schwab called down on a pretty much daily basis. Certainly, she didn't go a week without hearing directly from him about some problem that he or his mother or his friend had with the site or about something he thought could be better. So this guy is very engaged, very demanding. And the site works as well as it does because, from the top down, it's critically important that the site deliver a great user experience.

We come back to this time and again—the executives must understand the importance of the user experience to the business. Because no executives will put up their hands and say, "Let's do something that's bad for business" or "Let's do something that hurts our customers"—they won't do that on purpose. When they do those things, they do them out of ignorance.

You don't get widespread attention to user experience unless its importance is understood at the top. That's where the leverage is.

The executive helps to expand user experience design throughout the organization. Creating usable software can be essential to many different groups in the organization, or it may be the only way to keep up with the competition. Usability can save millions of dollars when there are large numbers of internal users. For example, the usability team at Sun Microsystems estimated that poor design of the company intranet cost the average employee 6 minutes per day, for a total of $10 million in lost time per year [Ward 2001]. A single second removed from the average call-handling time can be worth $50,000 per year or more in large call centers. With an application that has a large number of users, even benefits from small improvements can add up fast (Figures 1-3 and 1-4). It is no accident that the term "usability" is commonly discussed in executive suites now. Once the executive champion determines the specific value of usability to the organization, he or she must spread the word and keep people focused on the goal.

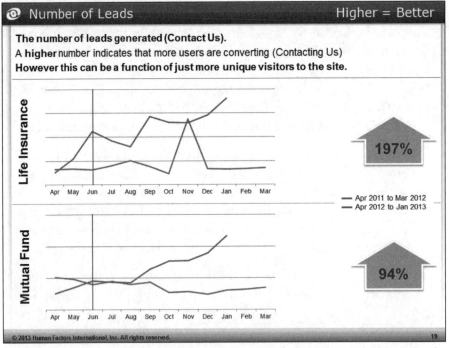

Figure 1-3: *Chart showing increased lead generation from a mutual fund and an insurance site reworked by an HFI user experience design team.*

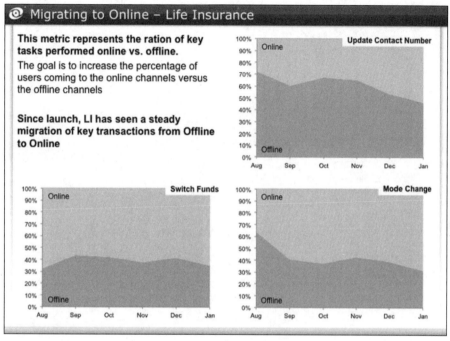

Figure 1-4: *Chart showing customers shifting from expensive human-intermediated channels to online self-service from an insurance site reworked by an HFI user experience design team.*

Chapter 2

Selecting a Usability Consultant

➤ Outside consultants are important to usability institutionalization—they can do things no insider can do.

➤ Retain a usability consultancy early in the process to provide infrastructure and jump-start the institutionalization process.

➤ There are many usability consultancies, and there are huge differences in their capability, resources, and fit with your culture. Pick the right consultancy for your organization.

➤ A good consultant will guide your strategy, set up your infrastructure, help develop your staff and internal organization, and smoothly transition to a role that supports the internal group.

A few companies invest in a solid internal usability group during the early phases of user experience institutionalization, but most companies start with a usability consultancy. The consultancy brings an integrated and experienced team of people and a complete set of resources. They can help your organization establish a well-tuned strategy and do most of the work of setting up the infrastructure. Consultants are skilled in supporting change management issues. As outside experts, their advice is often more easily accepted than internally made recommendations. Also, in the unlikely event that the whole initiative fails, consultants are easy and inexpensive to fire. For all these reasons, it makes sense to start with a consultancy.

In my experience at HFI, the cost of an effective initial setup for addressing usability concerns within a large company could be in the range of $800,000 to $1.4 million just for consultancy resources. This level of investment is required to cover the minimum set of activities, documents, and deliverables needed to get usability going.

You should select a usability consultancy that has a critical mass of staff, processes, tools, and specialists who can help with the startup tasks and the creation of the infrastructure. You want to select a consultancy that comes equipped with a full infrastructure because you do not want to create a methodology and toolkit from scratch. Also, be sure to select a firm with a good set of training courses so you won't need to build and maintain a suite of courses for your company—this can be a very expensive and time-consuming endeavor.

The consultancy's role changes over time. In the Startup and Setup phases, the consultancy guides the strategy and establishes the infrastructure. The firm may help with the design of one or two showcase projects. In the Organization phase, the consultancy helps with recruiting and supporting the initial projects for which internal staff members are not yet in place, experienced, and confident. During the Long-Term Operations phase, the consultancy's role changes yet again. The consultancy should continue to provide training and supplemental support where needed. This supplemental support may take the form of a very high-level consultant who performs audits and provides a second opinion, or it may take the form of specialists who assist the organization with uncommon technologies. The consultancy may also provide lower-level staff to help fill the ranks of usability practitioners. One particular advantage associated with some consultancies is the provision of offshore usability support. Done properly, the quality and low cost of an offshore group can make it possible to support all the projects that need usability work.

It is important to select the right consultancy, and this chapter will help you by describing what you should look for. Table 2-1 summarizes the selection criteria and suggests weightings for these items.

Table 2-1: *Weighted Criteria for Selecting a Usability Consultancy*

Criteria	*Description*	*Points*
Staffing	Has trained and professional usability personnel	17
Completeness of solution	Can provide a complete integrated solution, rather than hiring multiple vendors who specialize in niche areas	16
Domain expertise	Saves time and offers some special insights for your specific domain	11
Methodology	Follows a methodology that has clear activities and deliverables and is appropriate and comprehensive	10
Tools and templates	Already has an infrastructure of tools and templates in place	9
Size and stability	Is large enough to absorb your project requirements	8
Corporate cultural match	Matches or complements your own corporate culture	6
Specializations	Has a wide range of specializations in the field	5
Organizational structure	Has a clear and easy-to-work-with organizational structure	5
Change management ability	Helps you build usability into your organization rather than just providing usability consultancy	5
Quality control and feedback	Has a good quality assurance and process improvement program in place	4
Ongoing training for consultant's staff	Makes a continuous effort to keep staff up to date in usability knowledge and practice	4
Total points		**100**

While it is unlikely that any consultancy will score 100% on these criteria, you should try to find a company that comes close to this ideal. We have included a point system to reflect that some items are more important than others. This rating system should hold up well across different organizations, but you may want to adjust the weightings to match your needs and priorities.

Staffing

You should make sure that your consultancy has professional usability engineering staff. (Chapter 12, Staffing, describes the different types of usability engineering skills.)

Some of the consultancy's staff should have advanced degrees in usability engineering. These degrees can go by different names, including the following:

- Software Ergonomics
- Human Factors Engineering
- Engineering Psychology
- Usability Engineering
- User Experience Design

The staff members may also have backgrounds in cognitive psychology or sensation and perception.

Make sure that the staff members are oriented toward practical design work rather than research. If some staff members publish a lot, make sure that their firm also employs people who do the practical work. They should be familiar with the current research, but they don't have to author it all.

At least some of the staff members should have substantial experience in the field. It typically takes 10 years to develop solid competence. Although some of the staff may have less experience than this level, a consultancy in which most of the members have only one or two years in the field is likely not experienced enough to guide your organization.

COMPLETENESS OF SOLUTION   33

Without skilled staff, there will be little value added by the consultancy, no matter how good its infrastructure is. The people within the consultancy must be at the vanguard of the field and become role models for future growth within your organization.

Completeness of Solution

Some companies can provide a few pieces, but not all, of your usability solution—some may perform only usability testing or training, while others may offer expertise in projects or do high-level change management consulting. You can try to piece together a solution, but the parts will never be perfect matches. Certainly, all good usability consultants have a similar philosophy and work from similar principles. However, even small discrepancies in the interpretation of research or nomenclature can reduce credibility and confuse internal stakeholders. Therefore, you should select a consultancy that can provide a complete and integrated solution, including the following elements:

- **Support for institutionalization:**
  - *Strategic consulting*—consulting on the strategies for usability within the organization
  - *Expert reviews*—evaluation of existing technology products, such as applications or websites, to see which usability problems they contain
  - *Introductory training*—training on the basics of usability
  - *Detailed skills-level training*—training on more detailed skills for in-house usability professionals
  - *Methodological standards*—standards for a user-centered design process
  - *Design standards*—standards for the visual and interaction decisions for projects
  - *Templates and tools to support the standards*—tools to make standards easy to implement
  - *Recruiting of usability practitioners*—help and advice in finding qualified practitioners

- **User-centered design on specific projects:**
  - *High-level user interface design*—consulting expertise in high-level design for critical and showcase projects
  - *Graphic design*—graphic design expertise that dovetails with usability
  - *Detailed design and functional specifications*—user requirements from a usability point of view
  - *Usability testing*—consulting and help with the design and implementation of standard usability test protocols
- **Ongoing support:**
  - *New research updates*—a strategy for keeping the staff up-to-date on the latest work and research
  - *Usability audits*—periodic audits of standards and processes
  - *Mentoring*—mentoring of both executives and practitioners to advance their expertise

These criteria are very important because the effort required to manage a fragmented solution is significant. Even simple problems such as discordant terminology can slow the process. (For example, is the description of the user's workflow called *task design, scenario creation,* or *storyboards?*)

Domain Expertise

Organizations often overestimate the importance of specific domain expertise when selecting usability consultants. What is more important is that the consultant can augment his or her general domain knowledge with exceptional usability expertise.

The consultant should have general expertise in your type of applications and high-level domain expertise—that is, the consultant should understand the general domain of your business. Extensive specific domain expertise in the unique focus of your organization is not necessary. If your organization is in the financial industry, for example, it is important that the consultant have experience with financial products. If your organization produces software for chemical engineers, your consultant should have experience with scientific applications. He or she does not need to have extensive knowledge about your particular type of chemical product or financial offering.

Consider how you might choose an accounting firm. It would certainly be helpful if your accounting firm had worked in your industry—after all, your industry has some unique conventions and special needs, so a certain level of familiarity with these issues could save days or weeks of time that would otherwise be spent on investigation and learning. But when it comes right down to it, the accounting domain is pretty similar across industries. If this were not true, there would be no large accounting firms; instead, all accounting would be done by specialty firms focused on narrow vertical markets. You might be better off with a firm that knows your industry less but has a better staff or a superior process.

Like accounting, usability work is relatively similar across domains. Consultants with domain knowledge can save some time and offer some special insights, but having this level of expertise should not be a critical factor when choosing a consultancy.

Methodology

Select a consultancy that follows a complete and systematic user-centered development process. This means that the process is fully documented and has specified activities and deliverables that can be modified as needed to meet each new set of project demands. It is also important that the methodology you choose be appropriate and comprehensive.

Many user-centered design methods are available. HFI has developed its own user-centered development process, which is outlined in Chapter 4. *The Usability Engineering Lifecycle: The Practitioner's Handbook for User Interface Design* by Deborah Mayhew [1999] describes another such process. A brief look at the evolving software usability methodologies would include the following:[1]

- *Gould and Lewis (1985)*—published one of the earliest usability methodologies
- *Manter and Teorey (1988)*—outlined a usability methodology that was integrated into a standard software development life cycle
- *Nielsen (1992)*—expanded earlier usability principles to 10 detailed steps that should be integrated into an overall development plan
- *Schneiderman (1992)*—introduced eight interactive stages for usability considerations across any interactive systems development process
- *Mayhew (1992)*—advanced usability methodology by offering more detailed specifications for integrating iterative usability techniques into the software development cycle

There is also some useful ISO work, such as "Ergonomics of Human–System Interaction: Specification for the Process Assessment of Human–System Issues" (ISO/TS 18152, first published in 2010). In any case, there is no need to try to write your own methodology. It is faster, cheaper, and better simply to customize an existing method.

Tools and Templates

User-centered design requires a lot of work, but the amount of effort can be vastly reduced if the consultant has a set of tools and templates that support the process. Templates such as questionnaires for interviews, screeners for usability testing, templates for documenting expert reviews, and usability testing reports are critical to ensure that deliverables are easy to create and standardize. Without

---

1. This list is summarized from *Cost-Justifying Usability* [Bias and Mayhew 1994], which presents information on these authoritative methodology texts in more detail. Please consult that source for full bibliographic information for the books listed here.

these templates in place, the consultant will spend a great deal of time reinventing everything from scratch—an expensive process that will extend the project timeline.

In addition to the templates, there is significant value in having a set of tools. The consultancy might have remote testing software, a portable or fixed usability testing lab, and software for tasks such as cluster analysis of card sort data. Working with tools and templates makes consultants more efficient and the deliverables and results more consistent. But it is even *more* important that you obtain these tools and templates for your own organization so that your company can use them in the future. It makes more sense to use a commercial off-the-shelf solution and have it customized to meet your needs than to invest in creating these resources from scratch. You can certainly create your own templates over time, but having a set to use initially saves months of effort.

Object-Oriented Approach

If you were looking for a systems integrator, you would never consider one that did not have an object-oriented approach to systems development. You would not hire a company that just coded flat files for everything, burying all the work and making reuse impossible. Unfortunately, as of this writing, most user experience design companies tend to just create slide decks, or perhaps documents. After a few years, you are likely to end up with terabytes of data, worth millions of dollars—lost forever in a document management system. A simple question such as "What do we know about high-net-worth customers using a bank branch?" becomes nearly impossible to answer, because the search to answer it yields hundreds of documents that need to be read slowly to determine whether they are even relevant.

Best practice today calls for creating slide decks that tell a story as part of a project, while breaking out most of the content into separate objects (e.g., user profile, scenario). At that point, UX practitioners throughout the company can grow and share a set of ecosystem objects that relate to your domain. Instead of jumbling everything together in a flat set of slides, the organization should separate its user profiles, scenarios, environments, artifacts, needs and opportunities, projects, specifications, standards, and methods.

It should be easy to know or quickly identify every project that usability-tested a given type of user. Otherwise, you will be paying to re-research and re-design the same elements. Being able to pull in and work with UX objects is far more powerful and efficient than building everything from scratch.

User-Centered Size and Stability

Many usability consulting firms have only a handful of practitioners—perhaps even just a single practitioner—and possibly some additional contractors. These companies can have significant limitations. If you are working on a usability institutionalization program in a large company, your company's needs may overtax the capabilities of the quality staff in a small organization. Even if your own organization is small, a one- or two-person consultancy will be quickly overwhelmed by the swings in demands during even a single project.

If a consulting firm has eight staff members and you hire all eight staff members for five months, at the end of the project you might find that the firm disappears because it cannot immediately find new work to absorb all of the resources released at the end of your project. That means the same consultancy will not be there to help later when your organization has further needs.

Needless to say, it is a serious problem to have a consulting company fold in the middle of your strategy. The time you have spent getting its staff members up to speed on your organization will be lost. If the consulting firm cannot meet your fluctuating needs, you will have to slow down or modify your process to accommodate its limited capacity and capabilities.

A large firm can provide a team of people to support your projects and won't collapse if you don't need that support for a while. Larger firms are also generally more stable. The fact that these companies are well established means that they will be more likely to be there for you over the long haul, and they are more likely to have specialists who can meet your needs and facilities that can support your effort.

Corporate Cultural Match

It is not easy to achieve a perfect fit between corporate cultures. You want to be sure that the consultancy's technical staff will fit with your company's environment. In some situations, it helps to have a strong figure who can walk into a confusing situation and provide order. In other circumstances, you may need a usability expert who can work with your team and smoothly create consensus. It is important that the consultants have some flexibility in style. It may be even more important that they can provide a variety of staff members with different personalities and working styles, so that the ones who best fit your corporate culture can work with your organization.

Many other special characteristics of organizations need to be considered. In some cases, uncomplimentary cultures present some advantages. For example, a very systematic and controlled culture might need a consultant who can break the mold, be artistic, and provide a different perspective. Conversely, if your organization lacks a systematic process, it helps to have a consultant who can inspire that structure. In most cases, however, similarity in cultures is more helpful and often leads to a more comfortable long-term relationship. If you have a scientific- and engineering-oriented culture, pick a usability firm that has a similar approach. While the consultant will work closely with you for a relatively short period, there will also be a less concentrated, longer-term relationship. Being comfortable with your consultant's organization has value.

Specializations

Hiring a consultancy that has staff with different specializations in the field offers a significant advantage. People who have focused deeply on a given topic can answer questions in an instant.

There are many different types of specialists. Some usability professionals have experience in meeting the exact challenges of specific populations:

- Cross-cultural and multilingual design
- Design for the visually impaired
- Design for children

Some have experience in specific technologies:

- Mobile and embedded applications
- Gesture interfaces
- Telematics
- Voice response
- Web and responsive design
- Workstations

Others have experience with specific technical areas and topics:

- Search strategies
- Natural language dialogs
- Representation of large networks

Some staff may have particular experience in different parts of the user-centered design process:

- Interviewing
- UX strategy
- Innovation
- Persuasion engineering
- Complex structural design
- Usability testing

- Graphics
- Prototyping

UX staff also may specialize in certain types of situations and businesses:

- E-commerce
- Intranets
- Shrink-wrapped software
- Emerging markets
- Bottom of the pyramid (poor people)

Having consultants with a wide range of experiences at your disposal allows you to draw on solutions from many contexts. For example, someone with cross-cultural design expertise would take one look and notice that your command abbreviation "S" may mean "save" in English, but "exit" (*sortie*) in French.

Organizational Structure

Look for a consulting firm with the necessary staff to fit your organization's needs. With a small organization, it may not be difficult to manage all the usability work that is occurring simultaneously. When a larger organization is the client, the consultancy may also need to offer a business manager to handle contractual relationships, an accounting contact to handle payment issues, and a separate legal person to handle nondisclosure and contractual issues. For large-scale efforts, you have to deal with more people than just the usability consultants.

There will always be a primary usability lead and perhaps some additional usability staff on the team. In addition, it helps tremendously to have an escalation channel separate from the usability lead. When only the usability lead serves as a contact, it can be challenging or awkward to communicate when difficulties arise in the consulting engagement—especially if the usability lead has created the problem!

Change Management Ability

The consultant must provide high-level strategic guidance in the organizational process. Organizations must often realign their operations to support a user-centered design process and they almost always have to manage resistance to change. The consultant will actually provide assistance in change management. *Change management* refers to making changes in a planned and systematic way so as to make the transition to new processes easy and effective. This kind of guidance should include pointing out pitfalls, helping to identify and manage specific areas and people in need of special attention, and opening communication channels. The consultant should directly support the organizational process and have many examples, case histories, and research to substantiate his or her position.

Select a consultant who will help you meet your essential political goals and will defend your best interests, even at his or her own expense—one who will "stand in front of a freight train" for you. The consultant should have the ability to talk as a peer to anyone, at any level of the organization.

For some organizations, change management may be an important but not critical factor in the success of the usability implementation. For other organizations with a history of change management issues—or with highly charged changes already under way—effective change management might be a "make or break" factor in implementing usability.

Quality Control and Feedback

Some organizations rely on the skills of a single practitioner to ensure the quality of usability process deliverables. In such a case, there may be no standard process, review, or oversight. This is like the early days of programming when the work was done in a garage by a master programmer. If he or she was good enough, the code would work, but there was usually no concept of a separate and formal quality assurance process. The only concept of process improvement in this scenario was trial and error.

Look for a consultancy that has good methods to ensure quality. Is there a method of certifying staff quality and knowledge? Is there a review process for deliverables? Is there a process for gathering feedback about the quality of the design and results and improving from lessons learned?

Make sure the consultancy has, at a minimum, a systematic user-centered methodology and actually follows it. Such adherence ensures a more reliable application of design. This methodology is just the minimum, however. You should seek out a consultancy that engages in ongoing process improvement. Provisions for quality assurance and process improvement indicate a more mature organization that will provide you with far better service and support.

Ongoing Training for the Consultancy's Staff

Earlier in the chapter, we mentioned that the consultancy should provide training for your organization's employees, but it is also important to know how current the firm keeps *its* staff. The usability field is constantly adding new principles and methods. If the consultancy does not gather and disseminate these insights, you will not benefit from current best practices.

For example, usability specialists once thought that the optimal limit on menu size was either 7 (plus or minus 2) or 10 items [Miller 1956]. More recent research suggests that the optimal menu size is more like 16–36 items, as long as they are presented in groups of not more than 10 items each [Paap and Roske-Hofstrand 1986]. Insights such as these, which are often presented at critical conferences, can be valuable to your projects, so you should be sure that at least some of the consulting firm's staff attend these meetings. Chapter 8 lists some of these top conferences in the field. In addition, a continuous stream of useful books, articles, blogs, and e-communications can provide up-to-the-minute information about the UX field.

Selecting a consultancy that keeps its staff up-to-date on the best practices in usability and user experience ensures that those staff members can bring those practices to your organization's emerging user-centered design program.

Summary

A good usability consultancy is invaluable in helping your organization transition to an efficient and thorough user-centered design process. It is worth spending additional time screening consulting firms early in your institutionalization effort to make sure that you choose one with the most appropriate capabilities for your organization.

The next chapter provides insights into how you can create a practical strategy for your efforts that includes the activities and resources you have begun to formulate.

Part II

Setup

The Setup phase establishes the infrastructure needed to complete efficient and professional usability work. Certainly, you could hire some usability staff members and put them into project teams. But completing this phase marks the difference between a real institutionalization effort and unprofessional puttering. Without an effective strategy, training, methodology, facilities, tools, templates, and standards, a usability practitioner is unlikely to be successful and efficient.

In the Setup phase, you create a strategic plan that includes specifically sequenced steps, resources, and activities. This plan helps you build an infrastructure to support ongoing usability work. The infrastructure includes training for everyone, which provides an understanding of usability as well as specific skills for the design team. The organization also develops a user-centered design methodology, integrated with the general system development life cycle. A user-centered process recognizes the design of the user taskflows and experiences as the first priority.

You also create a set of reusable questionnaires and templates, decide which facilities and equipment you need, and develop interface design standards. The Setup phase is about building the infrastructure so that ongoing user-centered design can be completed in an efficient, repeatable, and professional manner.

Quite a few components and interactions are included in the Setup phase. The methodology must work with internal processes, and the standards must work with the technology and the business objectives. With all these complex elements to address, you can't expect everything to work out smoothly the first time. That's why the showcase project is strongly recommended—to work out the kinks in the process and prove that it all works.

Chapter 3

Institutionalization Strategy

> ➤ Create a strategic plan that has an overall roadmap and a detailed description of each activity, including objectives, activities, and deliverables.

> ➤ Getting this plan right is critical. It is a very complex puzzle, specific to your situation.

> ➤ Select and sequence activities to optimize practicality, efficiency, and support for cultural change.

> ➤ You can bootstrap the usability effort. The benefits of the small early activities often can fund the larger tasks of establishing infrastructure and an internal team.

> ➤ Let's avoid these strategies that do *not* work.

With all the excitement and pressure around user experience design, it can be difficult to take the time to strategize. But we have learned that the old saying, "Well begun is half done," holds true with UX design. A strategy for the institutionalization of UX design will lay out the plan and ensure that every component of it happens at the right level of investment, with the right tuning of the deliverable, and the right timing (Figure 3-1).

Sample Strategy—Unisom Pvt., Ltd. Usability Institutionalization Strategy for January–June			
Projects	*Organized by*	*Details*	*Cost*
Training Plan	DESEC Training	Four open presentations of the Basic Usability Course (two in Washington office, one in Colorado, and one in Texas). Schedule ASAP.	About $40,000
	TNF Development T. Smith, Lead	Two presentations of Web Design class (Washington office). Openings for 25 people per course. Schedule ASAP.	$20,000
Methodology	TNF Development T. Smith, Lead	Purchase HFI Framework and integrate with current RUP process. Target completion by Feb. 1.	$30,000
Facilities, Tools, and Templates	TNF Purchasing F. Chavan, Lead	Agreements to use testing facilities in Washington and Texas. Target completion by Feb. 1.	None until used
	TNF Development T. Smith, Lead	Prepare customized set of testing and PET research questionnaires customized to our environment. Target completion by April 1.	$40,000
Standards	TNF Development T. Smith, Lead	Develop customized interface standard to cover our public Web presence, extranet, and intranet. Target completion by March 15.	$140,000
Showcase Projects	T. Lam, Development Manager	New expense reporting system for intranet. To be completed as Showcase Project. Expected start—June 1.	About $175,000
	S. Chandra, Development Manager	Public website module for new member registration. To be completed as Showcase Project. Expected start—June 15.	About $150,000
Organization and Staffing	Office of the President	Create initial concept for organizational structure and staffing levels. Target completion by May 15 for presentation at Director's Conference.	About $25,000
	Personnel Department D. Lang, Lead	Recruit head of central usability team. Target—start by April 1, sooner if feasible.	About $130,000 per year

Figure 3-1: *Sample strategy for institutionalizing user experience design*

Without question, the executive champion must outline and own a written strategy for setting up and maintaining the UX practice. Nevertheless, this executive will not be equipped to create the strategy alone. He or she may have insights into the range of possibilities for a user-centered design practice as well as the priorities of the organization, but an expert will be needed to help set up the program. That expert cannot just be a good user experience designer—you need someone familiar with the issues in setting up a practice.

In some situations, you may be setting up a practice from scratch. More likely, you will be taking a limited internal capability and evolving it into a more mature, effective operation. In either case, there must be a roadmap that defines the specific activities needed (Figure 3-2). Each activity needs clear and detailed descriptions (Figure 3-3). It is not enough to say to your team, "We are going to develop a methodological standard"; instead, you need to document the exact focus of the standard.

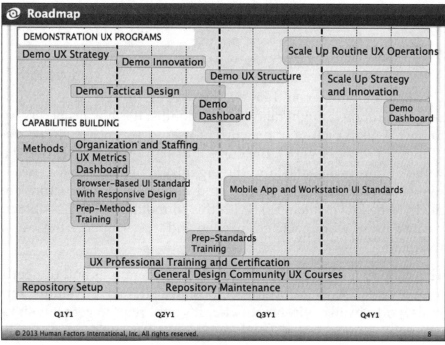

Figure 3-2: *Sample roadmaps for institutionalizing user experience design*

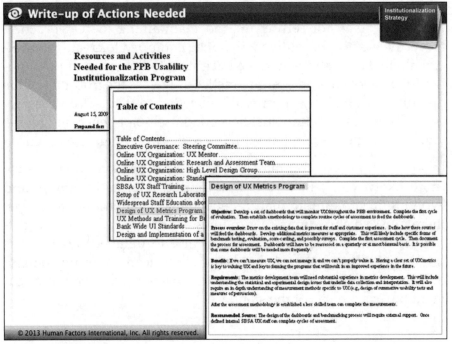

Figure 3-3: *Sample detailed write-up for institutionalizing user experience design*

Creating a strategy could take a few weeks, or in a large complicated operation it might take several months. It is always necessary to have a good picture of the current user experience design capabilities (to identify gaps), the current design quality (to prove the value of improvements), and the organizational culture (as executive championship, governance, and organizational structure are likely to be key challenges). With this foundation, it is possible to create a list of work packages needed and then sequence these as a roadmap.

This chapter indicates some of the key considerations and tradeoffs to be aware of when carefully composing a strategy. No simple formula works in all environments, but it's important to get your strategy right. A poor strategic plan can doom your institutionalization effort.

What to Consider When Developing the Strategic Plan

Putting a mature user experience design practice in place can be a lot like changing an airplane's wings while it is in flight. There is a blizzard of current projects that *have* to be supported. At the same time, you need to put capabilities into place. While this situation might seem daunting, it is actually a good place to be (assuming you have the resources to avoid getting buried under the immediate tactical needs). Ideally, you can have a real synergy between tactical programs and building capabilities. Recognize that your tactical programs can serve as showcases through which the value of mature user experience design can be demonstrated. It is odd: you can show a dozen industry examples of the value of user experience design to executives, but they never seem to have the impact of a single internal project. It is particularly useful when you have some programs that try to get by without user experience design, and perhaps others that a marketing firm and perhaps some good visual designers have attempted to help make customer-centered. When these efforts are compared with serious user experience design, the results usually make a compelling case for UX institutionalization.

Concurrent showcase projects also have value beyond conveying the value of user experience design. They allow you to refine and validate the infrastructure created in your capabilities-building program. You can apply the methods and standards and see if they work smoothly in your environment, and verify whether your staff can really complete designated activities. In the end, then, it is a major benefit to have parallel tracks of tactical work and capabilities building.

While it may take two years to complete your overall institutionalization effort, you will see benefits from your tactical work almost immediately. Moreover, the growth in user experience design infrastructure will start to pay off within a few months. The documented plan itself can be a short-term program with a duration of as little as three months or as long as two years. In any event, there should always be a written strategy covering the current growth path of the user experience design operation.

Your strategy must identify the planned activities, time frame, resources, and responsible entities in your organization and should address the following questions:

- Which sequence of usability initiatives will work best? Although some steps must be completed before others, you have choices with some of the sequence decisions you make.
- Have you considered your environment? How will your organizational culture affect the way you implement your user experience design practice?
- What are your most pressing projects, concerns, and objectives? As you begin the process of institutionalizing user experience design, you can have it unfold in a way that meets your most important issues.
- Are there people or units that particularly need to get on board? Pockets of resistance exist in every organization. Identifying yours and building them into your strategic plan is critical.

The strategy essentially describes *who* will be responsible in your organization and *what* they will be doing. This concept seems simple, but the decisions you make have significant implications. The following sections cover the main considerations involved in selecting the *who* and *what* for your strategy. Your usability consultant may be able to help you think about these issues and develop the best strategy for your environment.

A Proactive Organization

As you start the institutionalization effort, it is essential to set up a proactive effort. It is easy to start putting out the numerous fires of poor usability and have a small dedicated staff work to fix the tidal wave of bad designs, one by one. Be forewarned—this approach is guaranteed to fail. It is like having doctors administer to all the health needs of the community, from taking temperatures and applying bandages to transporting patients and performing surgery. The medical community can't work that way, and neither can your user experience design staff.

The medical community has paramedics, nurses, and physician assistants to help with the range of its activities. For your company's strategy, you need to build a similar set of facilities to create a pro-active organization. This is the only way to ensure routine usability.

Coordinating Internal Staff and Consultants

In Chapter 2, we described why your organization should consider using an outside usability consultant and how to choose one. Even with all the value that a consultant can bring to an organization, however, internal staff remain invaluable. Using internal staff costs less than hiring local consultants, to be sure—but there are far more advantages related to this decision than simply the cost. Internal staff members are the only people able to focus fully on business content and strategy within the company. They can learn the subject matter deeply, or they may already know it. As a consequence, they can be more efficient in design work. They can also develop a set of instruments and procedures that really fit perfectly with the issues the company faces. For example, if your organization is in the medical field, staff members will be aware of the latest FDA requirements. If your organization is in customer service, the staff will know the history of issues with workstation and voice response system integration. They know from first-hand experience what to attend to in the next release. Having the greatest familiarity with your customers, internal staff members can focus on building a shared model of the customers' ecosystem.

The global best practice for user experience design is to have it done primarily by an internal group, possibly with the supplemental support of vendors. Hiring a set of disparate vendors ensures a hodge-podge of incompatible, misaligned results.

Internal staff members also have an advantage when it comes to UX design institutionalization because they work in the organization on a long-term basis. They have established relationships with employees and groups within the company that are not involved in usability. Perhaps most importantly, they know the opinion leaders and sources of power in the organization, so they can often achieve a level of consensus and buy-in that consultants can't match. Internal staff also hold you accountable to your user experience design goals: while it is all too easy to tell a consultant, "Yes, we will accomplish user-centered design now," and then ignore the issue the next week after the consultant has gone, the internal group is in a position to deeply embed the usability perspective into the organization over the long term.

It is possible to have supplemental support from vendors. Organizations vary a great deal, so it is vital that your strategy fits your company culture. For example, some companies may be accustomed to having consultants work closely but independently, while others may want a consultant to just coach staff briefly or may prefer to do all the work with in-house staff. In every modality, however, there must be a strong internal user experience design group that maintains standards, methods, a persistent knowledge base, and strong quality assurance.

The Importance of Sequence

This book presents phases and activities for institutionalizing usability. Most companies modify this process somewhat. As you

Consultant and Internal Group Mix

Todd Gross, Ph.D., former Director—Corporate Statistics and Human Factors, Medtronic MiniMed

At Medtronic MiniMed, we used a mix of in-house and outside resources to complete our human factors projects. Outside consulting offered several benefits. Consultants could focus exclusively on our projects, whereas in-house personnel were often faced with multiple competing priorities. Consulting firms also offered greater depth of resources and expertise to dedicate to a project. This allowed them to complete the projects more quickly and with more comprehensive output than in-house staff can generate.

Another benefit of outside consultants is that they brought a fresh perspective to a project. Their experience with a broad range of products and applications allowed them to present recommendations in a way that was valuable. There's something about hearing opinions from an outside entity—the good news sounds better and the bad news has greater credibility than when in-house personnel present it. It's sort of like if a date tells you that you dress funny, you might give that greater credence than if your mother tells you the same thing.

In my experience, this mixture of outside consultants and internal staff can produce a powerful alliance to promote the use of human factors knowledge throughout the organization. I like the idea of having a department that provides core resources—I think that, on a long-range basis, manufacturers need to have that internal core. But the in-house staff can be complemented by a strong consulting relationship, especially for a company like Medtronic MiniMed, which makes devices with a broad range of human factors issues. Some of the devices are purely mechanical and others are electronic, with both hardware and software interface issues. This product diversity requires a corresponding wide range of human factors approaches in both design and evaluation. In addition, the FDA has continued to champion, and even mandate, the use of human factors during product development and usability testing. Knowledgeable consultants can supplement internal staff's experience with these regulatory requirements.

It is truly exciting to see the dynamic that can develop between internal and external team members, with in-house content experts providing the raw material, in the form of product-line knowledge and development history, and consultants helping tweak both product design and usability evaluation plans, combining to create a cohesive and effective strategy.

develop your own strategy, be sure to consider the sequence of activities that will make the most sense for your environment.

Many logical connections are built into the institutionalization methodology described in this book. For instance, keep the following sequences in mind:

- Have your strategy in place before the infrastructure setup begins; otherwise, you will spend money in an inefficient and uncoordinated way.
- Have standards in place before starting projects; otherwise, you will create a larger installed base of noncompliant designs.
- Get the upfront design process working before doing usability testing so that testing can fine-tune reasonable designs instead of documenting designs that are not even close to correct.
- Finalize your methodology and organizational design before you start the hiring process so you can be sure to hire user-centered design staff with the right skills and abilities.

These interdependencies are important and should always be considered when planning your strategy. It is also important to use the sequence to maintain flexibility. As in a chess game, it is unwise to move in a way that unnecessarily closes off options.

To demonstrate the value of considering sequence, let's consider when to hire usability staff. It's often better to delay full-scale hiring of usability staff until you have a formal methodology documented and the work within that organization allocated within the organization. You might find that with mentoring and oversight, trained business analysts can handle detailed design. This approach leads to a very different staffing requirement than large-scale hiring.

Reacting to Past Events

Many organizations have had bad experiences with consultants, making it difficult for them to work with a usability consultant. The new consultant may say that he or she is different—but then the previous consultant may have made the same claim.

If you have a negative history with outside consultants, it is critical to go about the relationship-building process more slowly. You may need to start with very small projects. Take time to gain trust and put the bad experience well in the past. The staff may also need much more explanation about the consultant's conclusions. There is never a time when people should take user experience design recommendations on trust—they should always be given the full rationale and research data behind each recommendation. Allow extra time for this.

Another past event that should trigger reflection is a difficult wake-up call for the organization when a design failed. This otherwise negative experience can be a resource that provides momentum for change in the organization. However, such challenges can also create too *much* drive. Overall, it is best to avoid strategies that are driven by a sense of panic. They rarely work well in the long term. If you are reacting to a wake-up call, avoid taking on lots of projects. Instead, select a few key programs and make sure they are completed successfully.

Targets of Opportunity

The greatest drivers for differences in strategy are existing tactical opportunities. It is important to establish a plan and shift the sequence of institutionalization to take advantage of the organization's current activities.

You might find that you can get training in conjunction with another company in your area, so training might be moved to meet this schedule.

You might find that you are installing a revised system development methodology. This is a great time to add a user-centered process to supplement the new method, instead of having staff members learn the system-centered method first and then learn about user-centered design separately.

You might select a showcase project because it is visible, or because the staff members are very interested in usability, or because the project is small and manageable and needs to start at the right time for the usability initiative.

Perhaps you have an opportunity to hire a very skilled usability specialist who is a good fit for your culture. Usability staff with skills and compatibility are very hard to find and may be on the market only for days. If unique opportunities are present, mold your strategy to hire sooner.

Clearly, as you establish your strategy, you must shape it to your opportunities and also expect some fine-tuning to occur as new opportunities arise.

Slower Can Be Better

Achieving a successful institutionalization program requires time and patience. There is an uncomfortable joke in aviation that captures this principle quite well. A plane called the "V-Tailed Doctor Killer" has a funny tail design, but is nonetheless a powerful and complicated aircraft. Many doctors have the money to buy such a machine, but they do not have the time or experience to use it safely. They can fly the plane under normal and comfortable circumstances, but in more dangerous and pressure-filled moments, they lose control.

It is much the same with a user experience design practice. You can buy a complete user experience design infrastructure. You can implement training, methodology, standards, tools, projects, and hiring. It takes a great deal of effort and money to put these elements in place, but until the organization has had time to fully digest each intervention and each component of the infrastructure, there is little value in it. It is all too easy to bite off too much and then think you are well fed. Take your time in implementing usability, and build that time into your strategy.

Phasing in Design Standards

In your strategic plan, make sure you get interface design standards in place early. Good design standards are so valuable that they can be justified almost anytime there will be significant and ongoing development. Standards save development time—and there is a real increase in expenses when developers must spend time reinventing the wheel. When there are no standards, it is as though you can hear a clock ticking. Also, developers do not have the time, skill, or attention to dedicate to creating a design that a standards team has. Therefore, developers' designs are almost certain to be suboptimal.

The biggest concern, however, is that current projects completed without standards will lead to a growing set of noncompliant screens. These screens must then be modified to bring them into compliance. This is a daunting task, and no company ever seems to do it all at once. Instead, noncompliant designs are grandfathered in. They are brought into compliance with the standard only when they are being revised as part of some renovation or enhancement program. This makes the conversion less daunting and spreads the cost over years. While this tactic might seem like the rational thing to do, it is quite costly to let developers keep churning out nonstandard designs while you delay standards development.

Aside from the costs of eventually converting the designs, working with a committee that represents an installed base of noncompliant and diverse designs can create a psychological drag on the process of creating standards. You can see each committee member judging the concepts based on how closely they match his or her own designs or the designs of his or her department. These committee members cannot see the ergonomic quality of the new, standards-based designs, and they cannot interpret the value of the new design to the company; instead, they are simply entrenched in defending their past decisions.

These groups can be hard to work with. You end up painstakingly having to take apart those past designs one by one. Typically, you have to show the ergonomic problems with the old designs, and the people involved must go through the process of accepting that they created an imperfect design and realizing that their designs need changes.

Providing a training class for the committee members leads to an infinitely smoother process. With training, they can see the problems with their designs themselves. Nevertheless, the larger the installed base, the more staff members have a vested attachment to the designs, and the more visceral resistance to making changes they are likely to demonstrate. Of course, you should avoid making unnecessary changes in past design conventions. Recognize, however, that people can develop powerful arguments for retaining very poor designs.

Key Groups for Support or Resistance

The institutionalization of user experience requires a set of discrete activities and resources, but the key to success does not lie in these accomplishments, but rather in the understanding and beliefs of the people within the organization. It is not unusual for companies to spend six figures on a usability testing lab, only to see it sit unused. Without the acceptance of user experience as a focus of concern by the people in the organization, there will be no real success.

The people in your organization can be classified into a number of key groups from the viewpoint of institutionalization. First, there are the early adopters, easily excited about usability, who almost instantly grasp the concept, methods, principles, process, and value of user experience. The earliest stages of the institutionalization effort need to focus on identifying these people and getting them on board. They will provide early momentum. As time goes on, you will need to worry about keeping them motivated and preventing them from feeling too frustrated with the pace of the overall organization. If they become bitter, they will alienate others, so keep them seeing successes.

A second key group is the power structure within the company. In a sense, the progress of institutionalization is wholly reflected in this group's level of understanding and appreciation. As user-centered design becomes a given from the perspective of the executive suite, impediments will melt, resources will appear, and success will be assured. If the executives are indifferent, long-term success is essentially impossible. Reaching these players is key. Put effort into including them in the design process (as experts in strategic direction and brainstorming), communicating successes, and providing education. You do not need these leaders to do the design work, but they should help you work on the organization's process of design.

When executives get involved in design, they follow several patterns. Some may attempt to micromanage the entire process or single-handedly reinvent the entire human engineering profession and literature. Others may drop into the design process periodically and make recommendations. This can be quite detrimental, but the worst situation is the executive who hands down design edicts from on high. These executives are the people who want to see "a big red area at the top" or "a tree view at the left."

These executives are usually so powerful that the design team feels forced to follow their orders precisely, rarely with a positive impact. Such executives become an all-powerful design constraint—and the design team already has enough constraints. Executives need to

Executive Support for Usability within AT&T

Feliça Selenko, Former Principal Technical Staff Member, AT&T

In an employee message to the people of AT&T, Dave Dorman, AT&T CEO, states, "AT&T has an important initiative under way to dramatically improve our 'customer lifecycle' processes. The intent of this effort is to drive higher levels of customer satisfaction and retention, and differentiate AT&T from the rest of our industry. By removing errors and the resulting rework, we reduce cycle time, improve customer satisfaction, and reduce our costs of doing business." That sentiment is reflected in every set of executive goals and objectives I have seen this year—that is, optimizing the customer experience is always one of the most important goals/objectives.

Although AT&T executives are using the term *customer experience*, which is broader than usability, goals/objectives focusing on the automation of manual processes, optimizing the customer's self-serve experience via easy-to-use Web tools, and removing errors from processes and interactions to reduce rework and improve cycle times are all aspects of the customer experience impacted by usability engineering.

reinforce the need for user-centered design and the value of optimizing user experience, performance, and design consistency, but they should never specify a design feature. Even with great experience and training, it is quite difficult for a consultant to select any substantive design decision that can be mandated in every situation, so executives should certainly not attempt to do so.

A third important group is the people who are against usability, or the "naysayers." It might seem odd to think that there could possibly be people like this in the modern-day business world, but there are. Down deep, they do not want to lose control of the design process. They want to continue to enjoy designing things *they* like, without needing to validate that the users can understand, use, or appreciate the result. There is a joyful freedom gained just from creating elegant code, while there is an unpleasant messiness to meeting the inconsistent, ambiguous needs of users. Naysayers won't admit to this type of thinking, but it is often what really drives their criticism.

Naysayers can come from different groups. Marketing staff members might think things will go well if they make sites that wiggle and dazzle users (although users often consider such sites "sales-y" and disreputable). Graphic artists might want to concentrate almost wholly on the beauty of the design and not worry about whether it can be navigated and operated easily. Systems coders might want to use the easiest technological route or perhaps the latest and coolest technological innovation.

Rather than seeing the benefit of referring to user needs and limitations as they create a design, naysayers will suggest that systematic user-centered design "takes too much time." Expect them to question the ROI of usability work. (In response, you might ask them if they have ever seen an ROI calculation for having a database designed by professionals instead of by amateurs.) Naysayers may suggest that, because their design intuition is so good, they can create better user interfaces than the ones based on ergonomic principles and user-centered design. Users will certainly like their designs more, these folks will claim. They will suggest that good usability cannot be achieved within technical constraints. If you point out problems in past designs, they will often reference past technical constraints that were recently solved by new technology.

Your strategy must eventually address these naysayers. They will listen to proclamations about user experience by executives, but think and act as if it is just the management buzzword of the month. (After paying it lip service, they will try to forget it.) They will pay some attention to presentations demonstrating the value of usability in pilot projects, and take more interest in presentations that include testimonials from other naysayers saying they saw value and practicality in the user-centered design process.

But one strategy works best. Most of these naysayers will be problem-solvers by nature. They will love to solve the most complex development challenges, and they will feel effective when they can break through these challenges and succeed. A breakthrough is possible when these people are tasked with finding a way to meet a customer need; they will find that usability is fun, and that it offers them a whole new set of puzzles to solve. No amount of ROI calculation or explanation will match that thrill.

The final key group comprises the masses in the development community—the mainstream developers. Once a strong core group is established to support usability, the members of that core group must begin the process of evangelizing and mentoring other developers. This effort will take some time because there are many mainstream developers, and they change slowly. Nevertheless, institutionalization is established only when this mass of developers has been reached. They will be swept up in new projects that apply user experience design practices. In addition, they will benefit from training and presentations. The mass of developers can also be reached by a set of online methods and tools presented on a company's intranet. Finally, consider including user experience as a part of your training program.

Training

While training is not a magic pill, it is a major pillar of the institutionalization effort. You may need several levels of training—for more information, see Chapter 8. Training provides widespread awareness of usability issues and instills a crucial element of motivation in the early stages of institutionalization. It can also be used to educate executives and evangelize the value of user experience.

Training provides skills for developers who must participate in user-centered design. It is true that the fine points of usability engineering seem to be best shared by mentoring, but without training in the basics, the mentoring process is long and frustrating. Skills-level training is really required.

Methodology and Infrastructure

It is common to see companies hire a few usability people and toss them into the design environment. It is like deciding that you want to have metal weapons and hiring a few metal workers. Certainly, they can set up a few huts with hand-driven furnaces and can begin work with a hammer and anvil. But if you want both efficiency and quality, you need to build a modern factory—*then* when you toss the metal workers into the factory, you can expect good results.

Without a user-centered design methodology, the development team members will end up working tactically. They will think of some of the right things to do, and they will have a positive impact, but a systematic approach will be more thorough and more efficient. For this reason, it makes sense to fit a user-centered process to your current development life cycle. Do this early, because time spent without a structured process is likely to be inefficient.

Once you've chosen a methodology, you can move toward establishing a toolkit that supports the methodology. Facilities, tools, and templates make work on the user experience design engineering process even more efficient. These "modern machines" lead to quality and efficiency. Chapter 4 provides more information on methodology, while Chapter 7 provides details on facilities, tools, and templates.

The Project Path

Selecting the showcase projects to work on first is one of the biggest decisions in the strategic plan. Obviously, you must select a project that is just starting so you can demonstrate the whole process. You should also select a project of manageable size and duration. It helps little to tackle a showcase project that won't be completed for many years.

It is equally important that the showcase project have significant user experience design objectives. Find a project with lots of users to whom user experience and performance is important. Chapter 13 covers in detail what to look for when selecting a showcase project.

Levels of Investment

User experience institutionalization, infrastructure, projects, and staffing are not free. It costs less in the long run to complete designs with the right methods and tools, but in the short run, an investment is required. It is valuable to calculate the ROI for implementing usability within your organization. Know the specific ways that user experience design will pay off.

The investment in user experience can be staged and progressive. For example, in my experience, the investment in an expert review or usability test will be in the range of $35,000 to 70,000 and can motivate managers to get serious about user experience design. The cost of the initial setup of a usability program for a large company by a consultant is typically about $800,000 to $1.5 million. The cost of establishing a UX design group and supporting it might be $1 million to $5 million annually.[1] Clearly, then, starting a usability program is a progressive process: each step should instill the

---

1. This figure, along with the others in this paragraph, is based on HFI's 20 years of experience with hundreds of clients across thousands of user-centered design projects.

confidence to go ahead with the next level of investment, and each step should fund the next.

Summary

Your attempts to make customer-centered design become routine will require significant changes throughout your company. A practical, high-level strategy will create the organization necessary to bring your decision making to the next level. This is the transition from a piecemeal and immature usability capability to a mature and well-managed process. The next chapter provides more details about the training element of your strategy.

Chapter 4

Methodology

➤ A methodological standard describes how to do user-centered design—select a good methodology that will work for your organization.

➤ You probably already have a system development life cycle in place, but it is probably not a user-centered methodology. You may need to retrofit a user-centered process onto or in front of the current technical methodology.

➤ Implement a quick test of your life cycle. Is it user-centered? Take the test in this chapter.

➤ Review The HFI Framework 7 as an example of a proven user-centered process.

Some people do not like standard development methodologies. They prefer to work with each project and figure out what is needed for that one project without thinking about standard practices. They may feel that any inefficiency and nonrepeatability are inherent to the creative process.

With a user-centered design process or methodology in place, the critical steps to make a product usable will not be missed. All projects will follow a similar method, ensuring a standard level of quality.

A methodological standard primarily plays the role of a memory jogger. It makes sure that you do not forget to complete some of the hundreds of major steps needed for good design. Implementing a methodology also provides your company with a mature process— that is, a systematic methodology that can be organized, supported with tools, monitored, and improved. A standard process of user-centered design is essential, and the methodology you choose or develop must enable you to be reliable, successful, and efficient in your design process.

A methodology is also the core of your institutionalization effort. Because many of the other steps to institutionalization are dependent on the methodology project, it is often the first thing that gets done. The methodology program will not only define what needs to be done, but also identify which groups and class of staff will do each type of work. If you decide to have your business analysts do much of the detailed design work (generally with mentoring from user experience design professionals), then you will need training for those business analysts. Doing the methodology first, as you might imagine, is often a good plan.

This chapter describes how to choose a methodology and outlines some of the challenges you may face as you integrate it into your current development process.

What to Look for in a User-Centered Methodology

Mature development organizations today use a defined system development life cycle for software development. That means they have a plan for developing software that includes an entire cycle spanning from feasibility to programming to implementation. Some of these are industry standards with software tools available, such as the Agile approach and the Rational Unified Process (RUP), while others are proprietary processes developed within companies. Although some software development life cycles may mention usability, none seems to provide the comprehensive set of steps necessary to follow a user-centered design process. Software development life-cycle methodologies concentrate on the technical aspects of building a software product, as they should. They do not make engineering the user experience and associated tasks the primary focus of development, which means they build applications from the technology and data, inside out. User-centered design is a different way to approach development: it concentrates on the user and the user tasks, rather than on technical and programming issues. Following a user-centered design process is the only way to reliably create practical, useful, usable, and satisfying technology products. In a user-centered process, you design the user experience first, and then let it drive the technology (as shown in Figure 4-1).

Almost all practitioners in the field agree on the general steps required to follow a user-centered design process. You can document these steps yourself and build your own user-centered design process. Accomplishing this feat, however, may be slow, expensive, and time-consuming. You should undertake this task only if you have senior usability staff with many years of experience, as that

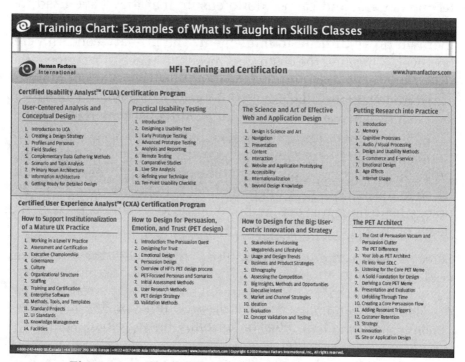

Figure 4-1: *The "old" technical-centered solution needs to be replaced by the "new" user-centered solution*

approach will ensure you are following industry best practices. In most cases, however, you are far better off buying a process and then customizing it for your organization.

Your user-centered process affects the way functional specifications are created. For example, you will craft the user taskflows before you worry too much about the database structures. The user-centered process will mostly bolt onto the front of your technology process. Then throughout the software development process, steps connect the user-centered process to the work that the technical staff is doing as well as to the documents that serve as input to the programming staff. In addition, many linkages ensure that the methods stay coordinated. Document handoffs need to be identified at a detailed level.

This is not to say that technical limitations are ignored in the early design phases. Interface designers need to know about the technical issues for a particular project. They need to understand what the technology can and cannot do to ensure that they have used the technology to the fullest extent and without designing something that will prove difficult to implement. The primary concern here, however, is meeting the customers' needs. You need to engineer the user experience and performance and derive the user interface structure to support this user taskflow. At that point, the technical staff can design the software to support the user interface design. This effort might require pulling together data from a dozen servers to provide a summary view when entering the site, using graphic preloads to shorten the download time on a website, or using cookies so that users get book offers that relate to their needs. The technology has a huge role to play, but it needs to remain focused on the needs of the users.

Select a user-centered methodology that meets the following criteria:

- *The methodology must be comprehensive.* It is not acceptable to have a process that relies on usability testing alone—it must address the whole life cycle.
- *It must be user-centered.* The methodology must be firmly grounded in designing for an optimal user experience and

performance first, and the interface design and technology must be based on user needs. It must take those user needs into account and must actually access representative users to obtain data supporting the design and feedback.

- *It must have a complete set of activities defined and deliverable documents required.* The methodology should not be a loose collection of ideas but rather a specific set of activities with actual documentation throughout the process.

- *It must fit with corporate realities.* Ill-defined or changing business objects are by far the most important cause of feature creep. The user-centered design process needs to include steps that bring together the diverse strategic views and ideas of your organization's stakeholders. There need to be activities in the process to ensure that all key stakeholders contribute and feel heard.

- *It must include more advanced user experience design activities, if appropriate.* Today, methods that simply ensure usability are usually no longer sufficient. As UX practitioners, we need to deal with the complexities of cross-channel alignment and integration—so there needs to be a UX strategy. We are often asked to participate in systematic innovation programs—so we need innovation methods and not just a general intention to be innovative. We need to design for conversion by applying persuasion engineering methods. For most organizations, all of these capabilities must be part of the current methodology.

- *It must be a good fit for your organization's size and criticality of work.* Large organizations that build large and critical applications should have a more thorough process and more detailed documentation.

- *It should be supported.* While it is wonderful to have a process described in a book, implementation requires much more. It requires training, templates, tools, and a set of support services. It is a daunting challenge to create all of these components or cobble them together from a diverse set of sources. You might find a pretty good user-centered design methodology—you might get it from the Web or from a friend. Then, of course, you need to determine what is required to support that methodology. Expect to devote a good half-year of work to this process if you have to create all the deliverable document formats, questionnaires, tools, and standards, and another half-year to develop training to support the standard.

- *It must be able to work with your current development life cycle.* This is no small task, and is discussed later in this chapter.

- *The methodology must have a cross-cultural localization process* through which the design is evaluated for language and culture issues (if you are doing cross-cultural or international development).

Integrating Usability into the Development Cycle

Janice Nall, Managing Director, Atlanta, Danya International
Former Chief, Communication Technologies Branch,
National Cancer Institute

We really want usability to be so integrated into the development cycle that it's just like graphics: It's just a process, and it's where you insert it into the process that matters. It's not at the end—when it's ready to go out the door—but rather at the very beginning. We just want to make usability mainstream and not constantly have to argue the cause. We are still in that mode; we feel like we have to prove ourselves every day.

If we can get it into the next realm where we can take it to the next step, where we are not spending all the time justifying why we need to do it, we can pursue research to get answers to the questions that don't have answers. I think there is a huge interest in really pushing the science—from our end certainly, but from across the federal government as well. We must make better-informed decisions and start advancing the field, sharing that knowledge and really disseminating what all of us are learning effectively.

An Outline of The HFI Framework

To give a sense of what a user-centered methodology should include, this section outlines The HFI Framework, a methodology based on the practices that have evolved at HFI over the last 30 years. Driven by cycles of data gathering and refinement, this method pulls in the knowledge and vision of the organization and harmonizes them with user needs and limitations. This solid process for ensuring quality design includes designing screens by using templates (instead of "reinventing the wheel" each time) and supports deployment and localization to different cultures. It covers the whole thread of user experience design work that starts with executive intent, and runs through UX strategy, design, and continuous improvement. If the thread is broken in an organization, sound executive ideas about what is needed for success will eventually fall to the floor, and the design will become nothing more than a set of functions only roughly associated with the intended organizational direction. We follow this process consistently at HFI and have integrated it in practice with almost every commercial system development process and hundreds of bespoke methods.

The technical part of our ISO certification is based on following this process.

Figure 4-2 shows an overview of The HFI Framework. The first column lists needs that are fulfilled, and the second column lists engagements we use to fulfill those needs. The last column outlines the business need that is being fulfilled. Not every type of engagement gets completed on every program. Instead, what is important is a coherent set of engagements ensuring that the thread between executive intent and design is unbroken.

Strategy and Innovation

The input into this work is the executive intent. Executives have various types of intent statements, as the following examples suggest:

- Reduce service calls and return of tickets in error
- Migrate customers to digital self-service channels

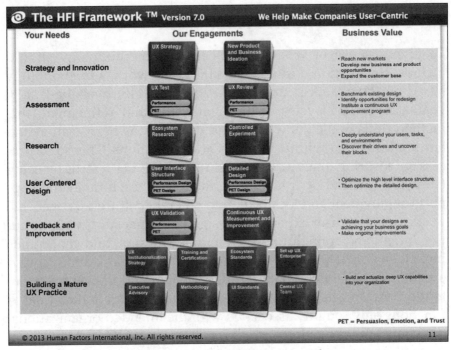

Figure 4-2: *The HFI Framework*

- Increase conversion and market share by 40%
- Gain a 20% share of the mobile market in Kenya

It is the executive's job to come up with these types of desires. But then as we start our **UX strategy** program, we must ask the hard question: "How is that going to happen?" We might want to migrate customers to digital self-service. But that won't happen by just creating a self-service facility. Nor will it happen—on a large scale—by just making the self-service website easy to use. First, we need to determine how to motivate customers. Where a decade ago the journey of a major development program might start with a discussion of the technological framework for the development, today it starts with work on the customer's motivation. Once the customer's motivation is understood, then we need to see how that target motivational experience can be supported with the wide range of available channels (Figure 4-3). Success generally requires coordination of applications, across various channels. There may be a physical

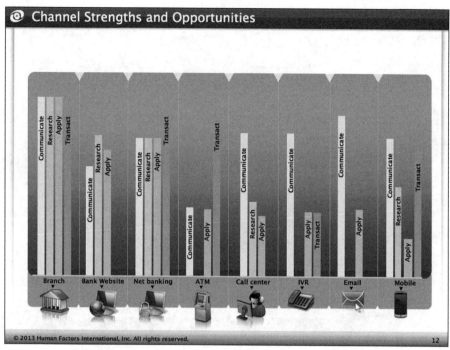

Figure 4-3: *The diverse capabilities of various channels*

store and a call center. In the end, the whole ecosystem solution needs to be simple to understand and a good fit for the capabilities and limitations of the various channels.

While it is common to find organizations that do strategy work, in the end they deliver only generalities—and those at a very high price. At HFI, we always illustrate a motivational and cross-channel solution with conceptual designs. This concretizes the recommendations. In the end, those concepts become the initial foundation for ongoing structural design.

The UX strategy is likely to spawn one or more **innovation** programs, identifying areas that need innovation in the business model or product design. Many organizations try to innovate by asking their staff to be innovative—they might provide a quick training program on "thinking outside the box," for example. In reality, a request for lateral thinking is quite different from industrial-strength innovation processes. Serious innovation takes a systematic definition of the context, including the capabilities of the organization and

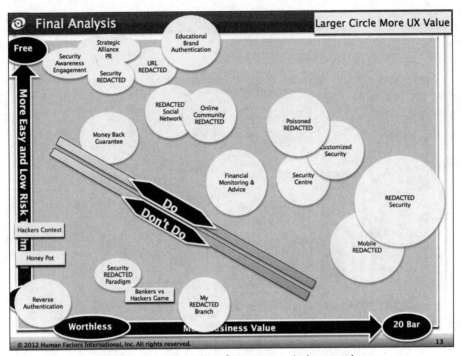

Figure 4-4: *Results of a systematic innovation program about online security*

the ecosystem of the customers (Figure 4-4). An innovation process creates many ideas and then determines those worth applying.

Assessment

If there is an existing application, it may make sense to evaluate the quality of the current design to justify the redevelopment program and identify areas that need special emphasis during redesign. During this phase, we also may perform a competitive analysis to understand the current best practices and identify competitive imperatives.

Two kinds of assessment methods may be employed. In a **usability test**, designs are evaluated by having representative users attempt to use the facility or be interviewed about the facility. In an **expert review**, trained experts in user experience design systematically investigate the design based on research-based principles and models in the field. You might think that the user research is much better than the expert review, but, in fact, the expert review is usually faster, cheaper, and better. User research might result in solid data that the user takes three minutes to complete a transaction. But what does that mean? Is three minutes good? An expert, in contrast, might immediately point out that default values can be used to slash the time requirement. In reality, the best application for usability testing as an assessment is when strong political issues are preventing stakeholders from listening to the expert.

You need different methods to investigate whether people *will* do a task as opposed to assessing whether they *can* do a task. PET is HFI's acronym for *persuasion, emotion, and trust*. The methods we use to check whether people get confused while using an application don't really work when we are trying to understand whether they will be motivated to convert. Today usability is no longer enough. It is certainly an expected hygiene factor to have a checkout flow that everyone is able to use, but assessing the customer's willingness to actually buy the product requires different methods.

Research

User experience design practitioners rarely do pure research, because they are too busy designing things. Nevertheless, there are two kinds of research that may be needed to perform. One is foundational **ecosystem research**. This type of research is performed to define the range of users, environments, scenarios, and artifacts for the target application (see Figure 4-5 for an example). You might do this research once, and then apply it to many ongoing projects (which is why we would think of it as foundational research).

The second type of research that user experience design practitioners undertake is a **controlled experiment**. This scientific research study, with proper controls and statistical analysis, is needed when a critical decision must be made between two different designs and millions of dollars hang in the balance. A controlled study is clearly justified when you really need to be certain which design is better. Controlled experiments are also appropriate to support marketing assertions. For example, HFI recently had a smartphone company approach our firm and tell us the blogosphere had proclaimed that they had the fastest keyboard. The company wanted scientific backing for the claim so it could own that distinction and make it the

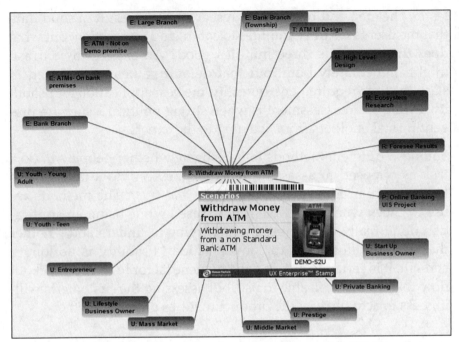

Figure 4-5: *Example of an ecosystem around ATMs showing scenarios, users, and other elements*

core of a marketing campaign. So we ran the study (the company's keyboard was the third fastest).

User-Centered Design

Once the strategy and innovation have ensured that you are building the right thing, then it is time to do the actual design work. It is best to think of this endeavor as two separate programs. The first deals with the user **interface structure**. Our years of experience at HFI have shown that 80% of usability is determined by a good interface structure: it ensures that users can understand what is offered, find things quickly, and navigate efficiently. There is also a PET aspect to the structure. Just as we have always designed the structure of the navigation, so we must now design the structure of the conversion as well. We need to know which drives, blocks, beliefs, and feelings we are dealing with. We need to know which set of tools will be employed to trigger conversion.

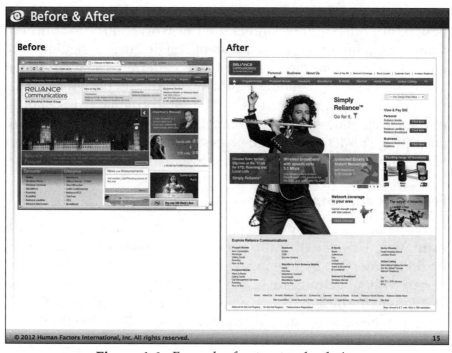

Figure 4-6: *Example of a structural redesign*

It is often best to complete the structural design before planning the detailed design. The structural design will create the overall container for the interface (Figure 4-6). It defines how the user will navigate, and if done well this structure will match the user's deep mental model. The result is that the design will seem obvious and laid out in a common-sense manner. The user will be able to find things. The navigational container must also be physically efficient. It must fit with the user's taskflow so as to minimize the time and physical effort involved. Finally, it must define the persuasion strategy and the style of the site.

The structural design takes a high level of expertise. Once it is done, however, it is easy to plan the ongoing **detailed design**. Each screen must be fully designed and specified. It is easy to find good structural designs that are built out with poor detailed design: they are good-looking and easy to navigate, but awkward and frustrating as the user proceeds through the interaction.

The detailed design work is easier than the strategic and structural design, but often involves quite a bit of work, and it is critical to maintain quality throughout this step. The detailed design must be guided by user interface standards (or patterns). Detailed design also requires staff who understand a wide range of design methods, principles, and techniques. It cannot be left to graphic artists or business analysts unless they are competent in user experience design principles. The detailed design process also generally requires cycles of usability testing, so that skill set is essential as well.

Feedback and Improvement

Once the design is complete and coded, it is a good idea to do a **UX validation**. This step offers an opportunity to ensure that the design works as intended by looking at the ability of users to operate the design without getting stuck, and by checking the users' emotional reactions to the design. This evaluation is a bit different from the UX testing involved in the design process. The testing during the design stage is "formative" testing focused on gaining insights into why the user is having trouble so that you can make design changes. The UX validation, in contrast, seeks to measure the user's performance to see if the objectives are met. It's a worthwhile step, as it can stop a bad design from being released as well as provide lessons on what might be done better next time.

The last phase of the user-centered design process, **continuous UX measurement and improvement**, is often neglected, but is potentially a great investment. If the design is for a large application, it pays to make ongoing improvements. At HFI, we once changed just one page on an office supply company's website and increased sales by an estimated $6 million per month. Ideally, you will create an ongoing dashboard that provides an array of UX measurements. This can allow you to track the impact of the ongoing work done on the design.

Generally companies have good business metrics on their sites and applications. And in a sense that is exactly the focus of UX work. We really care only that our work has increased conversion, saved time, and reduced call center load. Why, then, would you need user experience design metrics in addition to the business metrics?

A.G. Edwards' Usability Process and Methodology

Pat Malecek, AVP, CUA, Services Solutions Executive, Dell, Inc.
Former User Experience Manager, A.G. Edwards & Sons, Inc.

I've heard from usability practitioners at other companies that it's fairly common to have a formal and well-documented methodology in place but that it's not often followed to the letter. We certainly have a very well-documented methodology—whether or not it's followed to the letter varies from project to project, depending on scope, schedule, and things of that nature.

We have a summary version of that methodology that we are putting the finishing touches on. It is a product development life cycle that we've crafted, and it provides a much simpler view. This life-cycle document was developed by both the business and technical sides, and it puts forth a mutually agreeable methodology that calls for early attention to presentation issues and lots of opportunities for iteration and look-and-feel corrections. We are hoping to disseminate the life-cycle document to all the relevant parties because it shows in simple terms where various usability issues could be addressed.

In terms of examples of the usability practices that we put into the process—in the grandest terms, we do it all. We've completed projects in which we go out and interview users, and we do card sorting, and then we go to navigation mock-ups and move through paper mock-ups and test paper mock-ups, all the way through to a finished product. And when things are being done with great urgency, typically we do wireframing—and when I say "we," I mean our user experience designers. They have the proper skills and the proper knowledge, and—if time doesn't permit testing with the appropriate user groups—at the very least they will take those mock-ups to a cluster of people and do some informal testing to shake out some of the big bugs.

By having specific measurements for user experience design, we can tell if that design is likely to improve the business metric. If both the business metric and the user experience design metric yield poor results, then design improvements will most likely be helpful. If the business metric is poor but the user experience design metric is great, then the problem probably stems from something else, such as pricing, marketing, or even the executive intent.

A Quick Check of Your Methodology

You may discover that your current methodology has some user-centered design in it, but you might be wondering if it is a good process. The following exercise will help you test it. HFI developed this test based on feedback from 35 usability professionals with a great deal of cumulative experience in the field. They were asked to identify the most important activities in user-centered design. HFI then asked the participants to provide weightings for how much the activities influenced the quality of the results, and fine-tuned the rating system by working with clients. This quick check works for websites, applications, and any other software designs.

To take the test, look at the 15 design activities described in Table 4-1. Check which ones are included in your methodology, and then add up the points to get your Usability Quotient. The maximum rating is 100. If your methodology scores less than 75 or so, it is probably in need of enhancement. If it scores less than 50, you probably need a whole new process.

The Challenges of Retrofitting a Development Life Cycle

It is a rare company that does not have an existing system development life cycle. Your company may have purchased a method, or perhaps you built one from scratch. Someday every method will follow the user-centered paradigm, but today it is unlikely that either system does.

Table 4-1: *Calculate Usability Quotient*

Checklist Items	Explanation	Notes	UQ Value (if Complete)
1. Define brand, style, and tone	Define the character of the site with a list of adjectives (e.g., cool, high tech, trendy; stable, reliable, simple).	Use existing brand values where appropriate.	4
2. Define user	Describe the users in terms of skills, knowledge, interests, objectives, and simple demographics.	Also known as user profiles or personae, this addresses users' psychographics instead of population concerns.	8
3. Set usability objectives	List of specific objectives from the user's viewpoint (e.g., complete a trade faster than the competitor, or rate the site as easier to use than driving to store to buy product).	Usability objectives, goals, or criteria can be based on task time and error performance or the satisfaction survey ratings.	7
4. Define user environment	Describe the user's environment (e.g., interruptions?), pattern of work (e.g., uses once a month), and social context (e.g., needs to get supervisor's approval).	Base the description on interviews and observations made during a contextual inquiry.	6
5. Analyze current tasks	Understand how the site functions are done today. Draw a taskflow diagram.	Use contextual inquiry techniques. Develop user scenarios of use that can be derived from use cases.	9
6. Redesign tasks	Develop a story of how the functions and tasks will be done in the new application. Describe the scenarios and make them simple and easy. Optimize use of new technology.	Reengineer and match the taskflow to the limitations of the technology used in the application under development.	13

(continues)

Table 4-1: *(continued)*

Checklist Items	Explanation	Notes	UQ Value (if Complete)
7. Verify useful with unique value	Check that the site will offer substantial benefits, beyond other sites, applications, or manual facilities.	Does the site offer compelling value to make users return? Is it sticky?	4
8. Verify practical	Conduct a formal walkthrough of the taskflow design to ensure that it will be practical in the real-world environment.	Is the site practical from a common-sense point of view?	3
9. Test navigation	Run a short usability test to make sure people can find things on the prototyped main navigation pages.	Use low-fidelity paper or similar prototypes.	9
10. Test aesthetic	Run the test that validates the positive appeal of the visual design. Also check that the design supports the branding objectives.	Use the test of brand perception appeal to measure that the design is aesthetically pleasing and supports the brand.	2
11. Use page design standards	Design most pages by copying from sample templates.	Use generic or customized best practice page templates.	7
12. Complete detailed design by staff with training in usability	Get at least basic training in usability before designing pages.	Can be an HFI-Certified Usability Analyst.	8
13. Review all pages systematically for usability	Review the pages for usability and consistency. Do this with someone who is *not* on the development team.	Do a walkthrough of the site using the most important user tasks and user profiles.	7

Table 4-1: *(continued)*

Checklist Items	Explanation	Notes	UQ Value (if Complete)
14. Usability test site	Perform a simulation test where users complete a set of tasks and see where they have problems. Fix the major problems.	Use in-person, one-on-one testing "think aloud" protocol. Can be supplemented with remote online testing or with the application.	7
15. Monitor initial usage	Review initial usage with click stream analysis and user data. Fix significant problems.	Establish success metrics and monitor them.	6
Project's Usability Quotient			(0–100)

Occasionally, a company needs a whole new development process. This scenario occurs not just within brand-new organizations; a new development process may also be needed when there is a major change in the technology or scope, such as the switch from simple Web brochures to complex Web application development. Usually, however, the organization already has a software development process and needs to deal with the relationship between the existing process and the newer user-centered design methodology. The methods have to be interwoven with proper communication and handoffs between the different types of development staff. There may need to be particular stage-gates to verify that the required user experience design work has been done in one stage before proceeding to another.

There are three likely scenarios when there is an existing process: classic methodologies that are not user-centered, patches where some user-centered activities have been added, and classic methods that just have usability testing added. These same situations tend to appear in commercial methodologies that do not have an ideal user-centered process. The following subsections explore these three scenarios in greater detail.

Using Classic Methodologies

Most software development methodologies seem to follow a classic process. One such method is the waterfall method, in which the steps follow logically and build in sequence. Another classic approach is the spiraling method, in which design cycles are more iterative. Increasingly, there is some sort of rapid development method (e.g., Agile), which moves quickly to prototyping and tends to work well only for small projects. All of these are classic methods because they fail to put the user first: they identify business and technical functions and database design and middleware in progress, before the user tasks and actions are identified and taken into account. Therefore, in this context, *classic* means *old*, but not in any way *good*.

Retrofitting a Method That Has Added User-Centered Activities

Sometimes there has been an attempt to add user-centered activities to a software methodology. The problem is that while the attempt is always well intentioned, it is often not well done. Instead of a thorough user-centered design process, the end result is a software methodology process with a few usability activities added here and there. The effort is neither thorough nor sustained.

Both software methodologies and user-centered design methodologies have many steps. These steps are important for each methodology, and they need to be completed in a certain order. However, the steps are different. Trying to retrofit the steps of one methodology onto the steps of the other methodology does not work, just as trying to force the tools, templates, and documentation of one to fit the other does not work.

Retrofitting a Development Process That Has Only Usability Testing

In still other cases, a team has created a user-centered methodology by simply adding usability testing to its software development process. This is a common practice, though, not surprisingly, an ineffective one. Disappointment in the results is like being surprised at reaching the wrong destination when you travel without being given maps, a compass, or navigation tools for the journey.

Without a full user-centered process, performing a usability test at the end of the development process merely serves to highlight the unacceptable nature of the design. It's a sad and frustrating result, but there is usually little that can be done except to release the poor design.

With a user-centered process, the usability test becomes a source of useful, easily implemented changes. These changes are not radical because the structural design has been solidly built and tested; there is no need to throw it out when problems crop up. The insights provided by the usability test tend to be small—in the form of minor changes to wording, layout, and graphic treatment—and easily implemented. Yet this type of final usability testing is well worth doing.

Implementing full user-centered development can be compared to creating a wooden statue. In the early phases, there is sawing. Then, you need to switch to a chisel. Finally, you apply sandpaper. The final usability testing becomes the fine sandpaper. Without the full user-centered process in place, the development effort is just like trying to create a wooden statue by *starting* with fine sandpaper.

Templates

The methodology reminds practitioners about steps that must be taken. As such, it is helpful in planning projects. Once the methodology is created, however, you can build templates for the various forms and deliverables required to complete the methodology (Figure 4-7 provides an example). It is far faster to edit a template than to create each item from scratch. It is fair to say that "professionals don't start from scratch." It is hard to convey this lesson to staff fresh out of school, who have likely been threatened with disciplinary action for copying. In the user experience design group, though, you are not trying to prove you can do it all yourself; you are trying to put out a design that is fast, cheap, and good.

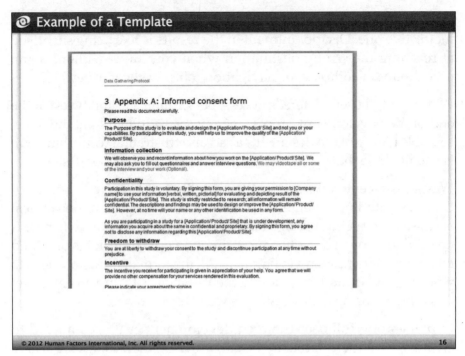

Figure 4-7: *Example of a template*

Summary

Following a user-centered design methodology makes your design activities reliable and repeatable. Without a methodology, it is difficult to produce high-quality designs. The maturity of your methodology is a reflection of your organization's commitment to user-centered design, so be sure to invest in the most effective methodology available. The next chapter outlines the interface design standards you will need to design efficiently and consistently while following the methodology.

Chapter 5

Interface Design Standards

➤ You can have interface design standards for browser-based applications, mobile devices, USSD (low-end phone), voice response, and other platforms.

➤ If you look at any application or environment, you can likely identify a few screen types that account for approximately 85% of all screen development. Templates are representations of these key screen types and can be used as the "DNA" on which the entire application is built.

➤ In addition to templates, a design standard should include general presentation and operation rules.

➤ Interface design standards save development time, maintain consistency in designs, improve usability, and make maintenance easier.

➤ There are a number of ways to create a design standard. Developing one from scratch should be a last resort.

➤ Design standards can be applied to a website as well as to all of an organization's public sites, extranets, and intranet.

➤ Don't develop standards unless you have a clear plan and resources for disseminating, supporting, and enforcing those standards. The completion of the standards is the beginning of the real process.

When teaching classes on design standards, I always start by asking how many people are excited by the prospect of doing all their future design work under a strict set of standards. Few people respond with enthusiasm. Many feel that design standards will be a terrible restriction, and implementing a standard feels like eliminating creativity. In reality, standards (both methodological and design) are like the well-known melodies in jazz (which musicians also call "standards"). Jazz standards provide a baseline melody, which the artist uses as a starting place from which to begin tasteful improvisation. Interface design standards are essential to provide a similar starting place and format. But it takes a great artist to work within the standard and make something worthwhile, just as it takes a great musician to work within the standards in jazz and create something special.

This chapter explains what interface standards are, explores why they help a usability team be efficient, and describes the content and characteristics of effective standards.

What Is an Interface Design Standard?

As you create a user experience engineering infrastructure, there is probably no more critical component than *interface design standards*. Done right, these standards help users who visit your page feel like they have interacted with a page like it before. With standards, the development is faster and maintenance is easier. But these design standards are *not* methodological standards, *not* software coding standards, *not* style guides, and *not* design principle documents.

Methodological standards, such as those described in Chapter 4 on user-centered design methodology, describe the process for design but do not specify precise design conventions.

Software design standards apply to the design of the underlying software. They do not address presentation-layer design conventions at all.

Style guides are usually like the style guides for writing a manuscript—they document specific fonts, colors, and the proper use of images and may even state the tone for the text. They may make suggestions on other topics, but they do not ensure full design consistency. These types of guidelines are useful, but they are not synonymous with design standards. Basically, a style guide documents rules for presentation style, but it does not get down to the level of specificity necessary to give the user the experience of real operational consistency. The style guide does not dictate the navigational and operational details of each screen, nor does it indicate which button is used to go forward—and we do need rules down to the level of selecting OK, Enter, or Continue for the button names.

Organizations often want to document **design principles**, essentially in the hope that such a document will tell designers how to do good interface design. In reality, design principles do not address the specifics needed to ensure design consistency. In any case, people rarely read documents of that sort. It is usually better to spend money on training rather than on writing a design principles document.

Interface design standards establish very specific requirements for the way screens look and operate. The key to these standards is the idea of a reusable screen type, pattern, or screen design template.

Types of Standards

You do not need a different standard for every system. You can create one standard that covers an entire range of applications in a given platform, such as a browser. A browser, for example, is used for both public and private websites—but that does not mean that you need different standards for each of those environments. A form can be designed with a set of conventions (such as how to show required fields), and those conventions can apply nicely across a wide range of systems and environments. If the interactive environment is different, however, you will need another interface standard. For example, a browser interface has different conventions from a thick client, a mobile application, and a voice response system. Each of these requires a separate standard. The browser standard can be extended to cover browser-based interactions on tablets and smartphones using responsive design, but then you need a browser standard that covers responsive design.

You do *not* need a different standard for each type of application. There might be cases where you have very different users and scenarios between applications, of course. You might find that you have scientists using one application and high school students using another. Do these two populations need a different design for data entry forms? They really don't need different standards. We can pick one name for Enter and decide if the field labels will be followed by a colon. Such a decision can be applied across both of these populations without difficulty. There may be some screen types in the standard that are appropriate for scientists but not for students. A complex tree view, for instance, might be a bit difficult for the students to understand, in which case we would simply not use that screen type for a younger population.

Screen Design Templates

If you look at any given Web environment, you will find a limited number of page types that account for approximately 85% of the total development time.[1] Some of the most common page types are home pages, forms, wizards, and database maintenance pages. The number of page types is not infinite; you might need a total of 10–15 page types for an entire environment.

Ideally, you will develop templates of commonly used page types and then modify them to create the specific instances you need. For example, on a form you would change the headers and field labels, but you would not need to change the Enter button name or the conventions of left alignment and required field marking.

The templates you create will become the foundation of your template-based standards; these standards can be developed for computer software screens as well as webpages. Figure 5-1 shows an example of a template for a wizard. This template reflects good

---

1. This figure is based on HFI's 20 years of experience in user interface design and standards development.

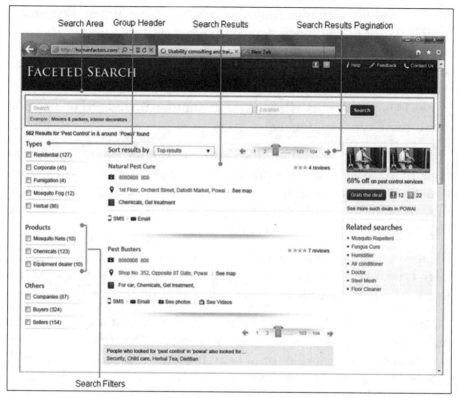

Figure 5-1: *Example of a reusable standard page template for a faceted search, taken from UX Enterprise*

design practices, even for the parts of the interface design that are not standard, and will be customized by developers when using this particular wizard. A template should include accompanying documentation on when to use a page type, rules for the parts of the page that are standardized, a prototyping tool (allowing the template to be quickly converted into an individual page or screen), and reusable code.

Instead of creating each page from scratch, the developer can consider the user's task and then select the template page or pages that support that taskflow. As a consequence, he or she can work at a higher level instead of a very detailed level. Identifying the type of page needed and choosing the best template, the developer can decide whether to use a menu, a display table, or a wizard and then copy the conventions for the page type. If necessary, the developer can create hybrid pages that combine multiple types. Without a design standard, developers must invest time in creating everything from a name for each button to navigational features. The names and features they select are often ergonomically unsound, and the user is left to try to figure out the meaning of the buttons on each page. This problem is why a design standard needs to be specific about these types of details.

The templates serve as the "DNA" for all designs, so they must provide an example of quality design in all respects. At the same time, you need to identify and document those aspects of the template that are actually standards. Standards fall into two categories: basic standards and optional standards.

Basic standards are elements that you must have to use a given page type. They include the features that will identify the page type to the user and the universal ways of operating the screen.

Optional standards are a little more complex, but are required to make the standards work. They are elements that may or may not be needed. For example, on a search page, you may or may not require a link for an advanced search. The optional standard says that if you don't need an advanced search, you can leave it out. If you do need this feature, then you *must* call it "Advanced Search" and place it in a consistent spot on the page. These rules need to be documented so that developers can look any item up and know what is actually required.

Improvements in technology for applying reusable code and content management have made the template concept work even better. These technologies make it easy to use program modules to support a given function on multiple pages. Once a defined page type exists, developers can readily write code to support it. In turn, designers actually need to do even *more* work if they want to violate the standard—they have to go into the reusable module and edit it.

Patterns

The screen template approach described in the preceding section works by describing overall screens and then having designers

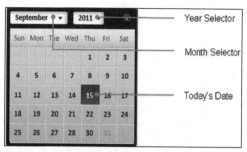

Figure 5-2: *Example of a reusable pattern for a calendar component, taken from UX Enterprise*

modify those screens with task-specific content. An alternative "pattern" approach attempts to provide smaller standard modules—an address, calendar, or carousel, for instance—that can then be combined to create a screen. While this design practice is certainly efficient, it comes with a catch.

Organizations that create a half-dozen commonly used patterns do very well. Other organizations, however, may try to create components to handle almost all of their interface design needs. In most cases, this amounts to hundreds of items. After some time, it becomes quite difficult to find the pattern that you need, particularly as you develop more variations of those patterns—with the result that the patterns stop being used. We recommend limiting your pattern library to a couple of dozen designs, not hundreds (see Figure 5-2 for an example of a reusable pattern).

Other Contents of a Design Standard

While page templates are the core of a good design standard, other sections and materials are needed as well. Some requirements and issues, such as those listed here, arise with all page types:

- Header and footer designs
- Error handling (pop-ups, inline error messages, embedded messages, graphic treatments, and formats for message wording)

- Button labels (guidelines such as "Use 'Next' button to get the following page" and "Do not use 'Forward,' 'Continue,' ' OK,' 'Up,' or 'Down' buttons to get the following page.")
- Justification of text
- Alignment of labels and data fields
- Formats for data (such as addresses and phone numbers)
- Fonts
- Restrictions on color usage

There is some overlap between style guide issues and design standards, of course. In many cases, the entire contents of the style guide can be incorporated into the general principles section of the design standard.

The Scope of Design Standards

It is important to note what is *not* included in the design standard. Except where there is a need to create a unified style and theme, it is best to leave significant design freedom to the developers. For example, an intranet may include hundreds of sites, and many will require different themes. The design standard should generally address only the elements critical to the user's recognition and the operation of each page type—or restrictions needed to ensure a consistent brand perception.

It is important not to mix up the design rationale with the research behind various decisions within the design standard; this would create an unmanageable amount of work and a vast body of information when developing standards. Such documentation can overwhelm developers and other users of the design standards. The design standard should describe only the *results* of all this research. The full research and rationale can be archived in books or explored in training.

Some design standards go so far as to document the windowing environment or browser operation. In our view, it is a waste of time to document third-party environments, operations, and purchased facilities like e-mail clients, along with anything you will build only once. For example, standards for the design of a staff directory aren't necessary because these standards apply to just that one application, and it is a one-time deliverable. It is far more efficient simply to develop specifications and build the directory instead of writing a standard that will guide the specification.

Another pitfall in this standardization process is the specification of underlying technology and coding practices. There is no question that technical standards are needed, but the design standards specify requirements for the presentation layer. While these requirements must be carefully reviewed to ensure that they can be implemented, there is no reason to make the presentation-layer standards dependent on the technology. It is wise to code the presentation layer separately. It is also wise to keep standards for middleware, databases, and coding practices separate from the design standards.

An interface design standard can cover a single application or a suite of applications, or a single Web site or a family of sites. For example, a financial institution might have a site for retail banking, a site for commercial banking, a brokerage site, and a corporate site. These sites might have different headers and footers. Different style guides might dictate different colors. But at the end of a form, all the sites should use the *same word* to say Enter rather than referring to the same function by different names (e.g., Enter, Submit, OK, Continue, Go). A single standard can cover a whole family of sites, such that when customers go from one site to another, they see that the company is consistent in its practices.

It is also possible to have a single design standard cover public Web sites, extranets. and the intranet. While some activities provided in the intranet could never be offered to the public—complex database maintenance, for example—there is a considerable advantage in using the same interface design conventions in multiple environments, such as for single functions or content modules. For example, current product features must be seen by the public—yet marketing staff, customer service representatives and suppliers must view those features, too. If the design standards are consistent, that page can be shared with all users.

You can also develop standards that work across different operating systems. While the controls for a form might differ somewhat in shape and style for each operating system, most of the conventions can be generalized successfully. While differences in hardware platforms do force some variations in page designs, you must make sure that a user who accidentally follows the wrong platform convention does not encounter any serious problems. If you make the Enter key mean "take an action" in one environment and "move to the next field" in another, for example, you will frustrate users and create significant mistakes.

Design standards can cover a very wide range of applications, but the one place where they cannot usually stretch is between platforms and technologies. For example, a standard for a voice response system cannot be applied to Web design. The standard scripting that works for telephone interactions does not apply to the Web. Also, as of this writing, it is difficult to develop a standard for both windowing applications and Web sites because the user expectations are quite different for each platform. Therefore, you need separate standards, although the page design, operation, and other attributes should remain as consistent and compatible as possible.

The Value of Design Standards

Design standards save development time. For example, instead of developers spending hours reinventing design decisions such as whether to call a button "Enter" or "OK" and where to place that button, they can simply refer to the design standards. This also ensures that all members of a team of developers can follow the same guidelines and makes the pages of an application or site consistent.

A design standard also saves development time by supporting the creation of reusable code. For example, if you define a single way for a search and list page to work, you can create reusable code to support that design. Applying that page type then simply requires making changes to the base code. This practice also reduces the need for quality assurance because the reusable code has already been debugged.

Design standards make applications more usable: because the designs are consistent, users can generalize their knowledge of how one screen works to all the other screens of the same type. If the standard is successful, users will look at the screen and think, "Hey! I've seen screens like this before." The screen then works the way they expect. This consistency has tremendous value, even if the designs are a bit suboptimal or idiosyncratic. Standard designs are likely to be far superior to ad hoc designs ergonomically, however. Ad hoc designs are generally created by an individual with limited experience and limited time, whereas a standard represents the best thinking of an entire committee—generally including highly experienced usability staff. Also, because the decisions of that committee are leveraged across hundreds of designs, the committee members tend to work harder on each design decision.

Design standards make maintenance and upgrades easier, too. For example, the development of a new DHTML slider control might make some graphic display standards obsolete. Assume that this slider is so compelling that all designs really have to be changed to take advantage of it. This change requires that the standard be upgraded, with the change then being applied to designs across the organization—a lot of work. Without a standard, you must scan through a wilderness of different graphic display designs, consider each one separately, reinvent each design, code it, and then test it. With a standard, however, you can review page types and find those places where the slider is needed. These changes can then be systematically rippled across all those page types—a vastly more simple process.

A few other intangible advantages of standards are quite significant. In a standards-based design process, the attention and creativity of developers will shift to more productive areas. For example, instead of having to worry about how to reinvent another type of menu, they can apply their creativity to understanding user taskflows and making improvements; instead of renaming the OK button, they can find a faster way to process claims.

Standards also support the creation of a unified brand—a critical element in a public Web site or private intranet site. The standard can provide a site with a sense of cohesion, organization, and reliability. Many customers become confused when they find that designs are different between modules of a single application or sections of a Web site. Consistent designs, in contrast, create a positive impression—a seamless experience that supports the brand.

While developers may initially resist the implementation of a design standard, it is essential to have one if you must do a significant amount of development. In fact, experienced developers are becoming more welcoming toward usable standards. They recognize that standards make it easier for other resources within a user experience design-centered organization to help them design pages or screens that allow users to run applications successfully.

The Process and Cost of Developing Standards

Standards development should be a high priority when creating a strategy, and it should be tackled early in the activities list. There are three ways to get a design standard: buy a generic standard, customize a generic standard, or create a standard from scratch.

If you have a small company or a lean operation with typical interface needs, it makes sense to start with a purchased, generic standard. Clearly, you'll eventually need to add conventions for your business area, special branding, specific user needs, and so on, but the off-the-shelf product will give your company a head start. You can start small, with customizations, and gradually build up your standard elements.

If you have a large company or your environment has many special needs, you need a full design standard, including a customized set of page types with specific designs to reflect your conventions and user needs, your brand (not just in color and logo), and the personality of your company—down to the style of interaction and page layout.

Purchased standards are a good starting point for a custom standard, even for a large organization. It is quicker to modify a standard than to create one from scratch. Full customization of a generic standard generally takes six to eight weeks.

In some situations, you will need to create a standard from scratch. The most typical case is one where your environment is so idiosyncratic that you can find no generic standard that remotely fits your requirements. The introduction of a new interface technology, for example, might mean there are no generic standards. Also, sometimes the corporate culture strongly values internally designed materials. If you decide to create design standards from scratch, be aware that this can be a long, painful process with many challenges. It will take a minimum of three months and perhaps even up to a year to do it right. The process will typically require $180,000 for a consultant's support.

If you are customizing a standard or creating one from scratch, you probably need to employ a committee-driven process with a usability consultant as a facilitator. This method starts with a review of your strategy, business areas, applications, and sites that seeks to determine the types of screens you need. The consultant then designs a good example of each page type (these prototypes may be based partly on your screens and partly on a purchased standard). This set of designs goes into a committee process. The committee, made up of the key opinion leaders in the development organizations, reviews the designs and decides whether the approach for each screen type is appropriate. This is a concrete process; the committee is essentially asked, "Is this the way you want to do a menu/form/wizard?" The final standard is based on their decisions. The process for customizing a generic standard takes usually takes from six to eight weeks and costs about $100,000 (for the modification of the standards deliverable, including the consultant's fees). If you can make your own design decisions without this level of facilitation and high-level guidance, however, your cost can be cut nearly in half.

No matter which method you use, here is one important piece of advice: ensure that your standards effort will not run out of steam by the time the standard gets written. Sometimes committees suffer from endless cycles of iteration during the standards creation process. After a year-long process, the standard may finally be complete, but committee members may by now be so sick of the process that they have lost the motivation to push the standard into adoption. In fact, the completion of your standards is just the beginning of the real process. It is important to pace yourself accordingly. No matter which method you choose to create a standard, be sure that you have the energy, will, and resources to follow through with its implementation.

Disseminating, Supporting, and Enforcing Standards

Before investing in a standard, be sure to plan for its dissemination and support. This means training, consulting, and enforcement.

Even though the design standard may strongly support creativity and improve an application's or Web site's usability, the resentment of standards is real. Thus, unless you work to evangelize and uphold that standard, nothing will happen after its creation. Your investment in developing it will be lost. You should not even develop a standard, in fact, unless you have a clear plan and budget for the standard's dissemination and support. Getting the standard written is just the beginning of the process.

At HFI, we have argued vehemently over the years about whether a paper or an online standards document is better. A paper document is easier to work with in some ways; the developer is already using the full screen for design work, so an online standard requires switching between windows. However, there is a significant cost involved in having a paper version of a standard—it must be printed and distributed. Updates will be required, and then it will be difficult to tell if you have the current version. Also, increasingly, purchased standards come with online materials such as reusable code.

If you have an online version of the standard, everyone has access to it. When the standard is updated, everyone gets the new version at the same time. Of course, making sure that everyone *has* the standard is very different from getting everyone to actually *use* the standard. You have to get the word out. Send notices of various kinds and highlight a link to the standard on the developer's intranet pages. Nevertheless, these efforts alone will not be enough to ensure appropriate use of the standard.

It is essential to provide training on the standard. Standards training differs in important ways from training on general usability engineering methods. Standards training needs to sell developers on the value of a standard. It needs to convince them that rather than stifling their creativity, the standard will actually make them more creative, effective, and professional—that there is still plenty of room for creativity with standards, but with a higher quality and consistency that make for better designs.

The standards training also needs to show people how to use the design standards. This means understanding the structure of the design standards themselves and ways to find things within them. Developers must be familiar with the different types of pages and be able to pick those that fit a given situation. They must also know how to use the general presentation rules. All this material can usually be presented in a half-day class. Done well, these classes increase acceptance of the standards and teach people to operate effectively within them.

Preparing reusable code is a powerful way to support standards. Often, a single standard is implemented in different environments: for example, your menu may be created in Macromedia Dreamweaver and Microsoft FrontPage, as well as by old-fashioned HTML coders working in Microsoft Notepad. It makes sense, however, to select the main environment(s) and create reusable code as a specific project. This may mean creating a template for each page type in a browser environment. The development process then becomes faster, and developers have to work harder to violate the standard. Maintenance is also easier because common code underlies the various pages. Alternatively, page designs may be placed in a content management tool. Whatever the environment, the introduction of reusable code will help move the standard into general usage.

With dissemination of the standard, along with training and tools that provide support for it, developers will start to try to follow the standard. They will sometimes have misconceptions or otherwise run into trouble when working with the standard. They might think that optional standards are required, might not understand which page to use for a given user task, or might even think that the content in the examples must be copied into the designs. Poor results like these can threaten the entire standardization effort. Designate one person or team as a resource to contact for help. The best way to staff this position is with internal consultants—key staff members within the central usability organization who can answer commonly asked questions quickly.

If a developer reinvents a page, however, there is no question for the internal consultants to answer. While the developer may be happy in such a case, the standard is undermined. Without feedback to the developer or immediate feedback to management, there is only a silent unraveling of your standards investment and, eventually, poor usability of the application itself. The only answer to this type of scenario is some type of enforcement.

Enforcement of standards is a hot topic. While it can be unpleasant in practice, some form of enforcement is required. The trick is to make this process fit the corporate culture. In some organizations, heavy-handed enforcement is natural and normal. In other environments, the very idea is abhorrent. In the latter case, don't call this practice "enforcement," but do at least institute feedback. Have designs reviewed by a usability engineer, and point out to developers specific places where they have violated standards.

The most common, worrisome problem is the reinventing of page types. Developers may attempt to create a new type of menu, for example. The review cycle for such elements is the time to point to the standard menu and suggest that developers use an approved page type to fit their needs. In some cases, all you can do is give feedback. In other environments, you might require changes, reporting the level of compliance to the developer's manager. The need for support of your standard is an ongoing requirement. At HFI, we have often created offshore teams that scan all screens for both ergonomic quality and adherence to standards. It has been a cost-effective way to ensure that standards are routinely applied.

Even after you have developed standards, they will continue to need attention. The standard is a living document. You will need to make improvements, add page types, and clarify areas that receive frequent consulting questions. It is also likely that areas where refinements are needed will be brought to your attention after your showcase project is launched. This refinement will lead to further improvements and greater buy-in from all users.

Summary

Implementing interface design standards should be a high priority for any serious, user-centered design strategy. The initial costs to create standards may seem high, but the return on investment in terms of branding, consistency, navigation, performance, and time savings from following template-based options more than offsets them. These gains will far outweigh any initial cost. Remember, the completion of the standards is the beginning of the real process—using them for actual UX design work. The next chapter outlines the steps for achieving a successful showcase project, which will also present an opportunity to refine your organization's standards.

Chapter 6

Standard User Profiles and Ecosystem Models

> ➤ Why knowledge of users and ecosystems is so important.
> ➤ Working with various levels of user knowledge.
> ➤ The imperative of a shared standard.
> ➤ Static versus organically growing standard models.

If you ask a good tailor to make a suit, the tailor is sure to ask you to come in for extensive measurements. Savvy executives know to hand the tailor a large tip to ensure that the job is done with great care—it's that critical. Of course, you *can* create a suit without any measurements. There are common features, after all (most of us have two arms and two legs). A "one size fits all" solution is seldom flattering, however, and is not really able to fit all. It is the same with user experience design. Some features are common to almost all users. Most users can see color in the way that humans see color, for example. Even so, we can expect that roughly 9% of men will have some color perception weakness, and we know that putting red on black makes an effect called chromosteriopsis (making the object look three dimensional). Thus we can design based on these general principles—but not well.

Before 1995 or so, usability specialists concentrated on designing human–computer interactions. To build these focused dialogs, we needed to know about the user population, their tasks, and the environment they worked in. That was really enough when we were working with a computer that sat on a desk and was used by a single person, in an office-like environment. Today, of course, computing is much more ubiquitous. Computers are used everywhere and in much more complicated and interrelated ways. We now need to employ ethnographically inspired methods to understand many different users (or "actors," in ethnographic terminology), interacting in diverse environments, using various artifacts (such as tools, art, and electronic devices), in a variety of scenarios. That makes it harder to "know your user"—but it also makes such knowledge far more critical.

I'm often asked why Apple Computer was so successful with the iPhone, iPad, and other such devices. Without question, these items are nicely designed. Apple also uses a lot of persuasion methods (such as keeping people waiting in line for purchases of new models). But the core reason for Apple's success is that the company developed an ecosystem solution. It is not just selling a smartphone or a tablet; it is selling a device that allows people to access material in a huge application vending website, and go to a physical store where Geniuses provide support. In the same way, the Kindle Fire, which was initially an awkward tablet, sold millions of units because it was a portal to the Amazon.com environment.

Today it is essential to know your user's complex ecosystem. However, that ecosystem is big, complex, and difficult for a single person to understand, much less research extensively.

The Worst Practice

Some user experience design practitioners are forced to design without good data on customers. Many have limitations because their organization will not invest in data gathering. This is particularly true with offshore operations, where the cost of travel becomes prohibitive. Some UX designers are just not trained properly. But the worst of the lot are those who think they already know everything and don't need to learn more to do their design work. In all cases, these designers are able to apply general principles, so the user experience design work is not without value. Unfortunately, the resulting design cannot be adjusted to the real needs, workflow, environmental factors, and cultural perspective of the users.

You need to know your users. Here are a few examples explaining why this is important from my own experience.

HFI was once approached by a medical device company that had a moderately complex device that was successfully used in American homes. The company wanted to adapt the device for sale in India, China, and Brazil. It asked if HFI could translate the instructions for these new markets. Soon, however, the company realized that those ecosystems are different and actually required a substantially different design. It was initially surprised to realize that a continuous power supply, clean water, and literate caregivers were not always available in the new target markets.

I once designed a website that claimed that it had great security—the organization's head of security taunted hackers to just try to get to his account. I thought it was a brilliant, persuasive design, but our research quickly showed that the design terrified local users. Rather than being more persuaded to trust the site, they were actually made more afraid by my design.

On another occasion, I was reviewing a Japanese website and was quite certain I had found a serious flaw. The user was constantly hounded by "Are you sure?" questions. The website included unnecessarily detailed instructions that went so far as to feature a downloadable PDF with a detailed description of each vegetable. Apala, however, pointed out that the Japanese have very high uncertainty avoidance. The level of detail and extensive instructions and verifications worked for the users. They even wanted the phone numbers of the company's officers.

Even very smart and experienced user experience designers will do poor work without solid models of the user population and entire ecosystem.

Thin Personas: "Jane Is 34 and Has a Cat"

Some user experience design operations proceed with only "thin personas." If you truly understand a set of people, you will understand the group in terms of many dimensions and characteristics. Most of these are best understood as distributions of data (see Figure 6-1). In the bottom distribution of Figure 6-1, we can see that substantial populations are focused on physiological, safety, and love/belonging needs. This is useful information—but in making a persona, you create a single fictitious person (occasionally a couple of them). A single person must represent the entire population. Such a persona is quite useful in sharing insights with armatures, but professional user experience design experts should always work with user profiles and not with personas.

It is also important to include the things about the user community that are important to design. In a thin persona, we often are given very little information of use. If we are told that "Jane is 34 and has a cat," what do we know that we can apply to design? We might suspect that our user population centers on an age of 34, but we don't know if it includes kids or seniors. Also, knowing that your population includes kids or seniors changes a lot in your design. Moreover, while pet ownership is a recurring theme in thin personas, it does not impact design (with the exception of a few pet management-related projects).

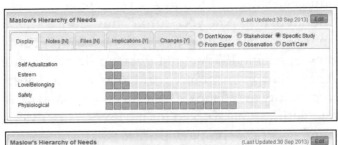

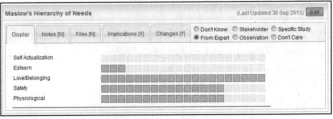

Figure 6-1: *Population distribution of needs, taken from UX Enterprise. Note that both of these charts show a few people focused on self-actualization, and many more people focused on physiological needs and love/belonging needs, respectively.*

Quality Personas

Even the richest personas have the problem of missing out on the insights you get from distributions. The good ones, however, can be a quick way even for a professional to grasp the user profile. An in-depth persona description will provide real depth in areas that matter to the design (see Figure 6-2). A good persona may also characterize the fictitious user with a simulated interview and even a DILO (Day In the Life Of, pronounced "die-low") model.

Quality personas are a bit useful, and we start to see the potential of having a centralized standard set. These centralized and standardized personas can reduce the amount of data gathering that teams have to complete. At least they start to reduce the amount of time spent repeating the same research over and over again.

While creating standard personas is useful, we hate to see this as a primary initiative in the institutionalization of a user experience design practice. Many organizations make this their first project, and at the end they just have a set of fictitious people. Someone always asks how that outcome has justified the cost of development. This is an embarrassing question, because those personas won't do anything until they are applied. In addition, the decision makers in the organization are unlikely to understand and feel good about the expenditure.

Figure 6-2: *User profile, on sale at UX Marketplace*

The Best Practice: Working with Full Ecosystems

Today's environment is characterized by truly ubiquitous computing. We develop applications that are used in a wide range of complex environments. We can no longer just look at one user operating one device. We need to design for complex ecosystems that have many user types (or "actors"), involved in many scenarios, in many environments, using many artifacts, and therein using our software (Figure 6-3). We have had to learn to apply ethnographically inspired methods to develop this type of understanding. Most real ethnographers, of course, spend months or years observing a culture—but we just don't have that much time. Even so, we can gather this type of widespread understanding on a given context.

The best practice of user experience design is to work from these ecosystem models and often design offerings that adapt to these ecosystems. Every organization has a range of ecosystems it tends to work with. To be able to claim that you truly "know your

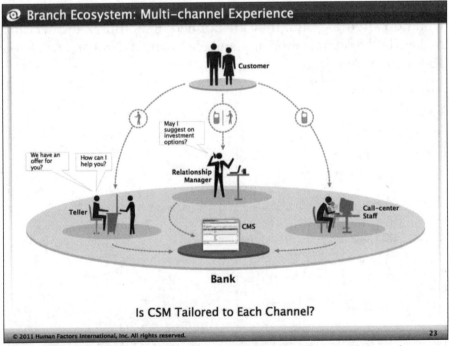

23

Figure 6-3: *A high-level ecosystem drawing for a bank branch*

customer," you must have a good model of all the major ecosystems that you target.

Standard User Profiles and Ecosystems

A thin persona takes very little time to develop, but you get what you pay for (though it might be better than nothing). In contrast, a serious user experience design team needs to get solid ecosystem models that can cost a lot to develop. Just studying one environment, such as an x-ray room in a hospital or use of mobile phones by middle-market digital natives in New York, can easily cost $250,000. Now consider how management will like having to pay this bill for each project. The costs become prohibitive very quickly. But there is a solution that makes it possible to work off of good data while keeping research costs to a reasonable level.

The answer to managing the cost of ecosystem research is to first maintain a shared standard for the commonly addressed ecosystems. Most organizations have a limited number of ecosystems that they address. A bank focuses on a branch, a high-net-worth client, a call center, and so on. An e-commerce company perhaps focuses on house renovations, with householders, contractors, families, and bankers as components of the ecosystem. A media company works on ecosystems of commuters, homemakers, and advertising buyers. There may be a dozen different ecosystems that are important—but the number is hardly infinite. In turn, we can create standard ecosystem models based on research and apply those findings to different projects for years. The cost of the research is amortized over dozens of programs, and now that $250,000 total cost for the research looks like $20,000 for each project, which is pretty easy to justify.

When we develop standard user interfaces, we always start with a generic set, if possible (see Figure 6-4 for examples). It is far easier to edit three generic interfaces than to develop those three standards from scratch. In the same way, a major benefit can be realized from the acquisition of baseline research that can then be fine-tuned to your specific environment.

By acquiring a generic ecosystem model for your domain, you will have a much easier time creating a model for your specific

Figure 6-4: *A generic set of health care-related user profiles available for $900 from www.uxmarketplace.com*

organization. You can focus your efforts on what makes your situation special, instead of wasting time documenting common knowledge.

Acquired ecosystem objects can even be merged to provide a more sophisticated starting place. For example, you might need to create a health care ecosystem for China. If you can get profiles for only American health care users, you might be able to merge those American users with Chinese cultural attributes and obtain at least a generic starting place that will be closer to the ecosystem knowledge you really need.

If you have complex needs, it becomes important to have ecosystem models that can be accessed using a relational database. As an example, let's think about a pharmaceutical company. It might need to see the ecosystem knowledge about a surgeon's use of a hospital pharmacy. There may have never been a specific study focused solely on this area, but a relational database can pull up all the ecosystem knowledge gathered from various studies that would apply. In the same way, a bank might need to know about high-net-worth customers' use of a branch ATM (Figure 6-5). It is unlikely that a specific study will have addressed this issue, but there might be enough parts to pull together to get a pretty good idea of that ecosystem. Perhaps the understanding will not be sufficient to create a design, but at least it can be used as a starting place to do more focused research.

At first glance, it might seem obvious which ecosystems will matter for your environment. A bank wants to know about branches; a media company cares about how people watch videos. In reality, the definition of an ecosystem quickly becomes very complex, because various ecosystems can be very different. The branch ecosystem consists of

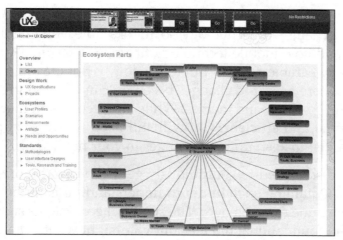

Figure 6-5: *Even though a specific study with this focus has never been done, we can still see everything we know about high-net-worth customers' use of a branch ATM using the UXEnterprise environment*

knowledge of everything around an environment; the watching videos ecosystem entails knowledge of everything around a scenario. In fact, ecosystems may be centered on almost anything. You might need to know everything about how a given design is used, or what a user experiences. You might need to know the focus of a previous study, everything around high-level design projects that have been completed, or everything around a strategic need (such as migrating customers to digital channels or reducing calls to the support group). And if this is not complex enough, you might need to know about combinations. For example, you might need to know about a user in an environment (e.g., a surgeon in her office), or about multiple users, using a device, while completing a scenario, in an environment (e.g., a family using mobile devices while watching movies at home). With these permutations, you can see why a relational database is almost essential for managing ecosystem knowledge.

Static versus Organic Models

Even if you have a very focused business, you will never really achieve a complete and final understanding of your customer. Your standard ecosystem models will always need to expand.

Today we live in times where every ecosystem is subject to change. There are changes in technology, so, for example, you might need to understand how mobile technology fits in, or near-field communication, or wearable devices. But technology is not the only source of change. There are rapid changes based on climate, and geopolitics, and shifting values, and memes. While your ecosystem models may be essential and efficient, you will still need to invest in periodic updates, just to keep up with changes in your field.

There is also a need to continuously get deeper and more specific insights. Obtaining such in-depth understanding is far better than doing the same research over. The standard ecosystems should provide solid foundational models, but you might want to conduct in-depth studies of how customers feel about using an ATM. That research will then need to be added to the existing ecosystem model. You will also find that good research tends to reveal a very complex and interesting set of driving forces, roadblocks, beliefs, and feelings. Beyond the obvious cost savings attributable to a shared and standard ecosystem model, there is value in letting research focus on more sophisticated issues.

Summary

Every organization should have standard, shared ecosystem models for the major user domains in its space. Development of such models eliminates the need for (and cost of) re-researching your customers. Even more important, it allows you to invest in research that gives a deeper and more specific understanding of your customers. You can also amortize the cost of the research across years of development projects.

For large-scale organizations, it is important to have these ecosystem models computerized so that they can be continuously upgraded. In addition, they must have relational database capabilities so that you can pull out just the knowledge of interest to your design project.

Chapter 7

Tools, Templates, and Testing Facilities

➤ If you throw usability staff into the organization without the right equipment, they are going to be slow and inefficient, and impractical in their approach.

➤ Get appropriate tools (e.g., lab equipment and prototyping software), templates (e.g., reusable questionnaires), and testing facilities. These items form an essential toolkit—the core infrastructure for routine usability work.

➤ Your toolkit can enable usability designers to efficiently complete the user experience design methodology. To determine the toolkit you need, review your methodology.

A well-trained staff in a room with nothing but paper can out-design a poorly trained staff equipped with a state-of-the-art facility. While in China, I was once given a tour of a half-million-dollar usability testing facility. It was impressive—very advanced looking. Later, in quiet conversations with the staff, it became clear that the team had no idea what to do with the facility. They had equipment, but no software to support the testing, and no methods or skills.

The main value of facilities, tools, and templates derives from time savings. Instead of creating a testing form from scratch every time a test is needed, a user experience design engineer can take an existing form and modify it for a client's specific test in approximately 20 minutes. By comparison, creating the concept and forms for a test from scratch may take days or even weeks. Clearly, it is advantageous to hire good staff members and supply them with the tools that can make a difference.

This chapter outlines the tools you need, the templates that are helpful, and the usability testing facilities that will help your staff be most efficient and effective. Of course, by the time this book is published, some of the tools and templates described here may be outdated. New developments are taking place all the time. For example, you might hear that usability testing labs have recently moved from "marginally useful in special circumstances" to being "a practical part of almost every test." Or you might learn that remote testing, which isn't used often today, is becoming far more practical and, therefore, much more widely used. **Remote testing** is usability testing performed at a distance; the participant and the facilitator are not in the room together (and may not even be on the same continent), yet the facilitator can monitor what the participant is doing and saying. **Unmoderated remote tests** are tests that are run automatically. The participant interacts with a scripted program that collects performance data and responses. Because the contents of toolkits will likely change, a skeptical attitude about these tools is useful—if a tool does not really make a difference in the design, spend your usability testing budget elsewhere.

Introduction to Your Toolkit

Your methodology points to the facilities, tools, and templates you need. For example, if the methodology specifies that a test of branding occurs at a certain point, you will want to have templates for reusable questionnaires and a standard template for the final report.

If you update your methodology, you may need to update the corresponding tools, templates, and facilities as well. Conversely, the introduction of new facilities, tools, and templates might lead you to change your methodology. Online prototyping has become easier, for example, so you might move it to an earlier point in the design cycle. Likewise, as remote testing becomes more feasible and useful, you might add it to your methodology and develop new tools and templates to fit it. Be careful about implementing these kinds of changes, however: some "amazing" breakthroughs are actually not particularly useful. Consider the new, crowdsourcing solutions that let many people review your design. While there are some known advantages to crowdsourcing supporting innovation, having a load of armatures be reviewed out of context may not be a valid methodology.

The following sections cover the infrastructure you should consider implementing at your company. They also explore scenarios and priorities for each facility.

Testing Facilities

Depending on the circumstances, testing facilities can range from a simple office setting or hotel room to a full-blown usability testing lab. Of course, a full usability testing lab is not necessary to conduct usability testing. If office space is at a premium, the office of one of the usability team members can be used for testing. There may not be a one-way mirror, special equipment, or videotaping in such a site; instead, you may have only a few chairs, a desk, and a computer at your disposal. Skilled staff members, however, can still successfully create and run the tests. Similarly, it is quite acceptable to use a conference room to run tests, but it is critical that the room be reasonably quiet and free of visual and auditory interruptions. For this reason, it is best practice not to use participants' workspaces for testing. You can observe them there, but workspaces are not good places to run tests.

There are a number of reasons for establishing a formal, dedicated usability testing facility. Notably, designating a space for testing shows a commitment to testing within the organization. While it is nice to have a room or perhaps a suite with that label, the practical value of a usability testing facility is less significant than the political statement it makes. Of course, the facility becomes an albatross if it is not regularly used—or evolves into a storage space.

While running tests in storage closets can still yield quite good results, it is best to have a testing environment that makes the participants and the facilitator feel comfortable and important. If you can make the test a relaxed experience, you will get more accurate and complete results. At the same time, you do not want the evaluation environment to feel *too* formal. Facilities that feel imposing and clinical should be avoided. Usability engineers call the people who engage in testing *participants* instead of *subjects* for a reason; no one likes to feel like a lab rat!

Facilitating a test is a very demanding activity. It takes focus, and it's difficult, if not impossible, for one person to simultaneously keep the test process running, observe the nuances of the results, and record data. There is no additional energy or time left to greet participants, provide the initial forms, and hand out the compensation once the testing is complete. Consequently, it is very useful to have additional staff available to handle these functions. Professional testing facilities, for example, have support staff.

In some cases, you will need a facility geographically separated from your offices. You might decide to do testing in a number of cities intermittently, or you might even need to complete testing in these different cities quite often. In this scenario, it makes sense to establish a relationship with a testing facility in each location. These testing facilities are generally set up for marketing studies, but they work well for usability testing. It is also possible to use a conference room in a hotel, but testing facilities come with valuable amenities such as a greeter, a one-way mirror, built-in sound and video, and usually a more comfortable atmosphere.

Whether you sign a contract with a professional testing facility or build your own testing space, there are a few other advantages associated with use of a professional testing facility versus use of a simple conference room for usability testing. Figures 7-1 and 7-2 show the appearance of a typical professional testing facility. Your facility may have a one-way mirror. Most people can tell when you have a one-way mirror, so if your facility has one in place, you should be

Figure 7-1: *Observer's side of a professional testing facility using a one-way mirror*[1]

Figure 7-2: *User's side of a professional testing facility using a one-way mirror*[2]

1. Photo courtesy of the Bureau of Labor Statistics.
2. Photo courtesy of the Bureau of Labor Statistics.

straightforward about it. With proper briefing, the mirror works very well. Developers, business owners, and marketing and usability staff can come to the site and observe the participants without disturbing the test. They can discuss what they see and send in their questions to the test facilitator. Alternatively, instead of a one-way mirror, you can use video feeds to adjacent rooms to allow others to observe without disturbing the test.

Recording of Testing Sessions

There is value in recording data-gathering and testing sessions. Professional facilities have video capability, and the new portable labs support video as part of their software.

Two types of recording usage may be employed. One common practice is to produce a full video recording of the session for the record. A continuous tape is made of the test, and you end up with many hours of tape. If someone later says, "I don't believe the user actually did that," you can offer to let him or her see the appropriate portion of the tape. In other cases, a much shorter highlights tape is culled from the full videotaping sessions. This edited video, 5–10 minutes long, shows key findings of the usability testing through the voices and actions of the participants themselves. Carefully selected examples on well-edited highlights tapes often can depoliticize the usability test findings: the finding is no longer the "opinion" of the tester, but rather the voice of the participant. Highlights tapes effectively grip the audience's attention when used as part of the final presentation (which, from a practical standpoint, cannot be done with the full, unedited video of the session). This is a very effective practice—there is nothing like showing video of the users in action.

In the past, recording sessions were prohibitively expensive, but the "shoebox" usability equipment available today (see Figure 7-3) has made the cost much more reasonable. Such equipment includes a TV camera, microphone, monitor, and a remote marker to make it easy to find interesting tape segments. There is actually no tape— just a high-capacity hard drive to save the data—so it is also far

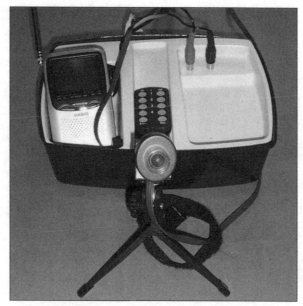

Figure 7-3: *Shoebox usability equipment*

easier to edit and present the results. This ease of use, combined with its reasonable cost, makes the shoebox lab a practical alternative to traditional equipment.

Most labs are using applications and hardware that make video editing increasingly efficient. With these new facilities, you can easily place parts of the video record in the report (see the sample of a test presentation video in Figure 7-4). The lab software lets you record the user's facial expressions and the activity on the screen. You can then add detail to reports with clear instances of user actions and reactions.

A few labs use an eye-tracking device, which identifies where the user's eye is fixating. You can gain a lot of information from this device. For example, you can see users scanning around the page because they are lost or scanning an image because they cannot tell if it is selectable.

Eye-tracking devices are very useful for research purposes. For example, studies have shown that people start scanning in the main area of a webpage and initially ignore the logo, tabs, and left-hand

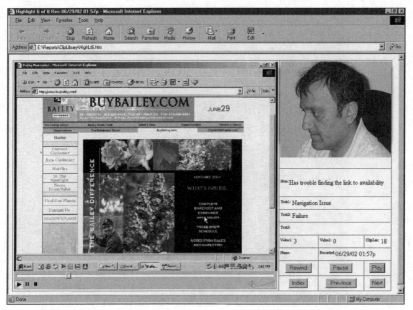

Figure 7-4: *Example of a video record from a usability test*

navigation [Schroeder 1998], and that people's eyes are drawn first to areas that have saturated colors (pure bright colors), darker areas, and areas of visual complexity [Najjar 1990].

You do not need an eye-tracking device to run an excellent usability test. A good facilitator can see where the user is looking and can supply you with very similar data. An eye-tracking device is expensive and requires setup time, so you probably won't use it for routine usability tests. It may come in handy in a remote usability test, however, because the facilitator will not be physically present with the participant.

Modeling Tools and Software

Most of the important usability work can be completed with a simple Microsoft Office suite and software for graphics work. It may help to have a flowcharting package, but that's about all the software you need. You also need to be able to use a word processor to document meetings and descriptions, and to have some kind of tool to mock up screens and pages. Which tool you use is not as critical as making sure that the usability staff members are comfortable with that tool and do not get distracted or waste time writing "code" to make the screen mock-ups work. Some people prefer a graphics program such as Adobe Photoshop, but Microsoft PowerPoint or other presentation tools work just as well. Some usability staff already have facility with tools such as Microsoft Visio. Whatever tool your staff members already know how to use that allows them to quickly mock up screens and pages is the best tool to use.

Selecting Design and Research Tools: Why the Rules Are Changing

*Michael Rawlins, Sr., User Experience Design Architect—
ESPN and President Emeritus, CT UXPA*

The options for selecting UX tools for creating wireframes and conducting research seem ubiquitous. Expect this trend to continue for the foreseeable future. UX teams will play a role in shaping the future proactively by revolutionizing the UX domain while opening the field up to more diverse thinkers and product visionaries.

Innovating the Trigger

Typically, UX teams start the innovation process in response to feedback provided by a new team member or some excitement generated out of a training class or conference demonstration. To innovate more effectively, we need to proactively experiment with software on our own using all trial periods offered by software vendors (take the tools through the paces).

Forget about the Traditional Software Purchase Matrix

Strategies are evolving for influencing funding stakeholders and corporate procurement/purchasing offices (getting them to "say yes") to acquire design and research tools. There are too many tools to perform traditional matrixes—rather, we should perform SWOT analysis (a diagram that maps strengths,

(continues)

Selecting Design and Research Tools: Why the Rules Are Changing (continued)

weakness, opportunities, and threats) to influence funding stakeholder decisions. This will enable you to establish criteria that are more salient:

- Who are the leaders?
- Who are the lagers?
- Who are the obsolete players, and why?

This evolution will continue for the foreseeable future—primarily because some smart product designers noticed opportunities to surpass the industry incumbents. Design and research tools have become vulnerable. Some are "too big to respond"—and some "simply out of touch." It's important to establish "direct" relationships with the software vendors—and join them as product creation collaborators. Tool choices are somewhat overwhelming. Here are a few recommendations to help UX grow and expand.

What Are the New Rules and Expectations?

New expectations have influenced the table stakes in software acquisition. As consumers, we are accustomed to the "no strings attached," full-feature, free-trial period. Here are a few expectations:

- Installation should be as easy as uninstallation.
- No invasive sales interaction will occur during the trial period.
- The software will work as marketed.

UX teams should merge traditional software acquisition strategies while aggressively moving toward a stronger role in influencing software product developers (vendor community).

Three Key Acquisition Strategies

1. *Perform SWOT analysis for research.*

- Why this software?
- Are demos available?

- What are the critical path features of the software—are they "must-have features"?
- Which optional features could be useful?
- Can we cost-effectively and efficiently build this in-house?
- What is the cost of this software?

Questions that lead to innovative thinking:

- Will the software disrupt the current process?
  - Example: Why do we need to sketch on paper, when there is prototyping software that looks like a sketch?
- Is the software easy to adopt—extending the type of resources that can use the tool?
  - Example: Can the UX team delegate specific user testing rounds to non-UX resources?
- Are the software makers/vendors accessible?
  - Will they openly share their product development roadmaps?
  - Are they including the team in ideation sessions?
  - Do they feel like partners?

Nailing this preliminary research is the first step in buying software successfully. Not only does it save you money in the long run, but it also allows you to fully grasp your company's future needs.

Take your time and analyze your company's needs. Vet your SWOT analysis with other UX teams in your company (and create scorecards for how features and capabilities align with the leading software solution).

2. *Costs: Low cost does not equal low value.*

There have been many exciting innovations in software as a service (SAAS) targeted toward enhancing our ability to develop and share interactive prototypes and perform product research. Many of the best tools are subscription based. I see

(continues)

Selecting Design and Research Tools: Why the Rules Are Changing (continued)

this trend becoming more pervasive going forward, with the leaders disrupting the current processes (becoming more "lean" and "time-to-market" focused). UX teams need to be pragmatic about asking cost-structure questions carefully—making sure that the vendor can sustain the long-term viability:

- How did the company form?
- What is the year-over-year performance?
- Are there any rebates available?
- Are you paying for other features that aren't necessary?
- How flexible is the individual per-seat licensing structure?

In an ideal world, cost wouldn't be a determining factor when buying software. Unfortunately, we live in a world where we need and want the price to be right. Making sure you pay only for the features you need is the number one priority when it comes to price.

3. *Learning curve.*

- Who needs to use this software?
- How difficult is it to use and grasp all the important features?
- How much will it cost to train employees?
- Will you have to outsource training?
- Are the time and resources available?

What is the time frame to learn the software? Minimally, there should be a demo version of the software available or a full-feature trial to download. If not, that omission is indicative of the vendor being out of touch.

Conclusions

Most UX professionals are facing the challenges associated with demonstrating our considerable value proposition to product design—especially in the face of shorter time frames and development life cycles. Tools enable us to disrupt the current mindset and contribute to the success of the product design and adoption. Here are a few implied takeaway messages:

- Select tools for prototyping that can be shared with non-UX resources (increase our effectiveness to focus on more valuable project activities).
  - Example: Balsamiq Mockups software allows non-UX resources, using drag-and-drop widgets, to create low-fidelity visual examples. This enables non-UX resources to disrupt the current work streams through collaboration and sharing visions.
- Seek research tools that extend the reach of traditional tools (e.g., remote unmoderated usability testing tools) that can be shared in social media channels.
  - Example: ZURBapps such as Verifyapp and Solidifyapp enable stakeholders to participate in constructing and seeing real-time responses to how people work with their product visions. This disruption to the typical business relationship builds more trust and credibility for the UX community—and leads to a greater understanding of why our methods work.

The rules for selecting software have changed. UX resources need to try as many tools as they can. Don't wait for the new team member, or the inspiration to come from a class or seminar. Download, subscribe, try, blog, complain, and influence!

Sophisticated modeling tools may or may not be necessary. Available software can assist in the development of very large taskflows and the modeling of taskflow behavior. An example of this type of software is Micro Saint (from Micro Analysis and Design, Inc.), which supports task modeling. This software has been used to good effect in very complex, critical applications, especially in the military design arena (although it has yet to be employed in producing commercial websites or applications).

Limited modeling tools are available for usability work. You may wish to create your own. At HFI, we built an application called the Task Modeler—essentially a specialized spreadsheet that adds up the number of clicks, mouse movements, and keystrokes used to complete a task. Using this application on a group of tasks that are representative of the work to be completed on a given interface provides a good indication of the time it will take an expert user to use the software. Such data are important because when measuring how fast users complete tasks during a usability test, you're measuring their speed during their initial usage, not their speed after extended experience with the interface. During the test, users spend only minutes with the software, so they will not be experts on using the interface.

In many cases, however, you may be designing for expert users. Also, you don't want to make the classic blunder of designing your software or application for first usage only. For example, while a menu design that can be used easily and quickly by novices is initially a much better choice than using keyboard commands, commands are usually faster once they are learned. If the software is to be used on a full-time basis, going with the "easy" menu can be a million-dollar mistake.

Many companies have purchased tools to track websites and provide feedback and statistics on usage. Some of these tools claim to provide usability information and are good choices for performing quick checks and validation. For example, some tools let you know if your alt text tags are missing (accessibility tools) or if your line lengths are long. Be wary, however, of tools that track download times for a page, the number of users who clicked on a page, or the amount of time people spent on a webpage, independent of other information. While this information can be useful to know, it can also be misleading. *Why* did a user spend only 3 seconds on a page? Was it because (1) the page is poorly designed, (2) the page is well designed and the user got what he or she wanted right away, or (3) the page *before* the current one was poorly designed, so that the user clicked on the wrong link? You cannot determine this underlying rationale just by reading a report on where people went and how long they stayed. Nothing can replace a trained usability professional for evaluating a screen or page or watching and interpreting users performing a task.

If you are involved in websites, you really should have an A:B testing engine. It is a psychologist's dream. When I was in graduate school, we would run perhaps 30 people through an experiment and we were happy to get that amount of testing done within a single semester. With A:B testing, you can run a comparison study and (for a large site) have 10,000 participants in an hour. The A:B test facility randomly sorts customers onto different versions of the site and then tracks their behavior, such as how much they purchase. It is just a great tool.

Like all tools, however, A:B testing has its limits. The "recipe" you are testing is critical. If you do not test a good idea, there is no way that A:B testing can magically recommend what to do. Companies that rely too heavily on this type of testing may think they are doing great work, but they may be uncompetitive in that their designs fail to innovate and may just have fragmented good ideas that don't hold together. Also, it is important to remember that with the large number of participants in these studies, it is easy to show statistically significant differences between designs that are in reality so small as to be trivial.

Data Gathering and Testing Techniques

Data gathering and testing are some of the most valuable tasks your user experience design team can perform. But the phrase "run a usability test" is a general one. There is not a single type of testing, but rather many different types. There are, for example, tests of

branding, early paper prototyping tests for conceptual design, and
later tests on robust working prototypes. You must select the type of
test needed for where you are in your development process and
then create the correct type of test questionnaires to support it.

You can save a lot of money and time by developing an initial set of
questions and then customizing them as needed for each test. Defining and creating predesigned templates can save countless hours.
While no template for a given type of test works for all situations,
there is certainly value in having a template as part of your infrastructure. Some example template forms include those listed here:

- The **screener** is an essential questionnaire used to select participants for a study. It can help eliminate participants who
  are too sophisticated or too inexperienced. In some cases, a
  template can be developed and used repeatedly for each
  study that will access those types of users, although typically
  the template must be modified for each test.

- **Usability testing routine forms** are needed when running usability tests. While not exciting, they are quite necessary. For
  example, you must have an informed consent form to get each
  participant's agreement to participate. Without this form in
  place, you are in violation of ethics in human research and can
  be sued. You may also need demographics forms and forms to
  acknowledge compensation.

As mentioned, there is more than one type of usability test. Following are descriptions of several tests. Which one you use depends on
what questions you are trying to answer.

- **Brand perception tests** let you see how the user perceives the
  current site or application. One version of this test is for a single design; a variant of the test can compare your design with
  competitors' designs, or to select the best among suggested
  designs. Such testing can be conducted with designs from different graphic artists or even different agencies. Regardless of
  the scenario, the questionnaire for this test must be customized to reflect the company's target brand values. Which ones
  are you looking for, and which do you want to make sure to

avoid: trendy, warm, friendly, sophisticated, "tech-y"? You need to tailor the questionnaire accordingly.

- If you ask users if they want a given function, they almost always say yes. If you give them a list of potential functions and ask them to rate how important those choices are, they rate most functions as very important. But if you give users a list of possible functions and say they can have only three, you get interesting results. This test, called a **functional salience test**, is a great way to identify the relative importance of functions.

- A **test of affordance** determines whether users can tell what they can select on a page. In this test, you simply give users a printed copy of a page and tell them, "Circle the items you think you can select and click on." You will see if there are selectable items that users cannot tell are selectable. You will also see if there are nonselectable items that make users think they *can* select them.

- **"Think aloud" tests** consist of a whole family of tests in which the user is told to do a series of tasks, which are observed. Users are asked to read out loud as they work and tell the facilitator what they are thinking. This is a great way to find problems in a design. You can also estimate how long it will take users to complete tasks.

- The **card sort test** is a useful method if you are trying to find how users categorize the topics in a website or application. With this type of testing, you create stacks of cards with one item on each card, and then the participants group the cards in a way that makes sense to them. Software can help collect and analyze the groupings used by different participants. The software uses cluster analysis and gives results that can guide the information structure of the design.[3]

- While the card sort test can help guide the design, you can use the **reverse card sort method** to check whether the design

---

3. IBM's EZSort programs are an example of cluster analysis software. For more information, visit www3.ibm.com/ibm/easy/eou_ext.nsf/Publish/410.

worked. With this type of testing, you give the participants a list of items and see if they can figure out where to go to find them. If they can find the items, the navigational structure is self-evident.

- **Subjective ratings** are a large family of tests that allow users to describe how they feel about your site or application. They decompose or break down users' perceptions to help you more easily track the cause of problems. For example, you might find that people love the colors but feel that the site is very slow. These findings need to be carefully considered. Many users might say that they want a search facility, but this may actually indicate a problem with the structure of the site. The stated desire for a search facility is often just a symptom of being lost in a poor navigational structure.

Note: While standard tests help you quickly prepare testing, each test needs its own set of forms, such as video consent forms, facilitator scripts, task instructions, and so on.

Advanced Methods

In addition to the classic usability analyses, a range of analytical methods look at the big picture, meaning the ecosystem of the customer. Some of these methods were inspired by ethnographic studies, such as shadowing. In this approach, researchers quietly follow and observe participants. In designing a mobile phone for use in an emerging economy, for example, shadowing lets us notice the need for much louder, dust-resistant devices to handle the conditions on trains (Figure 7-5).

Other methods allow us to probe into the user's emotional schema. When designing for psychological influence, we want to be able to model the customer's drivers, blocks, beliefs, and feelings. The more deeply we can understand the user, the more leverage we have on influencing conversion.

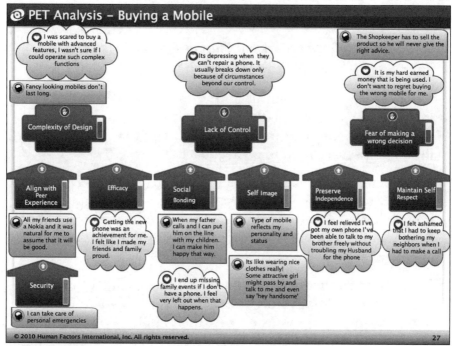

Figure 7-5: *A PET analysis (persuasion, emotion, and trust) created after in-depth gestalt-style interviews about buying a mobile phone*

The Special Needs of International Testing

International testing is far more difficult to coordinate and involves much more than just arranging for facilities and participants in many countries and racking up lots of air miles. Test procedures don't work cross-culturally; therefore, international testing takes special capabilities and infrastructure. You need to deal with translation issues and adjust the testing methodology based on cultural differences. For example, in some cultures it is not polite to criticize, so the usual methods of asking users to think aloud, expecting that they will say what they think is wrong with the product, may not work. If you are testing internationally, make sure you leave enough time to deal with these different and differing circumstances.

The Bollywood Method[4]

Apala Lahiri, Global Chief of Technical Staff
CEO, Institute of Customer Experience

The main challenge with usability testing in Asia is that it is impolite to tell someone they have a bad design. It is embarrassing within this culture to admit that you cannot find something, so it is very hard to get feedback.

I conducted a test on a site that offered airline tickets for sale. I used a conventional simulation testing method and got little feedback. I could see that users were not succeeding, but they would not willingly discuss the problems they were experiencing.

I then tried a new method I had developed, called the Bollywood Method. Bollywood is the Hollywood of India and makes far more movies each year than Hollywood does. Bollywood movies are famous for having long and emotionally involved plots. The movies have great pathos and excitement. In applying the Bollywood Method to this testing scenario, I described a dire fantasy situation. I asked each participant to imagine that his or her beautiful, young, and innocent niece is about to be married. But suddenly the family receives news that the prospective groom is a member of the underground. He is a hit man! His whole life story is a sham, *and he is already married*! The participant has sole possession of this evidence and must book airline tickets to Bangalore for himself or herself and the groom's current wife. Time is of the essence!

The test participants willingly entered this fantasy, and with great excitement they began the ticket booking process. Even minor difficulties they encountered resulted in immediate and incisive commentary. The participants complained about the button naming and placement. They pointed out the number of

---

4. Based on Chavan [2002].

extra steps in booking. The fantasy situation gave them license to communicate in a way they never would have under normal evaluation methods.

This method worked well in India and may even be able to be generalized to special situations in North America and other places where participants may hesitate to communicate freely.

Recruiting Interview and Testing Participants

Usability tests typically require fewer participants than marketing research studies because the findings in usability tests are usually qualitative, rather than statistically descriptive. In usability testing, you are not trying to generalize your results or estimate the numbers or percentage of people who feel or would react to a product in a certain way. Instead, you are exploring. You are trying to determine whether there are usability issues, what they are if they do exist, and how you might solve them. In doing so, you are trying to delve into the psychology of your users. This requires that the participants you test be representative of the target population of actual users. In other words, you need to find representative users for data gathering and usability testing.

In-house users, while easy to find, aren't usually acceptable participants because they probably care more about the company than real users do. They see the application as being worthy of additional effort and might exaggerate its value, or they might not flag aspects of the design that make it impractical. They are also familiar with the company's in-house language, concepts, attitude, and mindset, and they might even have different aesthetic values and perceptions than typical end users.

There is one case in which performing tests with in-house users is appropriate: if you are actually building an application for internal staff members. Sampling them is usually a very easy and informal process; staff members just need to be screened and scheduled.

Many market research and usability testing companies have entire staffs of screeners—clerical-level staff who call lists of potential participants and ask the questions included in a special questionnaire (also called a screener, as noted earlier in the chapter). The staff members use the questionnaire to select participants who fit the criteria for the study. Participants are typically offered a fee of $100 to $200 each, depending on how stringent the required match criteria are. Some of these testing facilities maintain databases of potential participants. This can be convenient, but the lists may be overused. (Some people seem to make a part-time job out of participating in studies!) You may want a fresher list.

To accomplish this, you may need to ask the recruiting firm about the people in their databases. You can shop around for databases and recruiters, and specify that the participants must not have been in any studies during the last 12 months. It may be more challenging to find these kinds of participants, which may make your recruiting more expensive. If you need general participants—for example, people between the ages of 20 and 60 who purchase goods from the Web at least once every 3 months—it may be relatively easy to find "fresh" participants. If you need people who work in a copy center who have never used a particular type of software, you will pay more for this type of recruiting. It is useful to have relationships established with companies that can help you recruit participants.

If your user group consists of current customers, it may be possible to develop a list of customers and have the staff screeners work from that list. This may be easier and more cost-effective than using a recruiting firm. In some cases, you can have internal staff work temporarily as screeners. This costs very little unless you need to hire in-house staff to work as screeners on a full-time basis. Using in-house screeners saves money over hiring a screener consulting firm, but the in-house screeners will need to be trained. Usability consultants, in contrast, are already trained and just charge you per project. In any event, having a smoothly running mechanism for obtaining study participants helps keep usability work progressing—problems with obtaining participants is the single most common source for the delay of usability projects.

A whole series of deliverable documents result from proper usability work. Some people approach usability without much of a concept of deliverables, thinking that by simply studying the user, good things will happen. That may be true—good things *may* happen. But making usability work efficient and repeatable requires an organized set of deliverable documents. The deliverables provide a clear focus and a set of milestones for usability work. As an example, Table 7-1 lists the major deliverables in the Schaffer Method.

It takes time to create good deliverables, but they offer several benefits:

- They document that steps in the methodology are actually completed.
- They allow work to be communicated to others—for instance, key stakeholders and development staff.
- They allow work and processes to be repeated.

Table 7-1: *The Major Deliverables in the HFI Framework Methodology (Version 5)*

Expert Review Report	Wireframes
Usability Test Report	Graphic Treatment
Kickoff Presentation	Simulation Test Results
Data Gathering Plan	Functional Specification
Insight of the Data Gathering	Developer Briefing
Contract for Design	Design Modification Log
User Interface Structure	Final Usability Test
Standards Identification	Plan for Process Improvement
Custom Standard	Post Release Evaluation
Module Definition	Localization Assessment
Module Requirements	Interface Translation Specification
Screen Flow, Functions, and Fields	

Most deliverables require several smaller deliverables to create the end product. In the end, there may be hundreds of deliverables. Imagine that you needed to create these deliverables from scratch for each project, determining the appropriate document structure and inventing the style of presentation. The level of investment required to achieve this goal would make usability engineering programs prohibitive in terms of both cost and time. If each of the 23 deliverables listed in Table 7-1 took just ½ day to create structurally, for example, then this task would add 11½ days to the project.

If usability is to be routine, standard reusable deliverables are indispensable. They help organize the project and save valuable time. Standard deliverables also make it is easier for managers to check a project's progress because they know the full set of deliverables to expect. Finally, using standard deliverables makes it easier to get oriented with and review an unfamiliar project.

Summary

The value of the tools, templates, and facilities outlined in this chapter lies in their ability to save you valuable time. However, it remains critical to pick the items most appropriate for your efforts. It is not sensible to invest in something just because it is a new technology. Refer back to your strategy often, and remember to let your methodology determine your toolkit.

Chapter 8

Training and Certification

➤ Training is an effective way to promote user experience design and ensure that key staff members have required skills.

➤ Provide knowledge training to educate most staff members about the importance of the process of user experience design. It is possible to train hundreds of people in just half a day.

➤ Provide skills training to development staff members who will be doing interface design work. Instruct them on how to do user experience design work throughout the cycle of development. It is possible to train dozens of people in 10–20 days.

➤ Encourage the most highly trained staff members to become certified.

➤ Use the sample training plan in this chapter as the basis for your own plan.

In the institutionalization process, training is a powerful tool, and a comfortable one to implement. The power of training is that it enables personnel to share insights and achieve shifts in perspective without the expense—and potential embarrassment—of learning while performing actual project work. The school of hard knocks is a miserable substitute for organized, research-based instruction.

Classes also provide a portal to the literature in the field. There is a billion dollars' worth of research in user experience design, but it could take a lifetime to read and digest the material that applies just to software design. Usability training, like any other educational experience, distills the literature into its key insights, principles, facts, and models. If you start the process of institutionalizing user experience design without training, you will soon find yourself back to doing design by intuition—or trial and error.

This chapter describes the types of training available and clarifies how training can fit into your overall program. It discusses certification programs and outlines a sample training program you can use as a basis for planning your own program. The examples in this chapter are from HFI, but many other qualified companies and schools provide similar classes (e.g., Nielsen Norman Group, User Interface Engineering, and Deborah J. Mayhew and Associates).

Types of Training

There are two distinct types of training: knowledge training and skills training. In **knowledge training**, participants gain an appreciation of the need for usability engineering, an understanding of what user experience design encompasses, and an ability to identify the types of tasks required in the user-centered design process. They do not learn to complete a development activity; however, it is in **skills training** that participants learn how to perform actual user experience design tasks. Trainees may practice accomplishing ecosystem research, detailed design review, or usability tests. They may need some coaching to get comfortable with a task and to fine-tune their skills, but skills training will provide them with the basic capabilities.

The Difference between Knowledge and Skills Training
Dr. Phil Goddard

There are two types of long-term memory: there's declarative memory and there's procedural memory. Declarative memory is a repository for facts—things that you learn about, that you can recite—it's information about things. The other memory repository is procedural memory. Procedural memory stores procedures or processes that you perform or do, and once learned they become automatic and are done unconsciously. In fact, you can't describe them verbally; you often have to struggle to describe them and resort to hand waving.

Expertise requires both knowledge and skill. For example, consider riding a bike—with a little knowledge (rest both hands on the bars, maintain steady speed, keep your feet on the pedals) and lots of practice, you learn how to do it—automatically. Once you've created the procedure for bike riding, it's ready for use anytime. So at the core, knowledge is often a combination of factual information and procedural skill that must be developed over time to result in expertise.

When developing a training program, we should recognize as user-centered designers that we can state factually some things we learn about design. For example, left alignment of all field labels and edit fields on a screen reduces the visual complexity of a page. But there are certain kinds of knowledge that aren't factual; they're more procedural—like performing a usability test. How to perform an effective test that doesn't give away the answer to a specific question, how to actually practice active listening—these things need to be learned over a period of time and assimilated, and sometimes they're just things that take more time to learn.

You must include both skills training and knowledge training if you want your training program to be powerful.

Knowledge Training

Knowledge training in user experience design does not have to take a long time. A single day of training is enough to convey the importance of user experience design and the scope of activities needed. For example, a half-day knowledge training class on Web usability can cover the basics (see Table 8-1). Because knowledge training does not require the level of close interaction and mentoring of skills training, large classes can be as effective as smaller ones. This is especially important if you need to train many people. While the course participants will not be ready to complete user-centered design work after knowledge training, they will better appreciate its importance, and a broad-based appreciation helps the successful implementation of user experience design.

Table 8-1: *Objectives of the HFI Half-Day "Essentials of Usability" Knowledge Training Class*

This Topic . . .	Will Help You . . .
Usability—the business imperative	Know when to use usability methods and how they benefit users
Information architecture	Organize content and functions so users will find them
Site and page navigation	Select the right site and page navigation model for your users
Writing for the Web	Write text that people can scan or will enjoy reading
Using color effectively	Add depth to your design by using good color principles
Standards and consistency	Consider using a standard to increase design consistency
Usability step by step	Create a usability project plan
How to keep getting better	Increase your skills

The best way to ensure a successful institutionalization effort is to get organizational support and acceptance. Knowledge training directly conveys the value of user experience design and the user-centered design process and provides a baseline of acceptance throughout the organization. Such training does not have to identify every activity and skill needed. Rather, it focuses on connecting with people's experiences and getting them to see how user experience design is an essential tool and can be a key competitive differentiator for their organization. A knowledge training class is a very efficient, organized, and focused method for conveying this understanding. If employees do not have this type of training, the user experience design staff must convey the same information and understanding on an ad hoc basis. It takes a great deal of time to explain this information on an individual basis and is inefficient and impractical to do so.

A good knowledge training class identifies the overall process of user-centered design and illustrates the value of standards, a good navigational structure, and good detailed design. It does not try to demonstrate every design principle and research-based recommendation, but rather just enough to ensure that participants understand that user experience design is not just common sense and should not be approached with anything less than a professional and systematic attitude.

Knowledge training can help make key transitions deep in the psyche of the organization. The entire staff needs to learn how user experience design is really the way to manifest the strategy developed by marketing personnel. Everyone needs to learn how UX design engineers ensure that the brand values are reflected in the design. Knowledge training can dispel myths, such as the idea that user experience design engineering goes counter to marketing or graphic design goals. Knowledge training can help move the development organization from design by opinions and superstitions into a systematic and scientific practice.

Who Should Get Knowledge Training?

Three groups especially benefit from this type of training: executives, members of the systems community, and new employees.

Executives benefit from knowledge training because while they do not need to be able to do a task analysis or complete interviews, they must understand what user experience design is about. These managers must make informed decisions about funding and support the user experience design staff when hard choices have to be made. Without this type of training, many executives won't have a basic understanding of user experience or an appreciation of its importance. While knowledge training is not always sufficient to instill a deep, gut-level commitment to usability, it should have a meaningful impact. Compared to other participants, executives in many cases require training that is shorter, higher powered, and more specific to their organization. They need to understand issues of investment and return, as well as the challenges of governance that they will be asked to manage.

The second target group is the systems community. Many different players are found at this level, including business owners, product managers, operations personnel, marketing staff, developers, and so on. Different organizations have different types of key staff, so your training program should have the goal of creating a core group of people who understand user experience design as a primary objective.

Regardless of which group you target as the most crucial, the knowledge must permeate the organization. Once this objective is complete, there will always be a few people in every important design meeting who will expect user experience design to be addressed as an essential success factor—systematically and scientifically.

It's also important to make sure that new hires are aware of the value of user experience design. Many new staff members may not know about UX design, and knowledge training ensures that they understand the focus on and the importance of user experience in the organization.

Although all these groups need to hear a similar message, it is a good idea to customize the presentation to best meet the needs and mindset of each group.

Skills Training

If usability testing were the only thing involved in skills training, this training would be straightforward. But such training encompasses much more than simply testing: skills training needs to provide the ability to participate in the entire cycle of development. Key user experience design initiatives must be completed at every stage, and this training must support a range of activities from strategic cross-channel design through conceptual structure, navigational, and detailed design.

When you look at the scope of what must be learned, skills training may seem daunting. In fact, it *is* daunting. Figure 8-1, which outlines course topics in the core HFI Web and application development skills training classes, gives you a sense of the scope and complexity of usability skills. Going through a training program provides a foundation, but given real-world constraints, challenges, and time requirements it takes more than that for most people to become truly competent at all these activities. The best results

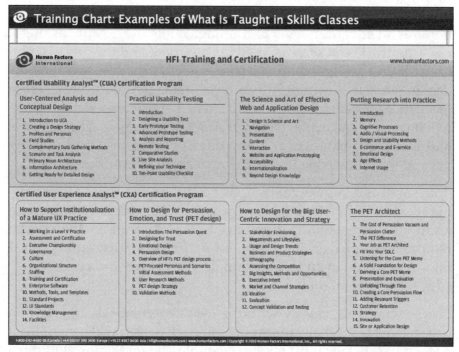

Figure 8-1: *Training chart: examples of what is taught in skills classes*[1]

---

1. Chart developed by Human Factors International.

generally come from having support for initial work experience. This support may include advanced training or a mentoring program for refining skills. Support programs can be completed before the start of real-world projects, or they can be incorporated into participation in showcase projects.

It is also important to have follow-up assistance for newly trained staff. It does not matter that the people are dedicated and determined—it is simply impossible for anyone to get everything right the first time. Just as there are residency programs for physicians, so there is a need for continued mentoring for newly trained user experience design staff.

Who Should Get Skills Training?

While all employees benefit from knowledge training, those who will actually perform the user experience design work require skills training. In addition, some managers must be able to evaluate the quality of designs and the design process in depth, which also requires an advanced level of training. While the executives might not actually design screens, they must understand the process, philosophy, and design rules to be able to evaluate and support the UX design staff. It is wonderful to have managers with very senior usability experience, but it is more likely that user experience design will be new to the management group. For managers who have not had extensive experience, a few days of more in-depth training beyond the knowledge training course should be sufficient.

Both small and large organizations need the same types of training, but they differ in terms of how many people need to be trained. In addition, large organizations need to train staff in the special requirements of working in a mature, process-oriented organization. This would include, for example, use of standards and knowledge management tools.

People who work closely with the user experience design staff on user-related tasks that support the interface design will benefit from a few days of skills training. For example, the marketing staff must provide strategic and branding direction, the technical staff must support the design's implementation, the graphic art staff must create the imagery, and the business analysts must consider functionality and business rules. User representatives may provide insights and organize data gathering with users, and other individuals may work in functional roles that surround the usability activities. With a more solid understanding of the design process, all of these personnel will be fully helpful, supportive, and aware of the importance of usability.

It is useful to pick a few of these individuals and put them through the same training that the user-experience design staff receives. Although they will not be actually completing design tasks, they will then have a clear understanding of what the UX engineers are trying to accomplish and will be more effective in working with them.

Some IT staff and developers may be involved in interface design in a serious way. They may not be dedicated user experience design staff, but often an organization does not have enough specialists to perform all the user-centered design work. In such a case, these staff members may be asked to perform usability engineering tasks. For lower-budget projects, or in smaller companies, they may have to handle the entire user experience design effort on their own, or at least with limited support. These people need about five days of training that provides hands-on skills in user-centered design, including user-centered design and analysis, user interface structures, usability detailed design, and user testing.

Some employees become dedicated user experience design staff and spend most of their work time on usability issues. They may not have degrees in the field, but they usually care a lot, have industry experience, and possess political skills. These individuals need a solid set of practical training skills. A foundation of a month of training is usually justified, and these dedicated user experience design staff should have ongoing mentoring and recurrent training every year.

Certification

You may want to consider certification for staff members who have received a professional level of training. Having trained staff certified helps instill confidence in them; coworkers will be more likely to respect their insights and decisions, knowing that the staff members who are making recommendations have a solid foundation in the field.

Different levels of certification exist in the usability field. There is the certification of a university degree, for example. Several universities and colleges now offer graduate-level degrees in a human factors field, and some of them are specifically for usability and interface design. Other colleges may not offer a degree but rather combine courses to offer a certificate. This is not the same as certification, however; it demonstrates only that the person took some courses.

The Human Factors and Ergonomics Society has spun off a certification body called the Board of Certification in Professional Ergonomics. This body grants a certification in general human factors engineering called either a Certified Professional Ergonomist (CPE) or, in accordance with the certificate candidate's choice, a Certified Human Factors Professional (CHFP) or a Certified User Experience Professional (CUXP). This thorough and practical certification program is not solely focused on software design, but instead includes the whole gamut of the human factors engineering practice, from cars and weapons systems to consumer products and power plant controls.

In the last 10 years, a few companies have started industry certification programs to fill the gap between a graduate degree and just taking a few courses. For example, HFI offers the Certified Usability Analyst (CUA) program. This certification program relies on a test specifically focused on software usability issues. This test, which is quite demanding, measures a person's understanding of user-centered design and usability engineering principles. It does not test the ability to work in groups or even directly sample design skill, but it does validate that the applicant knows many approaches to research as well as a wide range of principles and methods specific to software usability. The test was constructed systematically with item analysis from various test populations. It is available to all and does not require the participant to complete HFI courses. More than 4000 CUAs have been certified since the inception of the program. There is also an advanced certification from HFI called the Certified User Experience Analyst (CXA). This certification can be achieved only after getting a CUA, and it includes user experience strategy, innovation, persuasion engineering, and work within a mature practice.

A Typical Training Plan

Every company has its own training priorities and budget limits. Table 8-2 outlines a sample plan for the first year; you can use it as a starting point. If you work in a large company, you may want to offer each class in-house to your own people. If you work in a small company, sending a few people to a public course may be a better alternative.

Conferences

In addition to foundational knowledge and skills training classes, it's important to keep the usability staff up-to-date on the field as a whole. New ideas and insights occur in this field all the time, and new methods and technologies are being developed continuously. If your company does not gather and disseminate these insights, you will not benefit from current best practices. There are two critical conferences in the field, and each provides insights that will be valuable to your projects. Each person on the core usability team should attend at least one conference a year.

Each conference is different in terms of the size of the conference, the types of people who attend and the types of sessions that are offered. Visit their websites to get an overview of what each conference is like.

- Special Interest Group on Computer–Human Interfaces of the Association for Computing Machinery (SIGCHI) (www.acm .org/sigchi/)
- The Usability Professionals Association (www.upassoc.org)

Table 8-2: *Sample HFI Training Plan*

Class	Time Commitment	Description
Management Briefing	Four hours	In this knowledge training class, executives get an overview of the basics of user-centered design and many case examples. Class participants are acquainted with usability as a business imperative, and learn about the institutionalization effort.
Half-Day of Basics	Four hours	This class provides knowledge training for the general development community. Class sizes are large to get training to everyone who needs it.
Web Design Course	Three full days	This skills-level training focuses on screen design for usability staff, key development staff, and a few managers.
User-Centered Analysis and Conceptual Design	Two full days	Moving from initial concept to a user interface design is one of the most difficult challenges usability staff can face. This skills course covers how to move from concept to design.
Practical Usability Testing	Two full days	This class presents a synthesis of usability testing techniques for the practitioner. This skills course teaches you to choose the right test for any stage of design, from early to advanced prototypes and live sites.
Certification Track	Twenty days training	This training is for practitioners who will be the core of the user experience design effort.

Summary

Making training an integral part of your institutionalization effort not only helps educate your staff, but also provides an invaluable level of ongoing consensus and support. Training is one of the most effective resources available to enhance the knowledge, skills, enthusiasm, and commitment of your organization at the same time. The next chapter outlines the essential elements of a user-centered design methodology.

Chapter 9

Knowledge Management

> Large-scale user experience design operations are different from small ones. The key difference is their knowledge management requirement.

> Conventional approaches to knowledge management are associated with overwhelming problems.

> Good knowledge management requires object-oriented user experience design.

> Linkages are critical to accessing user experience design content.

> Putting an industrial-strength user experience design knowledge management facility in place presents challenges.

There is a quantum difference between doing user experience design with a small group on a small scale and approaching it with a serious, well-staffed team and/or across an enterprise. One of the by-products of a greater UX investment is an exponential growth in the workload, based on the growing recognition of the value of user experience design projects (see Figure 9-1).

When you approach user experience design in the conventional, small-team way, each project is represented by a set of documents—

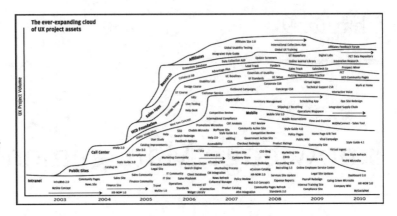

Figure 9-1:
Growth of user experience project load for a large pharmaceutical company

that is, you create slide shows and Word documents. At first, it might seem as if everything is going fine. But all too soon, you have terabytes of materials. Anything you want to know about is effectively lost in the black hole of your document management system. For example, you might have 40 projects that involve the "Digital Native" user group. If you want to collect what is known about the Digital Natives, you would do a search, only to discover that there are hundreds of documents to review. You find documents from the projects focused on Digital Natives—many of which are peripheral, containing perhaps a nugget of information about this user group. It becomes so difficult to read all the documents that most teams end up doing the research again.

Of course, you could make a special file for Digital Natives and keep the contents there—but user experience design work is not just about user profiles. It is about users and scenarios, environments and artifacts, needs, methods, standards, projects, and designs. You might need to know everything about an environment, such as a bank branch, or you might need to know about an artifact, such as an eye wash unit in a lab. (We call each of these items a *UX object*.) On top of that, you often need to look at the items based on linkages—and almost all of them are interlinked in some way.

With a small user experience design team, knowledge of users, scenarios, environments, and other UX objects is stored as a shared understanding within the team. Yes, the loss of a team member is a serious setback, but with just a half-dozen people focused on a limited domain, the organizational memory is usually not too difficult to retain. You can save methods and standards in physical or electronic folders. If the team wants to know something based on the linkages, such as which methods have already been applied to a given user group, someone probably remembers. If they want to find which applications have applied a given standard, they simply need to scan through perhaps a dozen different systems.

An organization may distribute the user experience design operation among a number of small teams, each focused on a single domain. The real challenges then come when looking at the way methods and standards are applied across the organization. It is a rare organization that has truly isolated domains: domain knowledge is so valuable that an organization's growth will almost always be based on an interrelated set of channels and business areas. As such, there is no good way to carve up user experience design work into small, siloed work teams without overlap—nor is there often a good business case to be made for doing so. Your retail and commercial banking operations might be fairly discrete from one another, and there is likely to be only modest overlap between the personal and business domains (e.g., your businesses owners have personal accounts that they would expect to have conventions similar to their business accounts). When your retail and commercial banking operations expand to a level that requires at least 50 user experience design professionals for each domain, however, you will have gone far beyond that easily managed small team—the one that kept all that knowledge in their heads and on their desks.

Why Conventional Knowledge Management Fails

Let's take a minute to break down the main methods used by conventional repositories to manage access to their terabytes of valuable data. Certainly, all repositories allow the author to affix meta-tags to each document. For example, you might create a report on *middle market* and *mass affluent* customers, using *mobile devices*, at *home*, in *branches*, and while *commuting*. In such a case, all the words in italics can go into the meta-tag. You can then easily find only those documents that are about middle-market customers using mobile devices. To some extent, that could be useful. Nevertheless, your search will not have given you a full picture of everything there is known about middle-market users or mobile usage. Instead, it shows only the documents that refer to both middle-market users and mobile usage. For your purposes, however, you might need to access the contents of a spiffy study on the emotions of middle-market users responding to high-pressure sales situations, or ecosystem insights into mobile device usage in emergency situations.

Another problem with meta-tags is that they are very much dependent on the diligence of practitioners in setting them up. To find the necessary content, you must resort to keyword searches—which finds relevant documents, but also gives you loads of irrelevant hits.

A strategy that many teams try is to set up a folder structure and to save documents based on that taxonomy. You can create a set of folders around different types of UX objects, for instance. You might have a folder of methods, for example, and a folder of standards. But what happens when you need to see all the projects that used a given method? What happens when you want to see only those middle-market user scenarios that take place in a given environment? When you have a little team and a handful of documents, this taxonomic approach works well. Once you begin industrial-size user experience design, it fails catastrophically.

The Cost of Failure

Most large-scale user experience design operations are like goldfish: they end up with a three-second memory. As a result, new studies are commissioned to research areas that have already been studied. At HFI, it's not uncommon to have a large company approach us with two or three requests for expensive international research. Each study is basically the same; the requests just come from separate, uncoordinated teams.

The cost of duplicate research is high, as a serious ecosystem study will cost at least $250,000. But that is not the biggest cost. Truly catastrophic costs are incurred by making design decisions without the power of the knowledge that an organization *could* apply—leading to suboptimal strategies, missed innovations, and suboptimal designs.

Consider the valuation of an organization. For many companies, the real value of the firm is how well it knows its customers. In today's business environment, an organization can no longer rely on the cultural memory of a team, with recollections about working in the field or doing projects for the customer segments. The workforce is moving toward shorter tenure within organizations and more free-lance staffing. Consequently, user experience design capabilities need to be more organized and sustainable. The result of object-oriented UX is a model of the customer, a key intellectual property.

Object-Oriented UX

The software industry went through a transition a few decades ago, in which it moved toward object-oriented programming. Originally, programs were written in a single flat file. This file mixed up screen calls with algorithms and data. Today, no programmer would use this method. Instead, programmers write modules of code for discrete tasks, and then call those modules repeatedly, so as to optimize reuse. In the same way, the user experience design field is starting to make its own transition to object-oriented design. Instead of doing all their work in a "flat file" or a document or slide show, UX teams are creating separate objects and then "calling" those objects inside of documents.

To see how it works, consider the UX Enterprise software service offered by HFI. To work properly, the user experience design team needs to work on the object and then, just as in programming, the practitioner calls the object when needed. Thus linkages are inserted inside of documents. Figure 9-2 depicts a sample "stamp" that is clicked to link to an object, Figure 9-3 shows a project report that uses stamps to reference the detailed objects, and Figure 9-4 illustrates a user profile object that contains everything that the team knows about one type of user.

Figure 9-2: *A UX Enterprise "stamp." Clicking on the stamp links directly to the object. Inserting the stamp in a project document links that project to the object.*

Figure 9-3: *A project slide deck that uses stamps to link to detail UX objects*

Of course, many different types of objects are possible—users, scenarios, environments and artifacts, designs, projects, methods and standards, and various types of training and research. The structure of each type of object is different (see Figure 9-5 for an example of an artifact), and to some extent the objects need to be customized to the domain of the organization (see Figure 9-6 for an example involving South African languages).

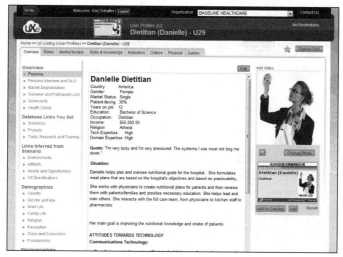

Figure 9-4: *A UX object holds everything the team knows about this user profile*

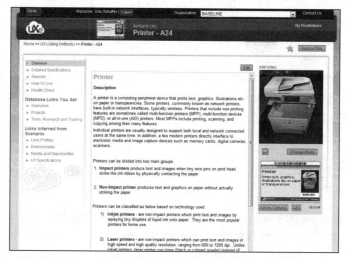

Figure 9-5: *An artifact is a tool or object that is used, but not designed by the team*

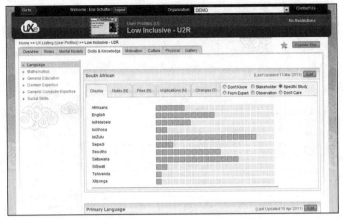

Figure 9-6: *An object customized for South Africa*

Professionals Don't Start from Scratch

One great thing about a "design by object" approach is the ability to copy objects and edit them, as opposed to creating everything from scratch. Why write a methodology when you can copy one and edit it? In making user profiles, we find the closest match we can and then edit it. For example, we might take an American surgeon profile and import Japanese cultural dimensions. There is no question that you can be far more productive when building on previous work. At www.uxmarketplace.com, you can find an open market for buying and selling all types of UX objects.

Linkages

Once a team starts working on a shared set of objects, instead of flat files of documents and slide shows, a valuable cloud of objects will grow steadily. But for this set of objects to be useful, the team needs to be a way to use the linkages between objects to view the data. For example, you might need to find the following:

- The projects that did usability testing on a given user profile
- The scenarios that a user completes in a given environment

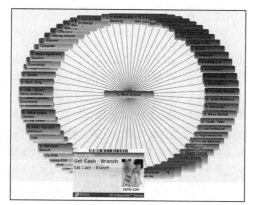

Figure 9-7: *An ecosystem of objects related to a bank branch (demo data only)*

- The scenarios that have a given need (or problem)
- The designs that apply a given standard

The only way to identify these subsets of objects is to store the objects in a relational database, and to create the linkages in as painless a way as possible.

With a relational database that allows you to access your cloud of UX objects, you can collect and view an entire ecosystem. Today the ecosystem view is critical, because we have to design for multiple actors, in complex environments, with embedded and ubiquitous digital channels. But what defines an ecosystem from a data structure viewpoint?

Practitioners draw charts of ecosystems, but charts have different centers of focus. They might show the ecosystem around a student, for example, or they might consist of the ecosystem around a mobile device. They might also depict the ecosystem within a given environment—or a single scenario. They can even illustrate the ecosystem of a need or strategic challenge (such as everything related to transitioning customers to a digital channel). Given the many possibilities, we must be able to let the practitioner identify the focus of the ecosystem model and then have the system concatenate the objects that surround the core focus (see Figure 9-7 for an example of an ecosystem model).

Summary

If your operation will be bigger than a small, manageable team of five to six practitioners, you should consider working in an object-oriented structure. That means breaking the habit of putting everything into slide shows. It also means having a toolkit that supports object-oriented user experience design. The result will soon be a valuable cloud of knowledge about your customers—core, corporate intellectual property that also makes the user experience design team stronger, more sustainable, and more valuable.

The transition from programmers coding in flat files and object-oriented programming took about a decade to accomplish. The transition to object-oriented UX poses a challenge as well. We have seen serious impediments around long-established habits, patterns, and vested interests. Given this reality, you shouldn't expect to pop in a tool and instantly change the way your user experience design practitioners function.

Part III

Organization

As the business world better understands and values UX, executive championship is becoming increasingly easy to obtain. The infrastructure can be bought and customized. The Organization phase—the people side of things—is where you will face the most serious challenges in institutionalizing UX.

No one wants a scenario where an executive wants excellence in customer experience and money invested in a UX infrastructure, but then finds that there are no people who can actually do the work. Having other people in the organization fail to include your user experience team in their projects would be equally problematic.

In Part III, we will first cover governance, which is how we ensure that the UX process is controlled, that user experience work is really performed, and that the institutionalization process is growing in maturity. It is all too easy to have a UX team sidelined, or called in only when it is too late to take advantage of their expertise. UX teams can also degrade over time and travel backward on the road to full institutionalization.

Some organizations have poor design quality simply because the organizational structure is inappropriate. There is more involved in a good UX process than just having a user experience team. The team must report to the right part of the organization—and it is important that they have the right structure and roles. Only in that way can the UX infrastructure be supported, and projects be completed effectively.

You will find that there is a huge demand for user experience work in your organization. But it is fanciful to think it can be done without enough UX practitioners! I recently talked to a major technology company. It was doubling their team size, which would give the company approximately 1.2% of the people needed to do the work. I reminded this company that there is no substitute for *trained* practitioners.

With the right capabilities in place, UX work can move forward. Initial showcase projects become large-scale programs that occur on a routine basis. Quality designs are produced. Outstanding designs may be produced. But the real measure of success and maturity is that user-centered design becomes a routine part of the organization.

Chapter 10

Governance

➤ Pay attention to governance; it is likely to be your biggest challenge.

➤ Understand your organization's culture and remove impediments to being customer centered.

➤ Create a meme that resonates with your organization's imperatives.

➤ Counteract the Dunning-Kruger effect with training.

➤ Design processes that close the loop so the executive champion can see if the UX initiative is working properly.

Today, there is rarely a serious problem with executive championship. Top executives are informed enough to know the value of a serious user experience design operation. They help plan the strategy to build an organization's user experience design capability, fund the program, and remove political obstacles that might hinder its evolution.

The infrastructure to do good user experience design is rarely a problem now. You can buy a coherent set of methods, standards, and tools. It is not that difficult to adapt them to your unique needs.

But risks to implementation of user experience design remain in the area of *governance*. Top management clearly demands great user experience design; these executives ask for world-class practices. But all too often those practices aren't put in place, or they are implemented inconsistently—that is, there is a degree of user experience design in some of the organization's processes, sometimes, depending on the charisma of the user experience design leaders. How does this happen? And what can you do about it?

The Roots of the Governance Problem

User experience design is reasonably straightforward. It is a practice based on a field of research and best practices—but it also represents a profound shift in the way things get designed. Organizations start out with a way that things get done. Just as there is an established process and established realities of political power, so there is an established focus for design (think technology, process, product management, or executive fiat). Changing this reality to a customer-centered process and focus not infrequently means pushing against years of organizational culture. It takes a lot of momentum to make such a change. Even when such a shift is made, there is a tendency for processes to snap back to their old configuration: take your hand off the design process for a moment—just blink—and you find everyone has reverted to the non-user-centered configuration.

HFI recently worked with a bank that had a long history of process-driven design, complicated by business staff inserting design ideas in a somewhat random and capricious manner. An HFI team spent 18 months on a showcase program. We developed a very advanced UX strategy, and then a solid and validated structural design. After just a few weeks away, I returned to find that the detailed design had been planned—but the planning process involved business analysts only, and the company was back to a process-oriented approach. Instead of designing screens that fit into the structural design, members of the bank's staff were picking processes based on a functional analysis and were planning to design each in isolation. If you do that, then you design recurring payment in isolation—and you tend to make an interface where recurring payment is a menu choice. The reality is that customers don't think of recurring payment, but rather see it as just one type of "payment." So the team had thrown 18 months of design out the window just in their planning process. We had to catch that, reeducate them, and get the design reworked.

Along with the inertia of the old process, vested interests may also thwart the transition to a user-centered process. User experience design is one of those fields where everyone is an expert. Making random and unsupported design decisions will be the highlight of some people's day. Those staff feel quite upset when you switch to an evidence-based, process-driven, validated process. In response, they will often work to marginalize the user experience design team. Excluding the user experience design team is one of the most common issues—or at least excluding them until the very end of the development process, when it is impossible to do much that's useful.

Memes That Kill

There are always ideas flowing around an organization that have the potential to derail a user experience design transformation. Organizations vary in their beliefs, but it is worthwhile to diagnose the specific, retrograde ideas prevalent within yours. You can then attack them as a part of the cultural change.

These memes are diverse (see Figures 10-1 and 10-2), but they share a few common roots. The first of these memes is that user experience design is not really important. People working hard on server efficiency may think that success is a function of fast response time. When you see everything in terms of milliseconds, user experience design objectives seem secondary. "Nothing works if the servers don't function," they will say. The fact is that all competitors have functional servers today—or simply use the cloud. Thus it is primarily user experience design that provides differentiation.

The second cluster of evil memes hovers around the misperception that everyone is a user experience design expert. It's a lot like the near-universal expertise in branding. There are numerous corollaries of this fallacy, such as it's just a matter of common sense! All you

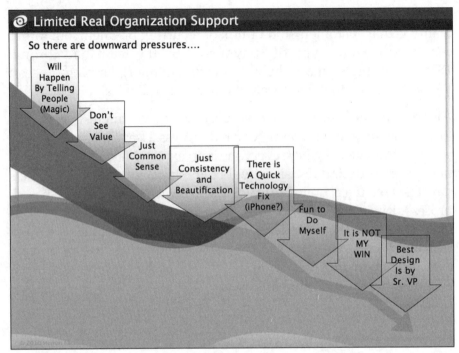

Figure 10-1: *Example of particularly numerous and problematic memes in a bank attempting a user experience design transformation. This organization did not create a practice that thrived.*

really need to do UX design is the motivation of your employees, this line of thinking goes. So the user experience design journey devolves into a motivational speech, bonuses around survey scores, or a few well-placed KITAs (kicks in the ass). Then there's the all-too-common notion that design can be done by senior executives based on intuition, anecdotes, and comments from relatives. Because being senior means those executives are exceptional people, this rationale states, it must also mean they are exceptional human factors engineers. For senior executives, it's a recreational break—especially when they are unencumbered by measurable assessments of their efforts—or, for that matter, by education, training, certification, or cracking a serious book.

The third and last meme insists that user experience design is inefficient and expensive. I like to say that "Usability is free." And that is true—it is the reason that user experience design is becoming so

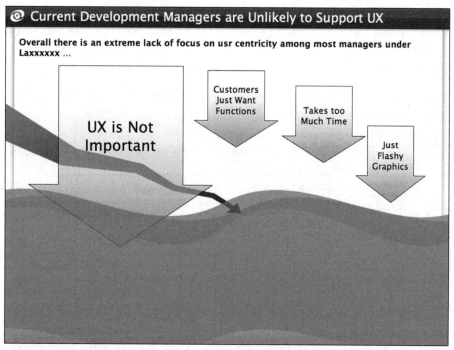

Figure 10-2: *Example of a more typical set of problematic memes in a product development company that was attempting a user experience design transformation. This organization succeeded nicely.*

commonplace. But many people have a very different experience: immature user experience design is expensive and slow. Taking someone with a limited amount of training; tossing him or her into a corner of an organization without accepted processes, standards, templates, knowledge bases, and team support; and loading that person with top-priority projects—that is not a recipe for efficiency. In other cases, user experience design consultancies are hired that contract for large research projects that yield volumes of shelfware—or solve the wrong problem altogether—because the organization has a culture of Ready, Fire, AIM! When these immature approaches characterize the UX effort, management hopes something useful and efficient happens. Of course, hope is not a strategy.

It is hardly surprising that many people experience user experience design as impractical. Mature user experience design requires that all the parts come together. You need an organization in which user experience design work is done on each and every project as a matter of course, and you need trained and certified staff working in a cohesive UX operation. Your staff needs access to methods, templates, standards, and the history of previous work.

The result of a mature user experience design capability is that the work becomes far more efficient than it is in an organization where the person making user experience design decisions is just guessing. You save time and money because the process is faster, cheaper, and better. You don't have to redo work. You discover changes that are needed early, when making changes is easy. Most importantly, you don't pay the price for failures.

Education Helps

One of the most universal roots of governance problems is the Dunning-Kruger effect [Kruger and Dunning 1999]. In the brilliant work by Kruger and Dunning, we see that people who know very little about a topic tend to substantially overestimate what they know. This gives rise to the frustrating and debilitating tendency of completely unqualified staff, often with executive positions in the organization, to make design pronouncements. A recent example is the insistence that the action buttons should be purple because that will cause more people to select them.

There is only one antidote mentioned for the Dunning-Kruger effect: education. As we make people smarter about a topic, the first thing that happens is they get a sense of what they don't know. Give people a day of training on user experience design and they will certainly not get a solid foundation to do the work. But they will gain some level of respect for the fact that UX is not common sense and not trivial, and that it cannot be addressed by random guesswork. At HFI, we have built training specific to that purpose (Figure 10-3). It was a departure for us, as we have generally built professional-level training to provide a solid set of stills. Nevertheless, we found that there was a need for the knowledge training that creates a general appreciation for UX, quickly.

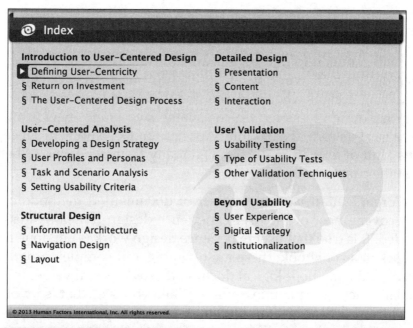

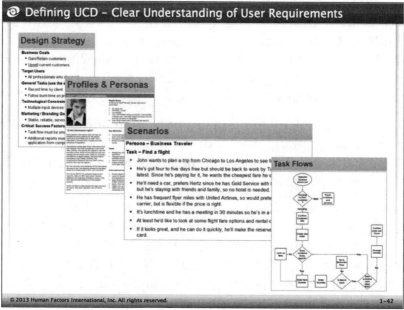

Figure 10-3: *Slides from training specifically geared to educating managers, instead of providing usable skills. Such training mostly helps executives appreciate what they don't know.*

Verify That a Methodology Is Applied

It is still common to find organizations with dozens of user experience design staff working on an ad hoc basis. They dash about, reviewing designs when they can find them and have time. They sit in group design sessions (which usually have a fancy new name for what is, at its core, the old Joint Application Development process). This kind of immature process is not any faster, cheaper, or better than the past techniques.

The organization *must* have a set of documented methodologies that covers most of the user experience design functions that are needed. It is true that user experience design work is not done from recipes in a cookbook; these are often big and complex programs. Even so, the methodological document provides real value. In particular, it acts as a planning guide. When you see what is involved in a best-practices structural design program, you are unlikely to ask for it to be done in two weeks. These methods concretize what has to be accomplished. Consequently, there must be a full set of methods that cover most of the user experience design work. The methods also make communication far easier. For 20 years at HFI, we have just said, "I'm working on a UIS" (user interface structure), and everyone basically knows what will happen.

Having a methodology in place is a baseline requirement, but getting a method is straightforward: you can buy one, or buy it and customize it. Making sure that the methodology is implemented is a more involved process.

Whatever your methodology, the question that should guide it is this: "Are the projects following the prescribed user-centered process?" Sadly, many professionals don't even know what that means! It does *not* mean that you care about users, nor does it mean that you have user experience design staff employed. It does not even mean that you follow your methodology. Instead, it means that the first thing you work on is the user's experience. Having completed that step, you then build out the processes, business models, and technology to make it happen. In terms of governance of such a user-centered design program, you need to have methods in place so that the first steps deal with defining the needs of the user and crafting a planned model of the future user's experience.

Even if you have a user experience design methodology, your approach can shift all too easily to *technology-centered* design (which starts with the database or the technical framework) or *function-centered* design (preparing a set of banking methods out of a high school textbook, for example, without researching what your customers and staff will really do). The staff might keep the user experience design team in the dark while performing the initial "preparatory work," and then ask for forgiveness for not starting with a true, user-centered process. It might not seem a significant misstep, but in effect, it fundamentally undermines the whole user experience design practice and assures that the user experience design team will not be able to succeed. In essence, the "old-timers" in staff and management, invested and comfortable with previous processes and systems, have consigned the user experience design team to screen beautification and cleaning up the mess.

In this scenario, things quickly devolve into a "finger in the dike" scenario, in which the user experience design staff dashes about, trying unsuccessfully to manage the cascading effects of a bad design. For staff resistant to a transformation toward user-centered design, that kind of chaos can be fun to watch. Of course, it might not be so fun to have their company fail due to lack of differentiation and a poor market position. That happens—and not infrequently.

Once the user experience design team is on board, engaged, and involved from the start of the project, it's essential to make sure that the work described in the methodology is the correct level of effort and is actually completed. A very general recommendation—the user experience practice burns approximately 10% of the budget and approximately 10% of the headcount on a given project—is a useful rule of thumb. In reality, of course, the question is more complicated.

It is difficult to figure out what is really needed to establish a user experience practice and transform an organization's development culture so that it is based on user-centered processes. At HFI, the people who decide what we bid on a project are highly skilled and receive special training. They have to be tested and certified. I meet with them weekly. Even then, they still have to kick ideas around with a client organization and ask lots of questions—and they very occasionally miss the mark.

Project planning in user-centered design means balancing cost and risk. There are risks to quality decisions, and risks to time-to-market decisions. The project needs to fit into the development culture and strategy of the organization. All the while, it must maintain good practices. The stakes for getting this right are very high.

In most cases, you can immediately spot the stupid stuff—for example, people wanting to test three subjects, major reliance on focus groups or surveys as a way of gathering data or assessing designs, projects proceeding without human performance or experience objectives, nothing done until a test at the end. Given that you have gotten this far in the book, we won't need to spend any time on these very basic mistakes.

The most important foundation for user experience design is a solid *UX strategy* for the overall cross-channel solution. This has two elements. The first part is the motivational aspect: why customers will want to convert and how they will be retained. The second part is the overall design and alignment of the multiple channels that customers will access (e.g., browser, mobile applications, call centers, stores). Without this top-level strategic design, you will almost certainly create a set of siloed and uncoordinated offerings, whose purpose and position will not align.

Today, many companies try to substitute "be like Apple" for a real UX strategy. On the face of it, that is not a bad idea. Apple has done a wonderful job at providing an ecosystem solution in which all the parts hang together. But Apple also has a unique position and style. Would that style be the best choice for a low-cost superstore? No, of course not. Thus the first challenge in developing a strategy is designing the right *emotional schema*—that is, understanding why people convert and are retained.

The second challenge is to identify how the various channels will be understood (Can users even figure out which channel to use?), interact (Are there places where the call center appears as a part of the Web site?), and align. We need to consider if there is a need for a

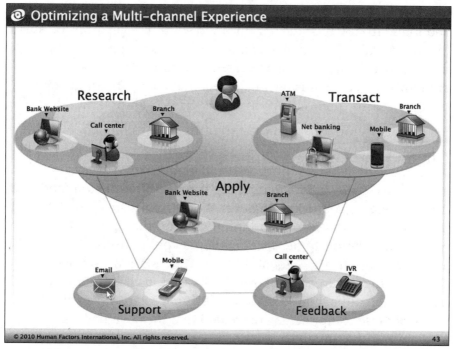

Figure 10-4: *Planning the role of various channels for a bank*

pervasive information architecture, where the structure and language of offerings and functions align between channels (Figure 10-4). For example, do the tabs on the Web site and the signs in the store have the same language and same sequence? There is also a need for interface standards to maintain consistency. Without a UX strategy, then, your methods will not be ideal. You may be designing "usable wrong things."

Once a UX strategy is in place, the key to successful implementation is maintaining a continuous thread through the rest of the design process. That doesn't mean simply having a series of user experience design activities at every stage; it's essential to uphold the innovation and logical progression defined by the UX strategy as you move toward increasingly specific and concrete designs. The structural design determines the detailed design. In turn, the periodic validation references the human performance and preference objectives defined in previous stages.

Governance means that there are documented methods, and it means that those methods provide a solid progression from executive intent to UX strategy, through the entire design process—a consistent logic and intent from which the organization should never stray. Be aware that there will be a tendency to marginalize these methods instead of making them central to the process. Governance must ensure that the organization retains this new user-centered design methodology.

Closing the Loop on Standards

At HFI, we have completed many hundreds of customized user interface standards. Today, I never worry about successfully creating a usable, effective standard. Our generic templates simply require adaptation to an organization's conventions and domain, and offer close to 100% reliability. Creating standards from scratch can be taxing. It can be an extremely hazardous chore for an organization to create a massive set of design patterns. Eventually, so many of these components are created that the designers can't really find anything. Conversely, organizations may try creating one template that will do everything (good luck with that). Outside of these odd cases, the main worry is about implementation.

I've asked many hundreds of developers how they feel about designing under a solid and strict set of design standards. They understand the value of those standards in providing consistency and speed of design. They understand that coding is faster, as is maintenance. Even so, it is the rare designer who really likes standards. Standards make people feel restricted and less creative. I have demonstrations that make it clear that this relationship does not hold. Nevertheless, an emotional resistance is still there—and you can count on meeting it as you try to apply your UX methodology across the organization.

To manage resistance to standards, you need to start with training. The design staff, including the user experience design staff, need about half a day of training on the standard. This training must share the templates, of course, and explain how to design using templates. Almost more important is training on why standards are really important. HFI uses all sorts of methods to drive this point home (see Figure 10-5), and to make clear that standards enable *more* creativity, as designers don't have to spend time reinventing the wheel. Yet despite how important and helpful this training is, it is rarely enough on its own.

Governance needs to ensure that standards are being followed. Just how that is done must be tuned to the organizational culture. In some organizations, it's a straightforward process to enforce standards and to require designs to comply with them. In these types of organizations, a review cycle can be put in place in which quality control staff ensure compliance and provide feedback. In other organizations, strict enforcement is impossible, because it goes against the culture. In such cases, the most that can be done is to provide feedback when

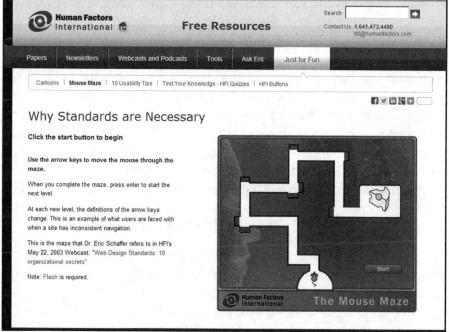

Figure 10-5: *The "Mouse Maze" is the most downloaded offering on the HFI site. It is a simple maze with three levels. In the first level, all the keys work normally; this maze is easy to get through. In the second level, the same maze is much harder, because the keys are switched around (so the left arrow goes up, for example). This represents poor design. In the last level, the keys are switched around, but also work differently in different parts of the maze. This third level is designed to be awful, and it shows what happens then there is inconsistency—when standards are not observed. We use this demonstration in our standards training classes.*

someone is not following the standards. At that point, compliance with the interface standard is the responsibility of the author.

One other cross-check we have started to use at HFI is a counter to check whether the online standards are being accessed. It is easy to fake access, of course. Even so, if you don't have anyone looking at your standards, it's an indicator to start worrying.

Checking If the Practice Is Alive

Unfortunately, a user experience design practice is fragile. Once you invest in methods and standards and tools, they merely need to be kept up-to-date. Other parts of the organization, however, can come apart quickly—particularly your staff. There is a strong market for experienced user experience design staff, so staff who have lost faith in your operation are likely to leave. Even if they are enthusiastic about your practice, they may be pulled away with various incentives (e.g., more money, a more important job title). The cost of developing replacement staff is substantial, and once you slip under a critical mass of technical specialists (generally about seven highly competent practitioners), it becomes difficult to bring onboard and integrate new people. Even with a mature, well-documented operation, your new staff need guidance from senior established in-house practitioners on where to look for materials and how to apply the UX infrastructure and facilities.

Yet even with infrastructure and staff in place, a practice can disintegrate. It is not uncommon for user experience design organizations that were mature and had sophisticated approaches to design to find themselves relegated to ad hoc tactical work because they have a new misaligned management. The stream of investment in training and evolving the UX practice can quickly shut off—at which point the user experience design organization begins to degrade.

How can executive sponsors spot these problems before they send the practice into an unstoppable downward spiral? Early detection and clear criteria are key elements to sustainability. Detection, however, can be difficult. Managers whose lack of understanding is destroying your UX investment will tout their improved efficiency. Even the staff who are voting with their feet and leaving the organization can seem to be part of normal attrition. For these reasons, it can be impossible for an executive champion to really know if the practice is strong. While you would think that an involved executive champion would quickly notice the downturn, failure to become deeply involved in the details of the team and a layer of management or two can combine to obscure a serious decline. As a consultant who specializes in institutionalization of user experience design practices, it has often been my job to walk into an executive's office and provide that warning.

You might not have a consultant who will be willing to put his or her relationship with the company at risk to protect the practice, however. Therefore we will outline three approaches that let an executive provide governance for team sustainability: measuring progress, tools support, and certification.

Measuring Progress

Metrics provide a classic method of governance. If you want to know if your team is alive and functional, you can get an indication by looking at customer experience metrics such as your Net Promoter Score, conversion, and customer retention. The only problem is that these indicators lag behind the actual UX design process. The work that the team does on designs takes time. Once those designs are envisioned, created, tested, refined, and documented, they still need to be implemented. Sure, some tactical changes may bump up your scores in the short run. Nevertheless, even these can mask a failure to create a solid strategy, to innovate, or to have holistic structural designs that fit into an ecosystem solution. It is not unusual to see good numbers for a year while your middle managers are effectively decimating your practice.

Metrics are a good way to make managers feel accountable and under pressure to attend to user experience design issues. Conversely, they are a very poor way to get an early warning of a disintegrating practice. The lag time is too long.

Tools Support for Governance

If the user experience design team is operating in an enterprise environment (like HFI's UX Enterprise), this environment is likely to provide a substantial increase in transparency. An even moderately trained executive is then able to assess the health of a practice in short order. The information used in design is instantly accessible, rather than hidden in voluminous documents and decks. Figure 10-6 depicts three different charts drawn instantly by UX Enterprise. Each chart shows the objects linked to a given design (UX specification). The number of links gives a good idea of the amount of supporting content guiding a design. Is the design evidence-based or a wild guess? It does not take an in-depth review of the documentation to tell.

HFI has been working on specific, governance-oriented reports and displays that let an executive gauge the quality of a user experience design practice in about 10 minutes. Certainly, a metrics system can be gamed with fake events and data. But if your design team is forced to fabricate the implementation of your UX program, it is probably running into other, possibly extreme problems that you are likely to notice without report—issues that major surgery will be required to correct. It is far better to find the problem early. To do so, we can check how often staff refer to methods and standards. As mentioned earlier, if your team has gotten out of the habit of referring to these core materials, they have reverted to an ad hoc approach to UX design far short of true institutionalization. We can also track how much data we have on user profiles, environments, and other objects. If objects are rich, based on observation and user research, we can be confident that the team is working in a serious way. If everything is based on stakeholder opinions, then we can be sure that the team is failing, because even the best stakeholders see things differently from customers (even if they were customers once).

Using Certification for Governance

It is hard for executives to get time to sit through briefings, monitor metrics, and explore data. This fact of life makes certification a great way to ensure that your user experience design practice is still operating effectively. When we created the Certified Practice in Usability at HFI, we did not really understand its potential role in governance; we simply knew that the need existed for solid, objective criteria for the maturity of a practice (Figure 10-7). We offered to police compliance with the criteria as well: a failure to renew your certification or a drop in certification level should sound a clear alarm that your practice is unraveling.

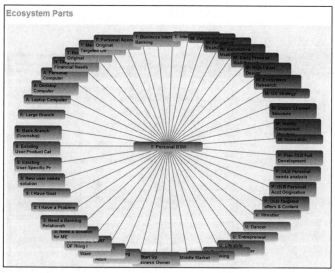

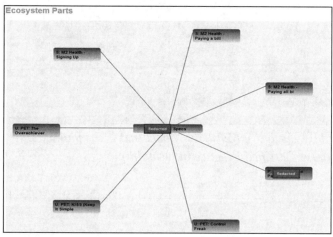

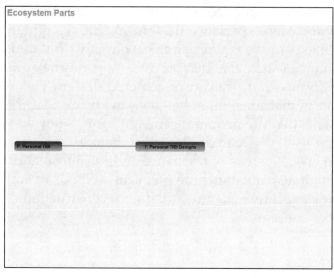

Figure 10-6: *These three charts show the users, scenarios, environments, and other elements that are the foundation for a given design. You can quickly see if a design is well supported, or just thrown together in a wild guess.*

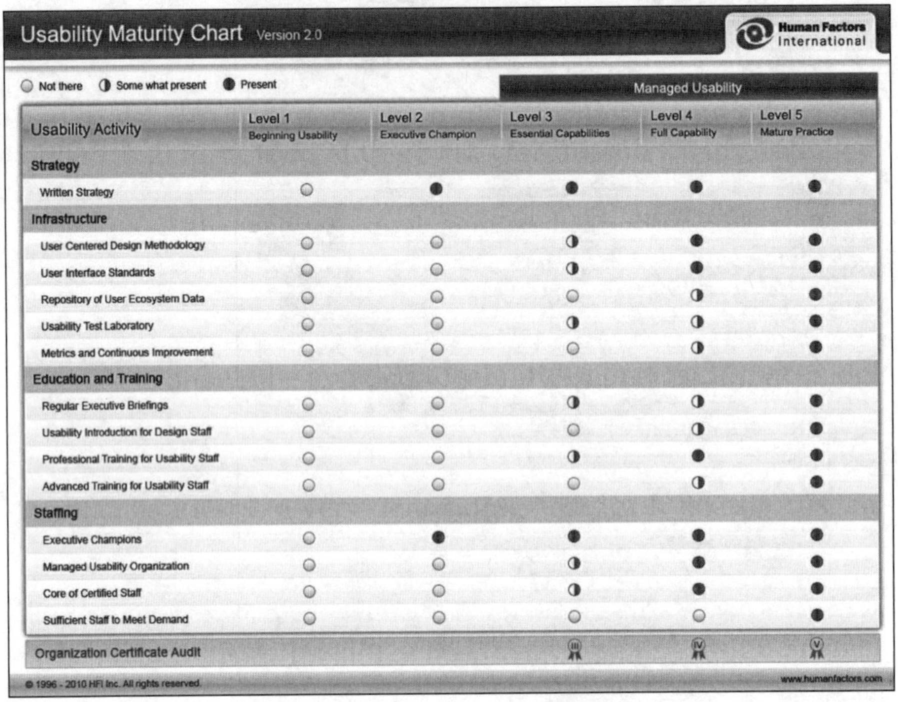

Usability Maturity Chart Version 2.0 — Human Factors International

Usability Activity	Level 1 Beginning Usability	Level 2 Executive Champion	Level 3 Essential Capabilities	Level 4 Full Capability	Level 5 Mature Practice
			Managed Usability		
Strategy					
Written Strategy	○	●	●	●	●
Infrastructure					
User Centered Design Methodology	○	○	◑	●	●
User Interface Standards	○	○	◑	●	●
Repository of User Ecosystem Data	○	○	○	◑	●
Usability Test Laboratory	○	○	◑	◑	●
Metrics and Continuous Improvement	○	○	○	◑	●
Education and Training					
Regular Executive Briefings	○	○	◑	◑	●
Usability Introduction for Design Staff	○	○	○	◑	●
Professional Training for Usability Staff	○	○	◑	●	●
Advanced Training for Usability Staff	○	○	○	◑	●
Staffing					
Executive Champions	○	●	●	●	●
Managed Usability Organization	○	○	◑	●	●
Core of Certified Staff	○	○	◑	●	●
Sufficient Staff to Meet Demand	○	○	○	○	●
Organization Certificate Audit			III	IV	V

Legend: ○ Not there   ◑ Some what present   ● Present

© 1996 - 2010 HFI Inc. All rights reserved.   www.humanfactors.com

Figure 10-7: *The HFI Usability Maturity Model that is the foundation of the Certified Practice in Usability*

Summary

Today, governance is the challenge most likely to emerge in the institutionalization of user experience design. Executives understand that customer experience is a key strategic objective, but middle management may not share that perspective—and may be quite resistant to a transformation toward user-centered design. Therefore, a combination of measures must be taken to ensure that the practice is sustainable: that the customer-centered focus is not sidelined or the practice itself dissipated. This must include education (ideally targeted at specific areas of resistance and misinformation in the organization). It also must include practical methods of surveillance to alert the executive champion before reconstruction of the practice becomes onerous.

Chapter 11

Organizational Structure

> Three types of organizational structures are commonly considered for the permanent user experience design team.

- *Matrix*—There is a central user experience design group, but rather than doing all the work, it supports user experience design practitioners working within different project teams. The matrix structure works well for medium-sized and large organizations.

- *Centralized*—All members of the user experience design staff are a single team, assigned temporarily to help on specific projects as needed. This structure works well for small organizations.

- *Decentralized*—User experience design staff members are allocated to specific projects and report up through the various lines of business. This structure has some inherent flaws; it is not recommended.

> All organizations need a central user experience design team. Although this team in reality is often found in many parts of the organization, it ideally exists under a chief user experience officer (CXO) or the head of marketing.

➤ Have an effective escalation pathway in place for problems with funding, staffing, and even specific design decisions.

➤ Graphic artists, writers, and other user experience design-oriented staff may best be placed in the same organization as the central user experience design team.

Once you have a proper infrastructure in place and a full understanding of your organization's needs, it makes sense to build a user experience design team. This team can be structured in many ways, and it is important to find the right structure to meet these needs and to place the people in the correct parts of the overall organization.

In the end, the success of the user experience effort depends very much on the quality and appropriateness of the staff recruited to do the work. Without skilled staff, the infrastructure will be of little benefit. Take care in assembling your team.

In the Organization phase, the benefits of user experience design begin to accumulate. You can start to make user experience a competitive differentiator and can expect to see well-engineered experiences become routine. The projects can begin in earnest and incorporate internal staff. This will, of course, bring new challenges in scheduling and resource limitations that will test your organization's ability to work smart within practical limitations.

The single most important organizational principle is that *user experience design does not reside in a single group.* Even if you have a team with that title, user experience design must permeate the entire organization.

Compare this situation with the health care model. In a health care organization, there are surgeons, doctors, physician's assistants, and nurses. All these people wear the "health care professional" title, have technology and training at their disposal, and are always aware of the latest research findings and tools. Although they form the official health care organization, everyone in society is a part of the larger health care system, because everyone has a basic understanding and a direct appreciation of health issues. Just as everyone must be responsible to some extent for his or her own health, so all employees should be aware of and feel responsible for user experience design issues.

It has been a common strategy to drop a user experience design team into an organization and hope for the best—which is about as effective as dropping a small group of well-meaning doctors into a foreign country where they don't speak the language. Let's consider the challenges. The user experience design team has its own jargon and perspective, which can lead to communication problems with the developers. When usability professionals talk about "personas," "scenarios" and "affordance design," developers won't have a clue what they mean. Those communications problems and different perspectives may lead the development community to mistrust the user experience design staff.

Interface design has also often become the *fun* part of the marketing specialist's, business analyst's, or developer's day. (And it *is* a nice diversion if you don't need to be rigorous.) Everyone thinks he or she is an expert in interface design, which lays the groundwork for a major power and control issue. The user experience design team must wrest control from other groups that are large, powerful, and entrenched.

Given these communication and control issues, the user experience design team often sees problems only when it is too late to fix them. This is a universal symptom of an incomplete institutionalization program. Developers are not sensitized to user experience design issues, so they do not realize that a problem exists until the users reject the application—or they find that the application's performance measurements are dismal. Developers proceed to create interfaces without knowing the basics of good design. They don't gather data from users, model and optimize the users' taskflows, apply research-based principles of good design, or begin routine user experience design testing at the early stages of the project.

Given the practices of many development organizations, it is no surprise that they build sites that aren't usable. Usability teams may feel helpless and ineffective in the wake of poor designs and end up clamoring for resources to fix broken interfaces. The solution requires a proactive approach: routine practices and perspectives must change throughout the organization.

The objective of the institutionalization effort is to ensure the user experience quality of all new sites and applications. This can be achieved only through a user experience design assurance system. When you consider implementation of this system, keep in mind that it should encompass the entire development organization, just as the health care system encompasses everyone in the community. Without this perspective, you will not have a successful operation, and the user experience design team will be ineffective.

I've participated in hundreds of meetings to plan the ideal organization for user experience design work. There are many nuances to attaining the optimal structure, communication, and task allocation, but really only one structure works well for large companies: a small centralized user experience design organization that supports user experience design practitioners who work in specific lines of business and are assigned to specific projects. For smaller organizations, the central user experience design team may be able to support the infrastructure and complete all the user experience design work itself.

This chapter discusses these organizational structures, the escalating problems that can occur, and means by which the user experience design team can work with user experience design-related groups.

Organizational Structures for User Experience Design Teams

You need to establish a structure for your permanent user experience design organization. However, the goodwill and the leverage of the people involved have as much or more impact than the structure on the success of user experience design. Air traffic controllers manage an amazingly complex task, occasionally handling crises where lives are at stake. Their systems are often antiquated, but they make the process work. Any structure can be made to work: people can scavenge resources and work out informal networks of support. Any structure can also be made to fail: if people decide not to accept the user-centered approach, they will sabotage it—whether willfully or inadvertently.

That said, it still makes sense to select an organizational structure that makes success more likely. We've mentioned three types of organizations that are commonly considered for a user experience design facility: decentralized, matrix, and centralized structures. Let's briefly review each of them.

Decentralized Structure

The decentralized structure allocates all user experience design staff members to specific projects. The UX staff then report up through the various lines of business. The benefits of a decentralized structure would seem to be that staff members become an integral part of the design groups. However, without a central group to provide a coherent set of methodologies, standards, facilities, and consultative support, or to provide a unified message to the executives, this type of structure almost always fails in the long run. Unsupported by a user experience design-focused leader, practitioners often end up doing software testing or some other activity needed to meet a project date rather than satisfy UX goals. The user experience design effort thus loses focus.

Matrix Structure

A matrix solution works well in mid-sized and large companies. In this structure, a small central user experience design team, as well as user experience design practitioners, work on projects and report to the various lines of business. The user experience design staff members are integrated and accepted within the project team, and they become deeply aware of the user experience design issues and techniques that can be applied to that team's initiatives. A matrix structure can be very effective as long as there is a small, central user experience design team to support user experience design practitioners on the project teams.

In the structure depicted in Figure 11-1, as the dotted arrow indicates, the central user experience design group has a reporting arrangement with UX practitioners on the project teams. The practitioners have a secondary reporting pathway, with the user experience design leader providing career counseling and input on performance reviews. The central group works with practitioners on the project teams. The central team members are responsible for methods, tools, facilities, training, and sponsorship. They help select new staff, advocate for user experience design practitioners when conflicts arise, and provide ongoing consultative support and mentoring. If the central team is not strong, the institutionalization effort will fail.

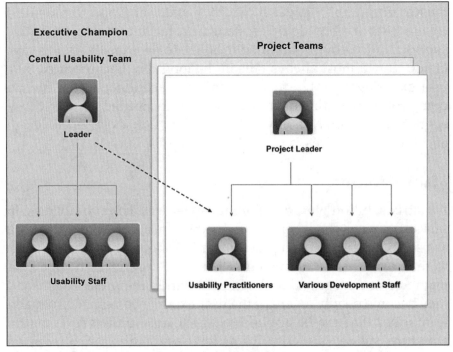

Figure 11-1: *A matrix solution for a large organization*

The central user experience design team must have an influential leader—his or her connections, political skills, and charisma are vastly important. In addition, the central user experience design staff (see Chapter 12) should include strong technical experts who can update standards, coach development teams, and operate as internal consultants. It is common for organizations with a central user experience design group to have three to five people working full time to support the methodology and consult with project teams. The team may also include a user experience design testing group that finds test participants and runs testing rooms and equipment. This group would include one or two people who can customize this process as well as other staff qualified to run tests.

For a large organization, the matrix structure seems to work well as long as the central group maintains momentum and provides a cohesive strategy. While the group doesn't have to be very large, it is essential to have one in place.

Centralized Structure

A centralized structure with all the user experience design staff in a single organization works well in smaller companies or in companies that undertake only a few development projects each year. In this structure, staff members are assigned to work on specific projects. It is relatively easy to maintain the user-centered perspective of staff members, upgrade their skill sets, and preserve the infrastructure needed.

In a large organization, however, the central group is likely to become disconnected from project teams and lines of business; in fact, they are often excluded from project work. Their staff are not understood and valued, and there is an unmet expectation that practitioners will deeply understand each domain and division. This disconnect explains why it is really necessary to have staff permanently assigned to design projects or lines of business in large organizations. That way, the complex domains can be fully understood and there can be solid integration with the working teams.

Being on Projects

Colin Hynes, President, UX Inc.
Former Director of Site Usability, Staples

A lot of making user experience design work is frankly just making sure we're on project teams. We are involved early in the process of every project on Staples.com, and part of our goal for next year is to do that throughout the catalog, corporate applications, and retail applications. We are "on the streets" with them—whether they're merchants or marketing folks, IS development folks or creative graphics people—showing our value to each project on a day-to-day basis. We don't swoop in and say, "Here's all the stuff that's wrong with your catalog, your application, your website, and good luck fixing it—we'll see you in another two months when we can do the same thing." We're integrated as part of the team.

I'm actually a business owner on some of those projects. For example, we're redesigning the registration process on Staples .com. I'm the business owner of that—I'm the client of that project as well as being the user experience design guy. So the user experience design group owns some of the action. We're not just staff advisors; we're responsible for some of the projects.

Placement of a Central Team in the Overall Organization

A centralized user experience design team provides central coordination, infrastructure, and support. This team must reside in a given part of the overall organization and report to an executive champion who will support that group over the long term. I have seen a centralized user experience design team placed within the quality assurance (QA) unit, the IT department, and the marketing department, but none of these solutions seem ideal. Placement directly under a CXO is the best positioning within a company. The subsections that follow briefly discuss these options.

Placement within Quality Assurance

The quality assurance group usually becomes the home for the user experience design team when user experience design primarily has a testing function. To ensure that quality is independent and uncompromised by the IT group's tough time constraints, the quality assurance team is usually not directly controlled by the IT organization.

When the user experience design team resides within the quality assurance group, the team functions as an auditor—a real positive for the summative user experience design testing process. The group can report tests of overall experience and performance with impunity. Group members may also be able to do consulting work with the detachment characteristic of an auditing organization. While this is an attractive solution in some ways, it can also be too removed from the organization's direct business imperatives. Placement within the QA group can keep the UX team focused on meeting arbitrary user experience design metrics, thereby losing sight of the real business objectives (e.g., making money) owing to the obsession with bureaucratic requirements. One solution is to have a small, specialized user experience design testing group within the quality assurance organization and then assign the central group elsewhere.

Placement within IT

Many user experience design teams are placed directly within the IT organization. It's a logical placement inasmuch as UX specialists are considered systems development staff. User experience design team members report to the CIO or more often to a second-level executive in the systems development division.

There is a downside to being attached to the IT organization, however: it makes the user experience design team completely dependent on the goodwill of the IT group. If the executive champion of the UX initiative works within the IT department, the placement of user experience design within IT may work very well. Conversely, if the executive champion works primarily in a different department, IT may be a tough place for the user experience design team to reside.

The IT organization is often focused on two main goals: meeting the schedule and eliminating bugs. IT group members often consider themselves successful if they get the site or application up in the time allotted. If the facility does not crash or have major errors in calculation, they celebrate a success—and are bewildered by users who say, "That may be what we asked for, but it is not what we want." When they hear this complaint, they blame the users. If this is the character of the IT group, it's not the right setting for an effective user experience design team.

Placement within Marketing

The central user experience design group is also sometimes made a part of the marketing organization. The marketing group is focused on making money—a goal it accomplishes by satisfying customers. Identifying a market niche, a unique selling proposition, and a brand, marketing generally has a strategy for moving the company forward. User experience design professionals then make sure that sites and applications support this strategy. Usability specialists ensure that the technology meets users' needs and accommodates their limitations in a practical way.

Marketing staff members quickly realize that the user experience design process is the logical continuation of their work. That can mean that people in marketing try to take on the role of user experience design practitioners. If they receive training and certification, such an approach works well; without the needed training, however, success will prove elusive. In the best scenario, the marketing organization becomes the greatest promoter of user experience design engineering.

Of the current most common options—quality assurance, IT, or marketing—the best location for the central user experience design organization is usually within marketing. The marketing organization has a vested interest in the quality of the user experience, and marketing staff members want to ensure that IT provides real value. They are determined to use IT expenditures in ways that really add value to customers. The user experience design team supports this process. In a sense, user experience design engineering is wholly focused on realizing marketing's vision. User experience design practitioners ensure that the marketing strategy is carried forward through the detailed design of the site or application.

Organizations without a formal marketing department, such as government agencies, may find their user experience design personnel distributed among various groups. However, an increasing number of these agencies now have entities that are very similar to commercial product management or lines of business. Divisions in government focused on specific functional objectives are an appropriate part of the organization for user experience design staff to reside, with the IT department being seen as the last resort.

Placing the user experience design team within the marketing organization may prove challenging in several ways. First, some marketing organizations are not concerned with customer interactions. That is, they are primarily focused on advertising programs that create offers for customers, but don't consider the customers' taskflows or process while evaluating their offers or getting them fulfilled. User experience design work will be a poor fit for the marketing organization in this type of environment. Even if the marketing team members do have a wider view of interaction, their expertise and focus are not usually directed toward design and delivery. They may set the direction for the products, but their primary concern remains getting customers to the point of sale. Product setup, normal usage, problem management. and other subsequent issues of customer experience are not the main focus of most conventional marketing organizations.

In any case, most marketing groups are responsible for more than just online customer interaction. They must consider many channels of marketing communication as well as the customers' behavior within a store, through the mail, and during interaction with company staff. This is, as a general rule, a good thing: usability work should be synchronized with the other modalities of interaction. While usability professionals do not design store layouts—marketers and consumer psychologists handle this task—synchronization is important. Problems can occur if sufficient consideration is not given to the online experience. Thus, if the marketing organization does not have a significant interest in online activities, it is a poor home for the user experience design group.

A second area of concern with the placement of user experience design teams within marketing groups is that they may not be clear on where marketing expertise stops and where user experience design work takes over. This is an understandable problem because both marketing and user experience design professionals gather data from customers, and both care about customer motivation and perspective. The key difference is that *the marketing group defines the target, and the user experience design group hits it.*

When members of a marketing group run group focus sessions, they are searching for a good product idea. They gather customer data to define the target market for the idea, and work to define a precise brand perception and selling proposition. With these elements defined, the user experience design team does its work with the development staff to ensure that the functional specification works for the defined user target. The user experience design team structures an interface and guides graphic designers to create that target brand perception, then engineers a taskflow that fulfills the unique selling proposition.

Some overlap may occur within this process. The marketing group often provides the logo along with the color palettes and corporate typefaces that are known to support the brand and are being used in offline channels. The marketing group may also select terms that describe a product offering, whether or not these terms mean anything to users. Members of this group provide feature lists that may sometimes be a close match for the real user needs. At the same time, the user experience design team may discover issues with brand values or the way the brand is presented. The user experience design team may suggest different descriptions of an offering or at least highlight those that will not work. It is important to be cautious when working in areas of overlap to ensure that the process remains smooth: a good user experience design team will be responsive to marketing throughout the design and implementation process.

Another challenge with placing the user experience design team within the marketing organization is that marketing may have almost no interest in systems that are not seen by customers. The user experience design team should work on the company intranet and customer service applications. It is certainly possible to have a separate user experience design team for internal applications, but it is a better use of resources to have a single user experience design group. This central group can then work on these projects. There is usually too much overlap in the work to be done on methodology, infrastructure, tools, and training to maintain separate user experience design teams.

Placement under a CXO

There is an increasingly common best practice (see *Outside In: The Power of Putting Customers at the Center of Your Business*, 2012, by Harley Manning, Kerry Bodine, and Josh Bernoff) of placing the central user experience design team under the direct supervision of a CXO. The CXO is placed high in the organization and has responsibility across every line of business. A single interaction with the user may, in fact, involve several different divisions. The CXO has the position, power, and responsibility to see that this interaction is a coherent success.

An interesting issue is emerging in organizations that have CXOs. The CXO focuses on the overall customer experience across all touch points. This includes the digital facilities and digitally supported facilities, of course—but it also includes analog, tactile aspects of the business process, such as the layout of stores and packaging and marketing materials. This multiplicity of platforms creates an interesting organizational dilemma.

Members of the user experience design group that works on digital channels must have very different skills than employees who work on store layouts. Improving manual workflows is much easier than creating digital solutions and can conceivably be done based on common sense. Some organizations create multiple groups, often with names that actually mean the same thing—for example, a Customer Experience Group and a separate User Experience Group. Although they have different skill sets, they need the same ecosystem data. Moreover, because all channels of customer interface interact, they must coordinate: point-of-sale facilities, for example, need to integrate with the store layouts. The central user experience design group needs to expand, accommodating somewhat different types of staff, to manage that integration.

Once created, the role of CXO becomes one of the key positions in an organization's power structure. It is certainly a position that

---

An Executive Must Champion Usability

Harley Manning, Research Director, Forrester Research

Almost every time we research organizational issues (including how the project is run), we find a project owner matrix-managing a cross-functional team. This project owner needs an executive champion who can make sure that he or she gets funding and gets support against all the organizational sniping that goes on. This executive champion should report to either the head of the division or the CEO. If not, the project has the potential to get derailed by efforts from other groups.

It's just as important for the champion to know what not to do as it is to know what to do. If you are an executive, it's important not to play other roles.

---

needs to be filled by an executive with considerable savvy and vision. The head of marketing has the responsibility for getting people engaged with the organization's products; the CXO is responsible for good things happening to the customer throughout that engagement. This is a huge responsibility, and one that is best placed with a single person who can oversee the entire range of engagements. For more information on the role of the CXO, see Chapter 12.

Escalation of Problems

When positioning the user experience design team, be sure to consider the chain of escalation for problems. With a new institutionalization effort, there are sure to be conflicts and difficulties over funding, staffing, and even specific design decisions. There may be a stubborn vice president who feels that a wiggly animation will really improve sales—especially when accompanied by a short, continuously looping music track. Project teams can bring these types of problems to the central user experience design group, and the leader of the central group can try to resolve them. Usually, a composite video of users complaining about download time and expressing annoyance with the design is enough to convince the well-intentioned executive. This approach does not always work, however. What, then, should the appropriate escalation path be? It is a critical question.

The CXO is the ideal path for escalation. Only the CXO has unambiguous responsibility for the user experience and a position high enough in the organization to successfully resolve these types of issues. When an escalation path to the CXO is lacking, there is a potential for problems to occur. A user experience design group in marketing may clash with the senior executive who has strong design ideas. A user experience design group in IT may clash with the executive who just wants to get the site up and running on time, regardless of user issues. A user experience design group embroiled in design problems may not get much help from a manager who is responsible for writing procedures, best practices, or quality assurance reports. The escalation path will inevitably go up through the area where the central user experience design group is situated. No matter where it travels, the pathway of escalation must be credible and effective.

Although the leader of the user experience design team should strive to resolve issues directly, a plausible and effective escalation pathway may exist when this approach fails. This is the primary reason for the leader to report to a position high in the organization. Otherwise, user issues will rarely win out over issues of schedule, politics, habit, and preference.

Graphic Artists, Writers, and Other Usability-Oriented Staff

A highly diverse family of specialists helps form the actual user experience. Graphic artists create icons and other graphical images, for example, while technical writers generate content and market research groups collect wide and varied data about users. How do all these different types of people interact within the organization?

If you have a CXO, you have someone in a unified position who can coordinate the disparate central groups that focus on user experience. Market researchers can raise issues to be studied by the user experience design team, and the user experience design specialists can bring challenges to the graphics team. A powerful creative synergy may emerge from such interactions. If you don't have a CXO, you need to consider placing these staff members in your central user experience design group. Despite the fact that they are not user experience design specialists, these other staff members have a critical role in supporting the user experience design engineers and/or creating a positive user experience.

Summary

The single most important organizational principle is that *the concern for user experience design should not reside only in a single group.* There should be a team with that title with primary responsibility and serious capabilities, but concern for user experience design must permeate the entire organization. The structure you choose should be appropriate to the size and goals of your organization, and it should take into account the best placement of the central user experience design team. The next chapter provides information on effective staffing theories and strategies that will help you finalize the structure you have established.

Chapter 12

Staffing

➤ The manager of the central user experience design group is the day-to-day leader of the central organization, and also manages the overall progress of user experience design in the company. It is better to have a good manager without much user-centered design experience than an expert who does not understand management.

➤ The central user experience design group needs UX professionals who play a number of types of roles. You may need to staff all of these roles and more:

- Infrastructure manager
- Mentor
- Topical specialist
- Ecosystem researcher

➤ The user experience design manager and practitioners do the actual user experience design work—they are generalists in user experience engineering and possess a solid skill set for the design process. In small companies, they may be a part of the central organization. In larger companies, they

> should generally report to the project teams within each line of business.

> ➤ Using an offshore model is potentially a partial solution for almost any organization building its user experience design staff.

This chapter describes the staff roles needed for the institutionalization of user experience design and explains what to look for when hiring people to fill them. These roles do not necessarily map directly to job descriptions, as one person may fulfill a number of roles. Conversely, one role may be filled by several individuals. Mix and match them as necessary, but the roles must be staffed. In a very large organization, greater specialization is the norm, and it is more likely that several people will work on a given role. In smaller companies, a single individual often must handle multiple roles. For example, in a very small company with only one user experience engineer, that person may need to fulfill *all* the roles described in this chapter (a daunting requirement), while a medium-sized company might have a specialist in cross-cultural design who also has graphic art skills.

Earlier chapters discussed developing the infrastructure of the user experience design operation. As a result, you now have the knowledge necessary to create a "user experience design factory" complete with appropriate processes and tools. But the success of that factory very much depends on getting the right UX staff in place, and this is not an easy task. Only a limited number of educational institutions offer graduate programs for user experience design practitioners, and many graduates of these programs still need real-world experience.[1] At the undergraduate level, there are some courses available in user-centered design but not degrees that focus on the necessary skills. Many countries are developing practitioner programs to meet this rising demand; thus an offshore model is

---

1. For a listing of the current university programs available, see www.humanfactors.com/downloads/degrees.asp.

another potential option for organizations to consider. In this chapter, I share insights gained during two decades of experience with hiring user experience design staff.

The Chief User Experience Executive

Once the institutionalization effort has succeeded, a central user experience design organization should be in place (as discussed in Chapter 11). This organization reports to an executive, who may be a chief user experience officer (CXO), the senior vice president of marketing, or the head of quality assurance. Whatever the title or position, the set of activities and responsibilities this executive must fulfill requires no user experience design skill. Understanding the field is certainly important—but this job is really about large-scale organizational leadership.

It is a common mistake for organizations to put practitioners into this position. Teaching a practitioner to be an executive leader is asking a lot. Practitioners generally do not know how to direct a large-scale organization, setting the stage for things to go very badly. Highly skilled practitioners frequently think that to develop a user experience design practice, more smart people like themselves should be hired. Without leadership experience, they don't understand the need to do large-scale, process-driven work.

In many ways, the user experience executive continues the role of the executive champion (refer to Chapter 1 for additional details on this role). It is essential to continue chanting the mantra of business focus for user experience design work and operating within the politics of the organization to ensure that support is obtained from key players. In some ways, these tasks are much easier to address now that the organization has been sensitized to user experience design issues and a foundation of support is in place. The initial strategy of institutionalization has given way to a far more complex set of projects and initiatives, and the executive must establish the balance among strategic activities, infrastructure, and tactical work. In addition, he or she needs to monitor progress, solve problems, and celebrate success.

During times of growth and prosperity, maintaining the user experience design team is not a problem. In contrast, during difficult times, the executive must make a solid case for continuation of the team. In the past, the usability organization was often cut early in a downturn—a development that can be discouraging for user experience design staff, and one that has prompted many talented people to leave the field. The executive needs to inspire a sense of purpose, commitment, and security in the organization. When a team is properly integrated and working in a mature way, then it will be sustainable through downturns and executive turnover.

No matter if you have just one UX practitioner or hundreds, you still need someone at an executive level playing the role of executive champion. The executive champion was critical in starting the process for institutionalizing user experience design, and a champion will be critical for continuing and maintaining user experience engineering practices. If you have a CXO, this person is most likely your executive champion. If you do not have a CXO, you need to clarify who your executive champion is.

The Central Usability Organization Manager

The executive champion or chief user experience executive provides high-level strategy and support. This role is essential, but the daily work falls under the supervision of the manager of the central user experience design organization, who has a very different job from that of the executives. The role of the central usability organization manager requires at least an understanding of user-centered design technology, along with very good connections in the organization. While the executive might spend a small part of his or her time on user experience design, the central UX organization manager is fully dedicated to the control and promotion of the user experience engineering capability within the organization. There is a rapidly growing set of skilled job candidates in this area, and an increasing body of knowledge about how to do that job well (see *User Experience Management: Essential Skills for Leading Effective UX Teams*, by Arnie Lund).

The central user experience design group has a whole agenda of projects and services for which the executive champion may provide overall direction, but the manager has to plan, fund, staff, and monitor each one. This job is a lot like running an internal consulting group—there is an infrastructure to maintain and a set of project offerings to design, create, market, and deliver.

The manager of the user experience design team is sure to spend a substantial amount of time addressing personnel issues—hiring good usability staff and cultivating them internally. Existing staff members also need to be mentored. Consequently, the manager should dedicate time to developing career planning and feedback sessions for this group.

The ideal qualities of a user experience design manager include in-depth knowledge of user experience engineering practices, a full grasp of the organizational dynamics, and a love of management. Such individuals have the expertise to chart the course for user-centered design work and contribute a great deal to the process. Owing to their in-depth understanding of organizational dynamics, even if they are not familiar with your organization, they will quickly familiarize themselves with it. The ideal manager is fully committed to user experience design and won't get sidetracked easily.

If you cannot find or afford a "walk-on-water" user experience design expert with management skills, what should you do? You may be tempted to promote a highly skilled user experience design specialist who has a deep understanding of the field. After all, he or she will understand what needs to be accomplished, will be able to assess the quality of work, and can help make wise tradeoffs when difficult decisions arise. However, placing a practitioner without management experience into a leadership role might lead to the collapse of your institutionalization effort. Without a leader who has the necessary savvy and political skills, the entire user experience design organization may be marginalized and eventually eliminated. While some cultures can be supportive of a technical expert placed in a leadership position, the specialist is ill equipped to run with the wolves in most organizations—or even to run from them.

As a second choice, it is better to select a street-smart manager who cares about user-centered design issues, providing him or her with plenty of training and support. This person's understanding of the management role and channels of communication is his or her most important capability, outweighing even limited user experience engineering expertise. The professional manager must be dedicated to user experience design and have the ability to build a team of experts—and then to grow that team and protect it. Ideally, the manager can mentor the team members in content as well as clear roadblocks for them. If he or she is not equipped to do so, the manager may need to delegate content mentoring to another staff person or an outside mentor.

The management role is the most critical for the team. If you have a manager who is not an expert, you will absolutely need one very key capability: someone who is able to select the methods that will be applied to each program and to estimate the scope of effort. This will take someone quite senior in the user experience design field.

It is often thought that the manager of the central usability team can also complete the work of the executive champion, but that misconception arises simply because many organizations do not appreciate the champion's critical role. You need a true executive to be the executive champion. The role should not be combined with that of the central manager. Refer to Chapter 1 for details on the role of the executive champion.

The Central Usability Organization Staff

As mentioned in Chapter 11, the central user experience design group comprises a small nucleus of staff members with user experience design expertise who coordinate UX activities for the company (Figure 12-1). This central group forms the dissemination point for best practices and success stories. It must also manage challenges to maintain progress toward an optimized user experience. This group rarely includes more than 6–10 people. (In large organizations, additional staff members are distributed in project teams.) The central

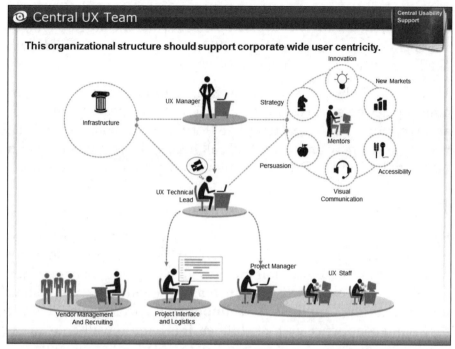

Figure 12-1: *A large central group supporting project teams*

usability team is essential to keeping the institutionalization effort moving forward while remaining coordinated—and dynamic.

We will define seven subroles that may be needed within this team to complete its centralized support functions: (1) infrastructure manager, (2) mentor, (3) topical specialist, (4) project planner, (5) project manager, (6) generalist, and (7) researcher. As with the concept of archetypes in mythology, there is usually a bit of each role in every user experience professional, although some people function well in only a limited set of areas, while others perform only one of these roles well.

The Infrastructure Manager

This role is far less proactive than that of the mentor, specialist, or generalist. The infrastructure manager spends much less time interacting with the constituent project teams. Instead, he or she is responsible for getting methods, standards, and tools in place—facilities that need to be maintained and disseminated as well. This has become an increasingly complex process. While the methods might not change much, the templates sitting alongside the methods will need to be refined and expanded.

There should always be a central facility to field questions about interface design standards and gather issues. A repeated request for an exception to a screen template, for example, could signal the need to add a new template. Tools all need to be administered and monitored. In addition, there is often internal training to provide.

The Mentor

People in the role of mentor reach out to guide and evaluate junior user experience design staff and provide selective support on many projects. Junior usability staff members have a lot to manage. They are often performing activities such as data gathering and testing for the first time, and they need support and encouragement while they build confidence in their abilities. It is hard to walk into a testing facility and face your first test participant—there is always a fear that you will not be able to manage the session. This fear is not unfounded. Some test participants repeatedly go off on tangents. Others harbor resentment about something the company did and want to talk about nothing but that one erroneous item on their bill. The consultant often accompanies junior usability staff members to a few sessions until their confidence increases.

Aside from emotional support, the mentor is there to provide an infusion of technical expertise when it is needed. Often, a few moments of attention from the consultant—noticing, for instance, that the task analysis documentation is too detailed—can help a junior professional avoid weeks of unnecessary work, averting real dangers to design quality. Seeing that the design concept requires impossible technology or could be accomplished with a simple, standard page type can also make future rework unnecessary. The mentor plays a key role in developing technical expertise through his or her guidance.

Fulfilling the requirements of this role can be great fun. A mentor gets to make a positive impact in many arenas, but rarely has to stay to complete what is sometimes considered difficult and uninteresting detail work. This role is the ideal job for the more aggressive and highly skilled usability generalist.

It is essential to have high-quality technical skills for this role. The mentor must be able to evaluate processes and designs without spending a great deal of time on analysis or reflection. He or she must be decisive and definite, and as the final authority in many UX issues, cannot afford to be wrong very often.

At the same time, mentors should be emissaries for the user experience design initiative, constantly educating the organization about the value of UX design and the resources available in the organization. Just like external consultants from a usability vendor's organization, these internal consultants must create positive impressions and bonds.

The Topical Specialist

The need for a specialist role depends on the type of work the company does. There are many types of specialists in the user experience engineering field. Software user experience is a specialty within the overall field of applied psychology, which includes transportation, military equipment, consumer products, aviation, and other subfields. Numerous subspecialties exist within software experience engineering. If your organization's core competency involves one of these subspecialties, it may make sense to hire a user experience design professional with expertise in this particular area. Following are some of the more common areas of specialization within the field of user-centered software engineering.

The Technology Specialist

Some user experience design specialists focus on particular types of software technology. These experts may specialize in mobile or Web applications, graphical user interfaces (GUIs), voice response systems (both touch tone and voice recognition), phones, and other handheld units. There is a lifetime's worth of detail in each of these areas. For example, a good general practitioner or consultant knows the basics of a voice response script and knows how to make menus short and simple. Nevertheless, complex strategies come into play when tuning a voice recognition algorithm; even the way that the software determines the end of a word is challenging [Kotelly 2003]. If the core business of an organization involves voice recognition software, it is worthwhile to have staff specialists who understand these nuances. If there is only an occasional, specialized area of need, however, it is best to find a specialist to hire on a contract basis.

The User and Domain Specialists

Specialists focus on particular domains or user types. Some focus just on the design of software for children, on financial applications, or on the presentation of graphic models for oil drilling. Every domain has its own language, insights, and challenges. While it is true that a good consultant can make a positive impact on almost any application, there is real value in hiring someone who has experience in your particular domain. For example, if the company is wholly focused on building gaming software, it pays to have a specialist familiar with the gaming industry, environment, and customer populations.

The same developmental activities are needed. You cannot just go to the specialist and say, "You have been building gaming applications for 30 years, so make one for me." This approach will at best result in duplicating the design, business strategy, unique selling proposition, and branding of a previous client. Instead, the specialist should go through a de novo, full, user-centered design process. This ensures the creation of a design that precisely fits your organization's competitive strategy. The specialist's expertise helps save time in understanding the domain and improves the quality of questions, thereby enabling your organization to avoid pitfalls. He or she will likely be able to accommodate design requirements that may not be obvious. Nevertheless, the full user experience design process is needed to create a competitive design.

The Developmental Activity Specialist

A good general practitioner or consultant in the field can complete the full range of developmental activities in the user experience design methodology. However, some professionals specialize in a limited part of the development life cycle, such as conducting usability testing. Developmental activity specialists are often less expensive to hire than generalists because their skill set is limited. These specialists may be very useful as members of project teams, or they may be collected in a service organization within the central usability group—which deploys the group's specialty more cost-effectively. You can apply their work across many projects throughout your organization.

Some specialists work on very sophisticated parts of the user experience design methodology. Developing an appropriate UX strategy is both critical and difficult. It requires someone who understands how to extract ideas from executives, who is familiar with business models, and who can envision large scale, cross-channel designs.

Other practitioners specialize in innovation. Everyone tries to be innovative in what they do, and you can certainly be trained to be more innovative—but serious innovation programs are entirely another matter. These programs are large-scale efforts that understand a business space and generate many ideas about new offerings and business models that are then systematically envisioned and evaluated.

Finally, specialists are commonly employed to run controlled experiments. If you need a scientifically valid comparison between designs with appropriate statistical treatment, you will need someone who has a solid experimental design capability—a characteristic that is somewhat uncommon among user experience design generalists.

The Persuasion Engineer

The rationale of making a design that is easy to use is essentially accepted everywhere. It is the "table stakes" of design—if you intend to be in business, your digital channels should be usable or you should not even try to be in the game. Today, however, the arena of competition is going well beyond simple ease-of-use. Don Norman [2002], one of the great thinkers in the usability field, has described how design must go beyond usability. We are now in a struggle to make interfaces that are enjoyable and compelling. It turns out that there is a whole set of research-based models, skills, and methods specific to *emotional design*. From UX strategy, through innovation and user-centered design, there are special activities that your persuasion engineering expert needs to complete to ensure a compelling solution. The design might need impressive graphics (we will cover that shortly), but being compelling is not at all synonymous with graphic richness. Consider two of the most persuasive interfaces online: those of Amazon.com and Facebook: though not graphically rich, they are quite compelling for more fundamental and powerful reasons.

The persuasion engineer is responsible for using a whole set of methods that shape emotion and trigger conversion (Figure 12-2). Of course, graphics can be part of the solution. Just consider two highly successful applications: slot machines and World of Warcraft.

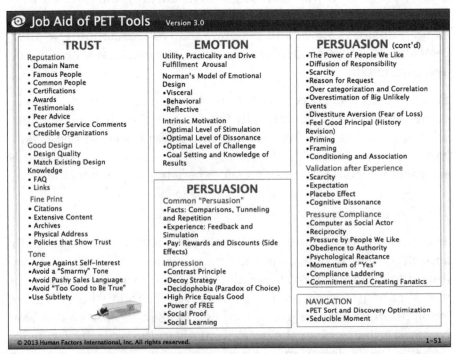

Figure 12-2: *Persuasion engineering tools from HFI's basic course on persuasion, emotion, and trust (PET design)*

The Cross-Cultural Specialist

Cross-cultural experts have a really in-depth understanding of how to adapt an application to different cultural contexts. All trained user experience design consultants are sensitive to the issues of globalization and localization of software and are aware of the challenges within this area. For example, a well-trained consultant for an American company would never approve the name "Morning Mist" for a perfume product destined for sales in Germany, a country where *mist* means *manure*.

A cross-cultural specialist will understand which principles of design make translation easier, such as "Do not embed variables in a sentence that will be translated because syntax changes will shift the order of the variables, making the rendering of translated sentences hard to code and maintain." Consider the following English text: "Thanks, [username]! That is [units bought] [color] [product] added to your account." In Spanish, it would translate correctly as follows: "Gracias, [username]! Eso es [units bought] [product] [color] agregado a su cuenta." Thus the programmer would need to reverse the sequence of color and product.

The generalist can do a credible job of avoiding many pitfalls in cross-cultural design. However, specialists in the field spend their professional lives seeking to understand the issues and processes of localization and have models that identify key differences between cultures that may impact the design. They know the characteristics of the target culture that will be of special concern.

If your business is defined by having a certain expertise, you will benefit from having at least one of these numerous types of user experience design specialists on board. The Social Security Administration, for example, will have accessibility experts. Large multinational organizations will have experts in emerging markets. A deep R&D operation will have theoretical cognitive scientists. A game company might have a positive psychologist (who studies fun and happiness).

Besides the specialists listed here, specialists may focus on areas such as multidimensional data, visualization methods, online search strategies, security, and font design. While it is important not to expect a specialist to be able to play a more generalist role within the usability team, if your organization is working within a very specialized domain, it may make sense to have a specialist on board.

The Ecosystem Researcher

As computers become more ubiquitous, we must consider a far more complex context for our designs. We can no longer just look at a person using an application. Instead, we have to consider many people playing different roles—that is, complex social and physical environments. So many of these contextual issues come into play that some businesses have started using cultural anthropologists and ethnographers to enhance their understanding. These researchers see things differently from classic applied psychologists. They look at the roles of various actors in a given setting. They are sensitive to the context, communication, values, and rules in a given setting. Their job is to study a given ecosystem, model the ecosystem, and then guide development of facilities that will effectively operate within that context. For many organizations, a central team—staffed with the right specialists—can perform this research and then share the results among many different design teams.

The UX Manager and Practitioners

In small organizations, the central group lends usability specialists to projects. In medium-sized and large organizations, practitioners work for lines of business and are assigned to specific projects. The project team may have only a single user experience design person, yet two different roles must actually be provided: a management role and a working practitioner's role. The manager is really the project manager for the user experience design activity. Fulfilling this role means creating a plan for user experience design work within the project. The company methodology lays out a generic project plan, but it is up to the manager to mold that plan and designate the specific activities and resources to make the generic methodology fit the project's time frame, budget, and key objectives. This takes a great deal of creativity and experience. It requires a top-level staff person with advanced degrees, certifications, and a proven track record. This person must address many issues and business decisions.

HFI has seen that an experienced project team manager with good planning skills can cut as much as 10–15% from the time and effort of the usability work. A poor planning job, in contrast, may make a usability project fail. Project planning is not composed of a single activity, but rather must be refined and revisited throughout the process. Project planning for usability work is mostly about finding shortcuts and avoiding traps, and the project team manager is instrumental in making such outcomes happen. The following list gives a sense of the level of planning considerations required:

- The current application is obviously bad, and everyone knows it. The manager decides to skip an initial usability test on the current application and go right to the design phase. This shortcut saves $60,000 and three weeks of time.

- The manager is told that users are hard to find but still does not agree to gather data from internal users. The internal staff, interviewed as surrogate users, would be biased by the company viewpoint, and several additional features might be mentioned that are of no interest to the real users. Avoiding this trap saves $250,000 in unneeded development and coding.

- During a project team discussion about the best width of the text, team members say they want to run a study to find the answer. The manager recalls seeing research, looks it up and makes a clear recommendation for a 100-character-wide display, thus putting an end to the discussion. This saves the team another two days of fighting and prevents an unnecessary study—a shortcut that saves three weeks and $30,000 to do the research.

- The team immediately wants to begin detailed page designs, coding them concurrently. The manager forces the team to make standard templates and reusable code. This cuts the final development time by three weeks and avoids customer complaints due to inconsistent, idiosyncratic designs—saving three weeks and $80,000. There are increased sales as well due to improvements in customer perceptions.

- The key business objective is to make the site self-evident. Rather than employing random or stratified sampling, the manager decides to just study low-end users. The team can test with just 20 users instead of 50, and still get better data. It's a shortcut that saves four days of time and $15,000.

Between avoiding traps and finding shortcuts, a good project team manager uses his or her experience to save the company time and money.

In the absence of a strong central user experience design manager, however, the project team manager may have to build the team. This means recruiting and screening the right staff for the group, attending to the career development needs and personal motivations of team members, and mentoring and growing the staff.

Finally, on an ongoing basis, the manager must support the project's progress. He or she must lead difficult negotiations with the other developers, track project milestones, unsnarl logistics, and allocate staff resources. Constant interactions with the other development team members are required, and adjustments in schedule must be made to accommodate them.

The project team manager role must be staffed by someone who understands the user experience engineering process well. Project planning is the toughest part of this role, but it is possible to get help for planning from the central user experience design team. Nevertheless, even if such assistance is provided for the management of the project plan, the execution of the plan requires someone who knows the details and vicissitudes of usability work. The person responsible for the usability of the project should complete the project planning. This is not the CXO, the executive champion, or even the usability team manager. This type of project management involves managing a specific project, not the user experience design group as a whole.

The Creative Director and the Graphic Designer

Traditionally, user experience engineers seek to make practical, useful, and usable designs. However, achieving these goals is often not enough. Designs must be satisfying, pleasant, inspiring, entertaining, and beautiful (Figure 12-3). This is the new frontier of the user experience design field. Unfortunately, today's usability staff

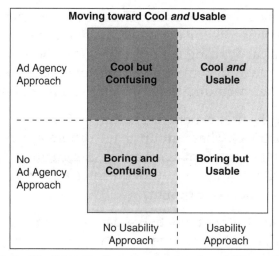

Figure 12-3: *Dr. John Sorflaten's matrix of usability and creativity*

members are often ill equipped to reach the visual design aspect of this goal on their own. Instead, to satisfy this requirement, user experience design staff must work with graphic designers.

When the design must appeal to the user's emotions, creative and artistic functional roles must be built into the project along with user experience design roles. Their degree of involvement and importance varies. If the site is an online brochure, the usability staff may have little to do, while the graphic design staff may need to do quite a bit of work on the creative design and presentation. Conversely, within a human resources site designed for an intranet, very little creative work may be required. For example, users of this site may want to see only their 401(k) account and benefits. While an appealing graphic skin on the site needs to be designed to support the company's brand, expenditures on aesthetic work should be limited. In most projects, however, there is a balance of these two perspectives. Public sites and shrink-wrap applications are two examples of projects that need a wise balance between user experience engineering and creative design.

To make a site beautiful, you need to bring in skilled people. There must be functional roles for both the creative director and the graphic designer. These people come from visual arts and design backgrounds, and many have also joined the interactive design field from advertising backgrounds. The creative director generally develops the concepts for the design, while the graphic designer does the physical drawing as well as creates alternative designs to meet the objectives of the creative director, and is responsible for decisions such as regarding color palettes and font families.

Integration of the user experience design and creative design efforts is some times tricky. These groups have different perspectives and methods, and they may not agree on the design. In a worst-case scenario, both groups want to control the interface structure, standard templates, and final page designs.

When bringing together these two separate viewpoints, you need to manage the situation. Each side needs to become sensitive to what the other is trying to accomplish. It is imperative to negotiate clear boundaries and roles to make this collaboration succeed. The right solution depends on the type of application being designed. To see how this plays out, let's examine in greater depth two of the examples mentioned earlier in this chapter.

If your organization is designing an online brochure, there is little need for complex interactivity; user speed and accuracy are also of less importance. In such a case, you can hire a creative director to run the project. The UX team can check the designs to make sure there are no obvious points of confusion and perhaps run a usability test to confirm that there are no places where the user gets lost or frustrated. Nevertheless, the focus of the project is really on its creative design.

Building a site for employees to set up benefit elections on the intranet poses a very different challenge, one that requires greater interaction. Users are not interested in being entertained by the site—they just want to get the job done quickly. In this case, let the user experience design team determine its process, and have a graphic artist complete a basic treatment of the design—there is little creative work to do.

You should also consider setting up an interdisciplinary team in which a user experience engineer, a graphic designer, and perhaps a technical writer work together as equals. The UX engineer will be responsible for navigation and interaction, the graphic designer for the graphical elements, and the technical writer for writing and editing content.

Outside Consultants

It may seem odd to hear this from a vendor, but the best practice in the UX design field is *not* to rely on vendors to solve your user experience design problems. Many companies have tried bringing in a bunch of brilliant consultants, with each creating a brilliant design. Everyone is impressed and applauds, and the vendors go home—but then the designs steadily become degraded over time. Most critically, the diverse vendors create a diverse set of misaligned solutions. While each solution might be lovely, collectively they don't fit together as a whole. It is essential to have a strong internal group to avoid these pitfalls. This group might contract for some work, but it controls the strategy, processes, and standards.

Vendors are quite useful in helping to set up a mature practice (after all, you set up the practice only once). They can also be a source of staff working for the central group. And there is one unique role that can be filled only by a vendor: because the outside consultant is not a part of the organizational structure, he or she can act as impartial arbiter and facilitator. This type of consultant can offer a unique set of services, and his or her impartiality can help break logjams while "saving face" for the internal staff.

The outside consultant can also communicate at any level of the organization. Within an organization, strong protocols usually prevent a staff member from walking into the CEO's office and raising difficult topics and concerns. The consultant, in contrast, is permitted and encouraged—and paid—to be critical. This type of service is an important part of the institutionalization solution.

What to Look for When Hiring

Hiring your first user experience design staff can be tricky. The market for UX personnel is poorly defined, and the people responsible for recruiting and hiring in your organization may not have experience or guidance in what to look for.

An organization hiring senior people for the first time may have a difficult time finding them. Senior practitioners in the user

The Social Security Administration's Usability Team

Sean Wheeler, Lead Usability Specialist, Social Security Administration

We currently have 18 people on the Usability Center staff at the Social Security Administration (SSA). Half of the staff members have their master's degrees, and one holds a Ph.D. More important than title, their training is consistent in areas directly related to usability. In addition to academic credentials, they typically brought 7 to 10 years of experience in usability when they joined our team.

We are a rather strange lot because our team is a well-integrated mixture of federal employees and contractors. Because the contractor staffing mechanism is available to us, the SSA Usability Center has team members with skills that would be impossible for us to obtain otherwise. As an example, we are able to do electronic prototyping within the Usability Center so we can get a reading on the accessibility of our designs early in the software development process—a high-value contribution to project teams within the federal government. Our federal staff members bring many years of experience as employees from SSA field offices with the corresponding knowledge of the laws and procedures of the agency, as well as the needs and expectations of our customers that comes only from direct public contact work. This combination of skills has served us very well.

We are really expanding our scope now. We're a much different organization now than we were a few years ago. Today, most of our staff has been involved in user interface design and human factors work for 10 to 15 years, with much of that experience taking place in the private sector. The team's skills allow us to support agency-wide process changes that put early focus on user needs and design rather than on the late-in-life-cycle usability testing we started with. This rapid infusion of skills allows us to support project teams in ways that would have been impossible when the center was established in 1996.

experience design field are still a small group, and they tend to be networked together through professional groups such as the ACM SIGCHI and the User Experience Professionals Association.[2] In terms of more junior staff, there are thousands of people in the field (and many thousands more who claim to be).

Most companies have a very limited number of user experience design experts on staff; many companies do not have one person with the entire user experience design skill set described here. In many cases, the bulk of the UX staff may have to come from outside hires, though this practice has its pitfalls. It is important for the user experience design team to be an integral part of the organization, so it helps to have team members come from within the organization. If most of the UX staff members are outsiders, it may be very hard for the team to be fully accepted. Insiders understand the organization better and may fit in better than new hires.

That said, collectively the pool of insiders from whom you are recruiting probably have very few user experience engineering skills. Consequently, these people will need a strong management commitment for their training, mentoring, and consultative support.

If your organization is new to user experience design, consider using recruiters who specialize in user experience design staff. They will be familiar with the best people in the field and will know when someone is ready to move. They can also help screen more junior staff. Your recruiter should have extensive technical expertise and testing methods to make sure you get the people who best meet your needs. Once you have a core of experts in your organization, you may be able to have them work their own networks and go to user experience engineering trade shows to track down potential new staff members.

Hiring user experience design staff is a big step that involves a huge investment in the form of salaries, benefits, management, facilities, and training. But these elements form only a small part of the risk. The far larger risk is in the opportunity cost for designs that are not competitive. A new employee will be at least in part responsible for

2. For more information on ACM SIGCHI, visit www.acm.org/sigchi/. For more information on the Usability Professionals Association, visit www.upassoc.org.

the quality of the user experience and performance of many applications over time. If this staff member is a poor practitioner, these costs can easily dwarf his or her loaded labor rate. The necessary skills to look for and selection criteria you should employ, based on HFI's many years of experience in hiring user experience design staff, are discussed in the following subsections.

Selecting and Training Skilled Professionals

As mentioned earlier in the book, user experience design work is not just common sense. If it were, you could simply tell your staff to pay attention, and the resulting designs would be successful. (Many executives have tried this with very limited success.) Without concrete user experience design skills, however, we consistently get designs that are suboptimal—or worse. To avoid this problem, you bring in professionals and train internal staff. But first let's explore what to look for.

A core philosophy and feeling for design is perhaps the most important prerequisite for a good user experience design professional. Specifically, the practitioner's philosophy should be user oriented. This doesn't mean simply asking the customers what they want and giving it to them—that is a sign of an immature or ill-trained practitioner. Rather, you should hire someone who sees the user's needs and psyche as something to understand, to design for, and to support.

The user experience design practitioner needs to focus on the practical viewpoint of the user and systematically bring technology to the user's service. To test for this orientation, check out how specialists react to the idea of a cool new technology that is clearly impractical for users. They may be polite about it, but they should exhibit a feeling of disdain. User experience design practitioners should act as a protective shield against flashy ideas that don't help people use your sites, applications, and software effectively and enjoyably. A bit of jaundiced skepticism goes a long way.

User experience design staff must understand human behavior and be able to predict how users will react to and operate sites, applications, and software. In a good training program, students read research articles and predict the results from the methodological description. They view designs and predict their success. In time, they should become adept at prediction, developing a sense for what will confuse users and which physical manipulations are awkward. They should understand what makes users uncomfortable or angry, and be able to predict the time it takes to complete an operation or learn a procedure. While these predictions may not be exact, when created by an experienced user experience practitioner they should be fairly accurate.

Many design decisions are based on the ability of the user experience design specialist to estimate user consequences quickly. To get a sense of this, it is beneficial to have prospective staff members review some page designs to determine whether users can quickly see the things that matter most. I have often used a terrible clothing site design for this purpose. The site is organized by brand; thus, while shopping, the user has to identify the brand and then see all the different types of clothes from that manufacturer. Good prospective employees immediately see that the user needs the site to be organized by male and female categories and then by types of clothes.

Potential candidates need to have a good overall knowledge of UX research and models within the field. Any good candidate should probably have a foundation of "top of mind" user experience design facts. He or she should immediately know, for instance, that about 7% of men and 0.4% of women have some color weakness [Goldberg et al. 1995], or that all displays can be seen as a competition between the signal the user should perceive and the surrounding noise [Rehder et al. 1995]—and that the work of a user experience designer is to maintain a signal-to-noise ratio that gets the message through.

User experience design practitioners should know that there are population stereotypes for how things work, and that they differ between user populations (e.g., pushing a light switch *up* in the United States to turn on the lights versus pushing the light switch *down* in the United Kingdom to do so). Practitioners should know that users see things in context and can make mistakes as a result. For example, if users expect to see a letter, a handwritten "13" can look like a "B." Users also make common keying errors, such as hitting the letter "o" instead of the number "0." Looking up each issue becomes tedious in practical circumstances. When he or she has a solid foundation in UX design, the practitioner already knows the answers to many common questions—as well as some that others may not think to ask.

Staff members also need to be able to find answers when they encounter things they do not know. It is not acceptable for a user experience design practitioner to simply make up recommendations out of thin air. There is a time to hunt for the right answer, and practitioners need to be willing to check the research. They also have to know how to use it. Research in the UX field is spread across more than a hundred different sources, so the practitioner needs online and print resources he or she knows well, and must know how to find other studies when required.

The good practitioner regularly reads the literature to learn from new research studies. Sometimes he or she needs to retrieve studies to determine the best design decision. Understanding research papers is not easy, however. Research can provide invaluable insights, but it must be evaluated with great care. The practitioner must understand enough about experimental design and statistics to be able to interpret the research correctly. Not every staff member needs to have this capability, of course—a practitioner can ask for help. Nevertheless, having the skill set readily available within your organization is quite useful.

It is important to be familiar with a methodology so that the design process can be approached systematically. Ask potential employees what they would do to ensure that a site is usable and persuasive. It is worrisome if they do not have a systematic methodology with clear activities and deliverables that build toward a solution. Any activity such as "We will listen to the users" is suspect. What comes out of that listening? How does it really help the design? If they cannot talk their way through a systematic approach, practitioners are unlikely to follow one—even if you hand them a copy of your methodology.

The development process requires a whole string of user experience engineering activities. The usability practitioner must know how to complete tasks like expert reviews, usability tests, in-depth interviews, task designs, wireframe designs, detailed designs, and functional specifications. Each of these tasks requires numerous subskills. For example, being able to "do" an interview includes the ability to stratify user segments, develop target user types, and develop a recruiting strategy—and that is just one small part of the overall process. It is worthwhile to inventory the applicant's experience with these activities and ask some questions about his or her approach to specific tasks. However, because it is difficult to really get a good sense of the quality of an applicant's work without direct experience, consider having potential employees work through a set of examples and evaluate the results of their work.

Being a user experience engineer is not easy. As outlined here, general practitioners need to know a lot, but beyond the core skills and knowledge, user experience engineers need to have a passion for crafting a customer's experience. They need to have communications skills such as the ability to excel in team interaction, and a sense of charisma that they can draw on when evangelizing usability.

Education

Although some highly skilled and effective people have a less formal education in UX design, most user experience practitioners have at least a master's degree in the field. Having a solid educational background is important. Many colleges and universities now offer usability programs. The Human Factors and Ergonomics Society (www.hfes.org) currently lists 72 graduate programs in the field in the United States, including all kinds of user experience design work. The professors in these programs may specialize in factory workspaces, consumer products, the biomechanics of heavy lifting, or military equipment, however, so you must check carefully to see which program actually provides appropriate skills for software design.

Senior usability people may have been in the field long enough to predate specific degree programs. Many of these people have master's or doctoral degrees in psychology instead of human factors, usability, or user experience.

Of course, a master's degree or higher does not indicate that the practitioner has a full set of skills. In fact, most programs typically cover basics such as general design principles or ways to read research. Some courses may provide experience in usability testing. Keep in mind, however, that education is truly only the beginning of the process of becoming an expert practitioner. Experience is a critical factor—and it cannot be learned in the classroom.

Another, perhaps more useful validation to consider is certification. Several certification programs exist. For example, the Board of Certification in Professional Ergonomics provides a very good certification with requirements for education, experience, and testing (there are three alternative certification types based on the certificant's preference: CPE, CHFP, and CUXP). In addition, HFI's certification program is currently used by approximately 10% of the world's UX design professionals. In either case, the certification gives you quick assurance of proven expertise.

Experience

In looking at applicants' experience, start with an assessment of the quality and range of their past work activities. There are obvious limitations to having worked on just a single application, particularly given that the applicant may have had a very limited role such as just running usability testing. Someone who has worked on a number of sites and applications has gained a wider perspective. Unless you are seeking someone with a limited and specific scope, look for a candidate who has completed many different user experience design activities. Once the new practitioner is on board, he or she can easily be drafted to work on the development team for a critical project. It is helpful if applicants have a wide spectrum of capabilities because—even though you may have hired them for a particular expertise such as usability testing—it is likely that they will be called upon to perform other tasks as well.

It is also worthwhile to consider the quality of the project experience. While it is not particularly important that an applicant has worked on "name-brand" projects, he or she should have worked on projects where user experience was valued and given a significant role. Some practitioners spend years in a reactive mode—they essentially sit in their offices and review designs, reacting to aspects of the design that are so obviously awful that they can be discerned without having to gather data or complete a user-centered process. These people do not have much experience in supporting a solid process and appropriate methodology.

While one can get a degree and read many books, maturity of skills within the user experience design field really requires explicit mentoring, so it is important to acquire staff members who have worked under a good mentor. Perhaps the least organized aspect of the industry, mentoring is critical nonetheless. A mentor can help a practitioner develop many different professional skills—team interaction, presentation style, and good writing, for example—as well as a fundamental design approach and the ability to perform specific user experience design tasks. If you are not familiar with specific mentors whom applicants have had, it can be difficult to determine whether the potential employees have been well taught. The best thing, if you have the resources to do it, is to set up your own mentoring program, either in-house or with an outside consultant.

A Background That Includes Design

User experience design work requires many analytical activities. The professional must be able to run studies, compile results, and make recommendations. There is research to be reviewed and assimilated, and valuable insights to be gained about user psychology and behavior. These activities, however, are very different from the synthesis necessary for actual design. It is common to find skilled analysts who cannot design well. They may be familiar with the theory of design and be able to make contributions, but they will not be able to synthesize their knowledge to generate good interfaces.

In evaluating staff candidates, questions about design principles may evoke excellent theoretical responses from analytically oriented people with no design capabilities. The individual may have worked on very successful design teams. However, other practitioners may have completed the actual design work. Thus it is essential to see each applicant do some design work yourself, and to evaluate the results.

There is a science to quality user experience design work—to the research, the methodology, and the many hundreds of design principles. But such work also has an intuitive side. The practitioner must pull these insights together in a "moment of magic." There is a huge disparity in candidates' abilities to perform this type of integration. Ideally, the practitioner should maintain a clear focus on the business goals and the overall context of the design. He or she must have a high-level model of the user's characteristics, limitations, and taskflow, and must generate the interface so that it fits the shape of those activities and needs. This is not to say that someone can do good design by pure intuition—process and science are needed. But there is indeed a step beyond the science. If you want staff members who are designers, look for the ability to take that intuitive step in synthesizing the results and creating the right solution.

Specialist versus Generalist

You might find someone with a doctorate in applied psychology who has a respected academic position, a long list of publications, and many years of successful experience working in a large company. This person may be the world's foremost expert in the psychological refractory period (the reaction time delay in stopping an action) as applied to handwriting errors. None of this background, however, guarantees that the candidate can do routine user experience design work. If handwriting is core to the business, this person may be a worthwhile specialist to add to your central usability team. Nevertheless, you should not expect him or her to be able to complete general usability activities, such as mentoring staff in development activities or developing quick tactical interface solutions under pressure.

It may be the case that specialized expertise in the field translates to general user experience design skill, but more often no such connection exists. Rather than making assumptions based on someone's CV, test applicants carefully for both general skills and design skills.

Real Skills and Knowledge

This chapter has discussed the skills and knowledge essential for effective practitioners. These essentials are not necessarily agreed upon, however, or even well known by those who consider themselves specialists.

Some people believe that if they have interviewed users one time before writing HTML code, they have done user experience design. Others feel that if they have gotten feedback from users about their design—or have read books and even attended conferences—they are experts. If you ask these people questions, they may be able to provide a strong series of impressive responses. They may tell you that they "weave a tapestry of user experience," provide examples of data gathering with users, and perhaps offer up a few buzzwords like "ethnographic research" and "user journey" from the latest magazine articles. However well-intentioned and forward-looking these people may be, they do not possess the skills, knowledge, methods, tools, and resources to deliver on their promises. Put in a position of control, they will create flashy sites with unusual designs. They seem to be plausible candidates, but their work will confuse and frustrate users. Their designs are likely to fail, creating a big loss for your organization and your user experience design department. Unfortunately, this lack of skills is often not evident until it is too late.

There are a few easy ways to detect this type of unqualified applicant. First, these candidates will rarely make any reference to research or describe how to access studies in the field. Second, they will rarely have a systematic methodology. They will talk in glowing terms of understanding users, but they will not have a process with clear activities and deliverables. Pay special attention to the lack of deliverables. Without concrete deliverables, it is very difficult to determine whether user experience design is being practiced properly. (While some tout "bargain" methods that are agile and drop the need for deliverables [c.f., Gothelf and Seiden 2013], these approaches are plausible only for very small programs. In almost all other cases, mature and systematic user experience design is faster, cheaper, and better for serious design work.) Finally, these applicants will rarely discuss concrete metrics. Good usability work is done to reach specific objectives. These results may take the form of a drop-off rate, efficiency, reduced training costs, and so on. Instead of describing the need for these kinds of results, this type of candidate will most likely offer flowery descriptions of a good user experience.

Interpersonal Skills and Level of Expertise

User experience design specialists depend on good relationships with the development team to perform their work effectively. A specialist may have deep knowledge, good insights, and a vast capacity for efficient design, as well as a thorough and systematic approach to his or her work. If he or she lacks good interpersonal skills, however, the organization will actually receive little value.

It seems almost unfair—there are so many requirements for good practitioners. They need knowledge of the literature, methodology, and design sense. On top of that, they must work well with others in a team. New recruits face real challenges in being accepted. If you bring in an experienced, high-powered practitioner whose expertise is far beyond that of other team members, he or she may be marginalized by the team as a defense tactic. Having a really brilliant professional on a mediocre team often makes other team members feel inadequate. What is the answer to this dilemma? The best solution is to ensure that you have a top-quality staff throughout your team.

In some cases, however, you will be hiring specialists for a team that is less than world class. They may be building fairly routine applications, or their work may be less than mission critical. In this type of scenario, consider recruiting a good, solid professional whose skills are not too advanced beyond those of the other developers. A mismatch in expertise relative to the rest of the team can cause problems, which may then be blamed on poor interpersonal skills. Remember that matching levels of expertise and good interpersonal skills are both important.

An Offshore Model

Given all the challenges that may prevent organizations from locating and hiring high-quality user experience design staff, other options may need to be explored. Once the benefits of good experience design are understood, its use may spread in a viral fashion. There is likely to be a rapid, project-level increase in demand for the application of user-centered engineering practices, which often puts unmanageable pressure on the user experience design staff.

The inability of the internal usability staff to keep up with the demand for support is a choke point. The model does not scale up easily.

Such understaffing typically occurs because, as mentioned previously, well-trained user experience design specialists are difficult to find or very expensive. Ramping up the expert internal staff required to meet the increasing demand can be prohibitively expensive and time consuming. Consulting companies may provide support for overstressed internal staff, but the cost of using consultant-based support for routine and sustained user experience design activities is prohibitive. The need, however, is critical. Without sufficient staff to do the work, institutionalization will falter. Companies could continue to apply user-centered design principles to a small range of projects, but the lost opportunity cost of such a strategy is huge. Finding cost-effective staff offshore can provide a scalable solution.

The Challenges and Success Factors of Offshore Staffing

HFI has been running large-scale offshore teams since 2000. Offshore staffing works well when you have a mature operation that follows systematic practices. It is necessary to have the offshore team properly trained and managed—and you must know what the team can do and how much it needs to travel.

You can avoid many of the communication challenges that can be experienced with an offshore model when you establish an organizational structure that meets the four core requirements for project success:

1. Effectively managing remote resources (both people and technology)
2. Ensuring an accurate and shared understanding of conventions, assumptions, and project goals
3. Maintaining quality of work standards
4. Delivering on schedule

Today's offshore models include components designed to help meet those requirements. Some elements relate directly to the specific development process and are explored in depth in other chapters of this book:

- *A systematic, trackable methodology* ensures that projects proceed smoothly.
- *Process-specific tools* reinforce correct use of the methodology.
- *Technical certification* through training ensures an understanding of the methodology and tools.

Factors unrelated to the specific development process are equally important:

- The *technical infrastructure* is secured with sufficient redundancy (e.g., backup generators and multiple internet access providers).
- Bidirectional *cross-cultural education* is designed to address both day-to-day interactions and critical escalation paths.

Communication between local and remote team members is improved when the project team includes the following roles:

- A single *company-resident project contact point*
- An *offshore project team leader* sensitized to native interaction styles

Communication between local and remote team members is not limited to interactions between these two individuals, but they should be aware of all communications flowing back and forth between various points of contact. This oversight ensures that collaboration is integrated and that the priorities and efforts of the remote team stay focused. An object-oriented approach and a toolset that manages document sharing and will make communication more efficient.

At HFI, we have been able to demonstrate that offshore teams can successfully complete all of the following user experience engineering activities (there are a few points where staff will need to travel to complete key tasks):

- Expert reviews
- Usability testing (in person and remote)
- User interface structure design
- Standards development
- Prototype development
- Graphical treatment
- Detailed page design and layout
- Graphic library development
- Implementation/508-compliant[3] coding

Integrating a well-trained, well-managed remote usability team significantly increases the productivity of the organization as a whole. Furthermore, creating and training a remote usability team provides a cost-effective release for the staffing chokehold.

The Limits of Offshore Usability

Despite all the benefits that can accrue from use of effective offshore teams, they cannot maintain the internal momentum for user experience design work. These practitioners can carry much of the development load, but they are not in a good position to be evangelists. There must be internal staff to maintain momentum and ensure that user experience design is not marginalized.

Summary

This chapter outlined a few of the roles important to the ongoing efforts of your central user experience design team, and offered

---

3. "508" refers to Section 508 of the Federal Rehabilitation Act. Section 508 mandates certain accessibility guidelines for federal agencies. For more information, visit www.section508.gov.

strategies regarding what to look for when hiring staff. For organizations committed to making user-centered design central to the development cycle, a well-trained and -managed remote team can provide the capacity to scale internal resources while establishing an institutionalized operation that is practical, successful, and cost-effective. The quality of your staff will play a big part in determining the success of your efforts and the reputation of your team. The next chapter provides specific information on strategies that will help you manage increasing demands across a variety of projects.

Chapter 13

Projects

➤ With a solid infrastructure and good staff, user experience design work will be effective.

➤ All project directors will want user experience design work, so you will quickly be short of trained staff.

➤ Prioritize projects by criticality (gold, silver, bronze, and tin).

➤ Put the best people on the high-priority projects, and place new user experience staff on less critical jobs.

➤ Use developers and others trained in user experience design to help, if necessary.

➤ For critical projects, get contract staff from user-centered design consultancies.

➤ Use some top user experience design staff as consultants to help the newer staff (especially on higher-priority projects).

➤ Cut corners when planning user experience design work.

➤ Cut out functions.

➤ Focus user-centered design work on just the critical modules (forget the administrative interface).

➤ Carefully scale back data gathering and usability testing.

➤ There are several ways to estimate your requirements for user experience design staff. Make an effort to get close to the required level, or the entire institutionalization effort may be wasted.

With a mature practice in place, user experience design work will be quite different: it will be faster, cheaper, and better. The time in which the user's needs were not formally addressed in the development process will be over. User experience design staff will no longer run about wildly trying to make ad hoc improvements to projects that are in flight (the "finger in the dike" approach). Methods will be selected and assigned with an appropriate amount of time allocated to allow success. This is the efficient, effective way to do the work. Perhaps surprisingly, the very success of your institutionalization initiative means that you will run into another problem.

When user experience design has been instilled in the development culture of an organization, lines-of-business managers begin to look routinely for a user-centered process for their projects—and for skilled practitioners to do the work. The result will be a severe shortage of user experience design staff.

There is a natural tendency to react to the shortage of practitioners by spreading people thin and giving each practitioner many projects. This approach will cause their work to become less effective, with the result that personnel up and down the organization will wonder whether there is much value to this highly-touted user-centered initiative. Resist the impulse to overextend your staff! This chapter explores better ways to use a limited number of practitioners to good effect, assuming that your organization is unable to explore an offshore model similar to that mentioned in Chapter 12.

Doing It Right

Assuming you have established the methodology, infrastructure, organization, and staffing—and have gained organizational acceptance of user-centered design—it is now time to begin the routine application of user experience design in your projects.

A mature user experience design process has many hallmarks. The work starts automatically, very early in the development cycle, as soon as the business need and the strategy are identified. Trained and certified practitioners—the leads on the project during the early stages—ensure that the strategy is refined and fully reflected in the actual site or application. The user experience design staff harmonizes the needs of the organization with the realities of user needs and limitations, creating a user interface (UI) structure that makes the navigation simple and straightforward. Because the UI is not developed or tested by untrained staff, there is no need to make frantic attempts to repair a flawed design.

Managing by Project Importance

Any site or application worth building is worth making usable, but there are differences in the criticality of user experience design work. An intranet facility that will be used by a few internal staff to maintain management accounting information is simply not as critical, from an experience engineering viewpoint, as an e-commerce application that will be the company's sole channel for sales. Under the pressure of insufficient time and resources, it makes sense to do a bit of triage based on such priorities. You can assign a level to each project—gold, silver, bronze, or tin—and then give the most critical projects the highest level of attention.

- **Gold**—Give the most user experience design attention to projects that are mission critical to the company—projects that will make a big difference to the ongoing success of your organization. These gold projects have a lot riding on the user experience and performance. Usability may be important because there are many users, the users are difficult to serve, or the performance stakes are very high—large amounts of money or even lives may be at stake.

- **Silver**—It is likely that the bulk of your projects will be important but not wholly critical to the organization. These are usually not publicly sold applications or websites accessed by customers; instead, they might be extranets used to access vendors or internal systems used to track and manage work. For each high-profile public site operated by a company, there are probably 10 supporting applications (ordering, shipping, inventory, and so on). While these are not examples of mission-critical programs, basic user-centered design issues matter. You might apply performance engineering methods (which ensure that the application is easy to use) without attending to emotional design or persuasion engineering. The resulting ease-of-use may support the ability of hundreds of users in the organization to perform efficiently; improvements in such areas can limit the need for training, reduce task time, and control errors. Many projects also have an impact on the company's vendors, such as widely used accounting and management information systems, and need serious user experience design support. Nevertheless, they are less critical than your gold projects.

- **Bronze**—Many projects do not really need a major user-centered design process. They are simple facilities—perhaps an informational site with only a few users, where user experience and performance are not really in jeopardy. (A very simple site is harder to make incomprehensible than a complex site.) It is not worthwhile doing much user experience design work on these projects, even when more resources become available in the future.

- **Tin**—User experience design practitioners should probably do no work at all on some projects. Occasionally, a project has almost no user interactions to worry about because it is entirely focused on internal database processing. In addition, there may be some legacy "disaster" projects that have been poorly managed, have not had user-centered design methods applied, and are in trouble. You can decide to intervene and try to save the project; however, it is often wiser to let it go without completing it because the chances are good that the project will be scrapped.

Who Will Do the User Experience Design?

Ideally, all user-centered design activities can be completed by fully trained, experienced practitioners from the central team (in small companies) or by practitioners reporting to lines of business (in larger firms). There are some alternatives to these approaches, however. If the quality and timeliness of work cannot be allowed to lapse even briefly, consider using contract staff from user experience design vendors. This is the common solution for an insufficiently staffed gold project. Contractors may not know much about your organization, but they are experienced with design activities, can adhere to your specific customized standards, and should do a good job.

For silver projects, trained staff members who are not professional user experience design practitioners can complete the user-centered design activities. While it is not an ideal situation, business analysts, systems analysts, programmers, and user representatives may perform credibly in this role. The usability of the site or application is likely to suffer to some degree, but you can take measures to minimize the problem.

If other staff members stand in for user experience design practitioners, they should have solid training. Without it, progress will be slow, and the work will likely be of poor quality. This training can and should take place both in the classroom and on the job. Practitioners with more experience and training can act as guides or mentors for newer individuals as they work on projects. This ensures that the work does not stray far from the chosen path. Even a few days of mentoring from an experienced consultant can prevent well-intentioned teams from taking expensive detours.

For bronze and tin projects, less investment is justified. You might have project staff members undergo a few days of training in basic usability design, but the project is unlikely to merit much consultative support. Developers must then make do with their training and the organization's overall user-centered design infrastructure.

Different Strategies for Practitioner Involvement

Some companies advocate that the best way to deploy practitioners is to make them part of a development team that designs by committee. If this is your corporate design process, it will prove helpful to have a user experience design professional in the mix. For significant development efforts, however, designing the user interface by committee is remarkably inefficient. User-centered design work is best done in cycles of data gathering and quiet work. While it is important that this work involve others (e.g., developers, graphic designers), for significant development efforts, the user experience design practitioner must be able to complete design work without interference by committees—that is, by studying users and finding out how they react, digesting these insights, and then making design changes individually or in a very small group. It is painful to see committees discuss the wording of a link for a full hour. With 15 people working, that link costs 15 person-hours to draft! It is fine to have a committee participate in a walkthrough, but this approach is a poor way to do design, even if plenty of experience design practitioners are available.

It is also unlikely that a good UX strategy and interface structure will evolve through the scrums and sprints of a rapid development process (such as Agile). It is imperative to do your structural design before beginning the rapid development process. With this approach, the chances are far better that the detailed design can be executed within the rapid development process.

When working on a silver or bronze project with limited resources, the user experience design staff can take an evaluative role. In other words, the project team creates designs, and the user experience design staff reviews the work and provides feedback. The project team analyzes the feedback, makes changes to the designs, and returns them for another usability review if necessary. This process involves risks, however, and it may be inefficient. For example, if the data gathering with users is poorly done, the staff might spend valuable time on unneeded or incorrectly structured screens. Many review cycles may be needed to reach a good design, which can be frustrating and even a bit adversarial. (In time, the developers will flinch just seeing the user experience designers.)

While this is not an ideal strategy, limiting his or her involvement to evaluation of the project team's work does use less of the experience engineer's time: you can support an entire project with just a few days of help from a practitioner. Although this approach may be feasible for a silver or bronze project, it is not acceptable for a gold project.

For silver and some lower-end gold projects, one alternative often has great success: the user experience design practitioners take full control and responsibility for the development of the user interface structure only. This means that they do not design every page or screen, but simply the critical structure. To accomplish this, they may have to review or test the original application or site. The practitioners use data gathered from users to structure a site that is practical, simple, and efficient to navigate. They then test this design to confirm that it is self-evident and that the graphic treatment supports the brand values of the organization. At that point, the design can be given to personnel with basic training (e.g., business analysts), who can use the standards to proliferate the detailed pages needed under the structural design. The user experience design staff can provide coaching and review the detailed designs created by the developers. This approach brings scarce practitioners in only for the most critical work.

Recall that 80% of usability is determined by the structural design.[1] If the structure is right, not much can go seriously wrong with your detailed design. This is particularly true if the work is done under standards. The detailed design requires less demanding work (but often takes 80% of the time), and it can be completed by staff members who are more numerous and may actually be more familiar with the detailed requirements than new user experience design practitioners.

For high-end gold projects, there is no alternative except to employ skilled and experienced practitioners. They must certainly do the

---

1. This figure is based on HFI's 20 years of experience with hundreds of clients, across thousands of user-centered design projects.

structural design work, and it is also advisable to have them complete—or at least lead—the detailed screen design and usability testing. This yields the best-quality designs in the shortest time.

Working Smart

When the shortage of user experience design practitioners is acute, a number of strategies can help alleviate the pressures on those personnel. While it is easy to become alarmed by the magnitude of the problem and frantically try to do everything at once, this is the time to get organized and plan carefully. Staying up late on the project just makes you inefficient; you will have to fix fatigue-induced errors in addition to handling the onslaught of new work. Instead of panicking or pulling all-nighters, work smart.

- *Trim unnecessary functions.* User experience design practitioners can often identify functions that are not needed at all or are at least secondary. It is often possible to trim the size of the deliverable and still end up with a useful offering; many projects benefit from having excess features trimmed, in fact.

- *Focus the experience design on important modules of the interface.* You can apply the same project triage principles discussed earlier to the modules of an application, rating them as gold, silver, bronze, or tin. For example, you might find that the product display and checkout pages are gold, whereas a whole set of administrative screens will be seen only by a few highly trained, motivated internal systems administrators. Thus you can rate the administrative module as a bronze project and not worry too much about it. You can use the same schemes to assign personnel within the project as we have suggested for whole projects. A systems analyst might design the administrative module; the user experience design practitioner reviews this module, but is otherwise busy perfecting the checkout process essential to the project's success.

- *Use an effective but scaled-back testing strategy.* For example, you would not want to eliminate data gathering and testing early in the process—these tasks are essential and relatively inexpensive. You might be able to test fewer participants, however, or test in fewer locations. If pressed for time, you could eliminate the final usability testing; it is expensive and tends to merely fine-tune the design.

- *Consider using remote testing.* Being face-to-face with users during data gathering offers real value, as the nuances of facial expressions can give user experience design specialists important insights into directions of inquiry. Nevertheless, remote testing is often a viable alternative. Remote testing methods may even help cut the time required for simple testing. The methods themselves can be very simple as well. For example, you can simply send an image or questionnaire to the participants and then talk to them by phone.

- *Consider the possibility of sharing testing sessions between projects.* If more than one project is targeted at a given user population, it may be possible to test both projects at once. The main cost of a data gathering or usability test relates to getting the participants in the room, so extending a test session from an hour to 90 minutes may let you gather data to support two programs in a single session. Beyond 90 minutes, participants will be too fatigued to yield good results.

- *Scale back the number of participants in studies and the number of geographies tested.* You can get good usability testing data from as few as a dozen people, and testing in many different regions of the United States, for example, tends not to yield many new insights. These are reasonable areas in which you can scale back. Do not scale back by using internal staff members as stand-ins for actual users in data gathering and testing, however. Internal staff members are almost always different from typical users, and their input can lead you astray. It is also not recommended to reduce the number of participants to fewer than a dozen, because it is too easy to be overly influenced by an unusual person who just happens to show up in a small study. You'll also really know there's a problem only when you encounter the same failures repeatedly. If you test five people and one makes an error, you can't tell if it is a fluke or a significant problem.

- *Have a single practitioner work on a number of different projects.* This can be a great way to stretch your scarce user experience design resources. Having one user practitioner working on several different projects can pose challenges, though, and not all practitioners can juggle projects well. A practitioner in this role should be providing guidance/advice only.

Efficient Project Planning

Much can be done in the project planning stage to make the work faster and more efficient.

- *Use standard project planning techniques to track phases and activities.*
- *Watch for cases where a critical path can put the whole schedule in jeopardy.* For example, when working on an interface structure, start working out the details of participant acquisition for the data gathering sessions the day the project is approved. Although data gathering is the third or fourth activity in the sequence of user experience design steps, lining up participants can take weeks. If this task is not started immediately, filling your sessions could delay the whole project.
- *Work concurrently.* Experience design work often allows for concurrent activities. For example, graphic artists can be working on designs while user experience design practitioners are writing questionnaires. Similarly, results can be tabulated for the first day of testing while the second day of testing is in progress.
- *Be ready to make adjustments.* User experience design work is often influenced by outside factors such as developer activities and business needs. Be prepared to review your project, plan often, and make adjustments.
- *Hold firm.* People tend to think that experience design is an area to modify or cut back when time is limited. Do not let others force you into agreeing to perform a task in less time than it will take. Produce less if you must, but make sure each deliverable demonstrates that value of the field.

Estimating Experience Design Work

As you plan and manage the flow of projects given a limited set of practitioners, it helps to accurately estimate the requirements for

Organizational Support for Usability

Dana Griffith, CUA, Web Consultant—Interactive Media, American Electric Power

The people at the highest level in my group believe in usability. For them, it has become part of the process of creating a new site or revising a site, so we probably have a little different approach to the question of institutionalizing usability. Because we manage the corporate website and the company intranet, we are able to address usability at the point when design decisions are being made, without holding up the project for any measurable length of time.

different projects. This information allows better allocation of the resources available and can provide a good estimate of the number of user experience design staff members you will eventually need within your organization.

For gold and silver projects, you can usually get a good idea of the level of effort needed for user experience design work by gauging the percentage of the overall project effort represented by that work. Very small projects end up with large percentages of usability work because there is a limit on the amount you can reduce the interface development effort. No matter how simple the project, for gold and silver projects, you need to access data from users and test the design concepts. That said, you are likely to see a maximum of perhaps 25% of the project effort spent on user experience design. With larger projects—say, a typical e-commerce site costing $5 million—you might spend 10% of the budget on user experience design. As projects become larger, you may be able to take advantage of economies of scale for a further reduction—down to about 7%. If your plan for a gold or silver project has allocated less than 5% of the budget for user experience design work, you are probably making a mistake.[2]

You can also make estimates based on the type of experience design work being completed, as shown in Table 13-1. This approach is more

2. The figures in this paragraph are based on HFI's experience with its customer base. In addition, the 10% figure is cited in a report by Nielsen and Gilutz [2003].

Table 13-1: *Estimated Time Frame for Usability Activities*

Activity	*Elapsed Time*	*Practitioner Person-Days*
Usability test of the current design	3 weeks	12–20 days
Expert review	2 weeks	10–20 days
User interface structure	6–10 weeks	45–65 days
Draft detailed page design (very roughly)	1 day per page	1 day per page
Quick, formative usability tests	7 days	7 days
Final usability test before release (one country)	4 weeks	40 days
Final usability test before release (five different languages and countries)	8 weeks	120 days

accurate than taking a simple percentage, but it is still an estimate; your results may vary. For example, an inexperienced team may take a much longer time to complete a task than a seasoned one. Other factors can affect boilerplate estimates, such as the complexity of the application or product, the number of different users, and the need to develop a product for use across different languages or cultures.

Summary

The efforts you have made to build an effective infrastructure with high-quality staff are sure to bring you a certain amount of success. However, managing projects carefully is still an imperative. By following the tips and strategies in this chapter, you should be able to maintain a good level of momentum. The next chapter elaborates on some of the ongoing activities and responsibilities of the established usability group.

Part IV

Long-Term Operations

In building a practice, we must always think about sustainability. In the words of Bob Dylan, "He not busy being born is busy dying." We have to design an organization that constantly moves forward—that constantly proves its economic value, and that protects its quality and capabilities.

The UX field will always keep growing. People are complicated, and their expectations and needs keep changing. Push your team to expand their skills and knowledge. A business needs to provide a better customer experience than the competition, and a mature UX practice is a key differentiator.

There is a whole set of new frontiers that our field will face. The globe is large and cultures are diverse, so we need to manage our design of international delivery. And the future will bring a whole set of new realities, new frontiers, and new technologies, to which we will need to adapt a human body and nervous system that evolved for life in the savannah.

Chapter 14

Long-Term Activities of the Central Team

➤ The central user experience design group is responsible for the overall corporate initiative toward user-centered design. Keep the user-centered viewpoint vibrant, effective, and respected.

- Don't be marginalized, ignored, or diverted back to a technology focus.

- Maintain momentum by building excitement and visible progress into your development and design plans.

- Evangelize user-centrality by frequently hosting events to share lessons learned and convey excitement about the value of experience design.

- Train new personnel to keep the knowledge of user-centered design in your organization. Also, enhance and update the skill sets of existing staff.

- Mentor staff working for project teams.

- Update the design standard and provide consultation to help developers follow the rules.

- Form a community of interest. Support formal activities, such as information-sharing sessions, that provide mutual support.

- Conduct usability tests objectively, as outsiders to the project team.
- Measure the value of user experience improvements to show your investment is working and to highlight areas for improvement.
- Take responsibility for experience quality throughout the organization.
- Report your progress and achievements to executives.

In the Long-Term Operations phase, the full infrastructure and the central team become operational. User experience design is now a routine part of every project.

- You have a solid UX strategy that describes what will motivate users to engage with your organization and how the various channels will align effectively into a coherent overall experience.
- You no longer build a site or application first and then merely hope it will be what users actually need.
- You do not let the technical design of a system alone drive the selection of controls for ease of use.
- You will be ahead of your competitors if they have not completed their own experience design efforts—this is a significant benefit to your brand and corporate efficiency.

The organization is working effectively at this point, but there must be an ongoing process of renewal, evaluation, and enhancement. User-centrality is not such a simple issue that the organization will continue to flourish without attention from the executive level and ongoing excellence from within the user experience design team.

Once you get the infrastructure in place and the organization built, the central group must maintain and grow the user experience design process, continuously reinforce the value of good experience design, and integrate the user-centered methodology. While working on projects, practitioners follow the methodology, use the best research and principles available at the time, call internal consultants and specialists from the central usability team for support, and occasionally demonstrate and promote the success of the user-centered perspective.

The executive responsible for the central group may provide resources and encouragement and may clear obstacles from the pathway to growth, but the heavy lifting of the continued user experience design process falls to the central team. This chapter focuses on the most important activities the central usability team can perform to keep the institutionalization current and vibrant.

Maintaining Respect and Negotiating Effectively

User experience design practitioners usually face some degree of resistance on an ongoing basis—it is the nature of the development process. User experience design groups need to maintain respect so that they can ensure that users' needs take precedence over prioritized technology or design function lists—and avoid being marginalized themselves.

For example, a user experience designer may tell a developer that users need a display that collects all their data in one place. The developer quickly sees that this display will require a lot of work to support: it will be necessary to link calls to a number of databases, and will require greater processing power. The developer wonders whether this practitioner knows what is going on. Will this feature really make a difference to the user? Will it benefit the business?

First, the practitioner and the developer should need to agree on a solution based on a mutual understanding of the user issues and technical constraints. If they cannot come to an understanding, a consultant from the central group needs to review the conflict and quickly decide whether the user needs are, in fact, critical. If they are not, the central team needs to be realistic and negotiate something different.

The central team may occasionally correct a recommendation from a practitioner on a project team. Once reviewed and confirmed by the central team, the recommendation must be supported with research studies or examples from the literature that demonstrate the effect. Usually, coming up with just a few studies earns the team a reputation for making research-based recommendations—so that eventually it will not have to defend many of its decisions.

Of course, that does not change the fact that practitioners will need to step in at various times and push the user's perspective against coding convenience throughout the organization. As such, the ability of the practitioners to manage claims about technical feasibility takes on particular importance. Developers commonly claim that a recommendation is not feasible when it is, in fact, possible to implement. The practitioner needs enough technical savvy to understand both sides of the interface. The user experience design staff should get in the habit of digging deeper into claims of infeasibility. What does "That will take too long" really mean? Does it refer to coding time, response time, or something else?

When the technical staff attempts to overpower a less experienced practitioner, the central consultants must step in. They must know enough about the technology to be able to accurately assess the situation. The practitioner might need a course in technical limitations so he or she will make fewer infeasible recommendations in the future. More often, however, technical staff members need to be shown that "technobabble" will not be accepted as a substitute for the hard work needed to meet the user's needs.

Respect is important for the competitive health of the user experience design organization. Organizations that marginalize user experience designers in favor of coding ease eventually get nasty wake-up calls.

Maintaining Momentum

It is critical to keep the momentum going to motivate the user experience design staff and the development team. The user-centered effort does not need to be too aggressive—companies that mandate an optimized user experience design and try to implement it

The Value of a Research-Based Approach to Usability

Janice Nall, Managing Director, Atlanta—Danya International, Inc.
Former Chief, Communication Technologies Branch,
National Cancer Institute

At the National Cancer Institute (NCI), we needed a research-based way to make decisions about the way we design Web sites.

We developed research-based guidelines, and that was the turning point. With guidelines in place, it's not a manager saying what to do, and it's not the head of the Institute saying it. It's the users saying it, and it's the research—the literature. In our culture, that's what it's all about. So it's making what we do work within the culture here that's important.

I think the guidelines have given us a much more powerful voice than we expected originally. We developed them from a research-based approach because we thought it was the right way to do it. We truly underestimated the power of having the data and having the user's voice represented. Very few people aren't willing to make changes based on the evidence-based guidelines.

The largest amount of hard-core resistance we see tends to come from programmers and some graphic designers. That's why we try to get them to attend training or observe testing. If we sense any resistance to usability from developers or designers, we test the current site or some other site and force them into the observation room so they can see people struggling, and it helps them understand the process. We try to do it in a very nonthreatening way so that they're part of the team helping us try to make it better.

instantly do not do well. Yet while disseminating a user-centered perspective throughout the organization takes time, there must be forward movement.

One trick to gain initial momentum is to stay focused on smaller projects as you begin your UX effort. Even if your resources are

Roadblocks in the Path to Good Usability: The IT Department

Harley Manning, Research Director, Forrester Research

One change that has to happen to make usability part of the culture is to get your IT act together. Otherwise, even if you design a great product, it won't materialize.

The IT department can be a big impediment to getting more usable digital channels. It's not intentional; rather, it's that "easy" means something very different for them. If you're an application developer, for example, you probably know three or four different programming languages and maybe have a good grasp of systems architecture—even the most opaque user interface looks easy to you.

So the IT folks are not exactly your typical business user, nor are they necessarily sympathetic to your typical business user. And they're not typically evaluated on how well they deliver usable software, either. They are—to steal a phrase—"the inmates running the asylum" [Cooper 1999]. They have different goals and different things they're trying to optimize.

We did a survey in this area a few years back, and you know what? The number one consideration for IT managers buying enterprise software was whether it was compatible with the rest of their architecture. Usability was near the bottom of their decision criteria.

Today IT leaders are shifting their focus from reducing costs to improving business agility, and from developing back-end "systems of record" to creating customer-facing "systems of engagement." But these trends are dangerous unless IT departments develop sound usability practices and engage with their business stakeholders.

The bottom line is that business leaders are not going to have good usability if they don't engage with their IT counterparts in a meaningful way—and that way is not the old "waterfall" approach, where they would send their prototype off to be coded, and it came back working differently and looking differently than what they sent in.

Orchestrating that level of collaboration leads inevitably back to the top of the organization. Because who is the common manager of IT, marketing, and the customer experience or user experience group (if one exists)? It's someone with a title like COO or CEO.

limited, you can turn one or two projects into showcases. In this way, even a small commitment becomes visible and motivating. After that percolation period, you can start to tackle larger projects. Make sure you don't have practitioners trying to work on too many projects simultaneously. If you have a small number of staff servicing a huge organization, your efforts will be invisible and you will lose momentum. The practitioners will find themselves dashing from one design session to another, making wild guesses, yet letting everyone feel that user experience design has been executed.

Evangelizing

The central group must provide information and share lessons learned on the value of user-centered design, which means making presentations on a regular basis. These presentations can share project examples, new research findings, and progress in the metrics of user performance and conversion. Beyond formal presentations, it is necessary to have a process for constant communication with individuals and small groups, including quiet lunches and personal exchanges at social gatherings. Practitioners need to exploit every possible venue for communication and sharing. Most importantly, team members need to convey their excitement about and commitment to the user experience design effort—they need to evangelize!

When missionaries travel to new countries, they translate their beliefs into the local language, making their ideas and value systems fit with local traditions and needs. In a similar way, the user experience design evangelist must speak the business language of the organization. He or she needs to translate the value of user-centered design so it meets the objectives of development teams and other groups. Dropping UX terms such as "cultural dimensions," "scenarios," and "function allocation" can be impressive, but particularly at the beginning of the institutionalization process, it's important to couch user-centered design ideas in the local language. With business people, for example, you should talk about conversion rates and call time.

The Role of the Central Usability Team

Arnold Lund, Connected Experience Labs Technology Leader,
Human–Systems Interaction Lab Manager—GE Global Research
Former Director of Design and Usability, Microsoft

My design and usability team should be a place where we learn and build our intellectual capital around good design. It should be where we abstract from the many projects we're doing those lessons and insights that cut across releases and products. The resulting intellectual capital should make us more and more effective over time, and I would hope that eventually what we learn would work its way outside of Microsoft and into the broader user experience field.

One goal we have in Microsoft is to build community across the corporation and then advance the community. As Microsoft design and usability managers, we are creating a long-term plan for the company about where the user experience practice within Microsoft should be heading. The plan is based on a view of where the company is going, how technology is evolving, which user experience methods and tools are emerging, and what that means for a vision of design and usability five years out. We are trying to figure out where we need to be to maximize our contribution to the business and to our customers in that time frame. We will then draw out the implications for career growth, for skills growth, for new tools that we need to develop, for design and usability, for techniques and methods, for hiring, for internal training—indeed, all the things we believe we will need to do to advance the community and practice of design and usability within Microsoft.

As I think about promoting an understanding of the importance of design and usability within Microsoft, I think about what we do already and what we can do in the future. There is a corporate newsletter, of course, where stories about product successes and individual usability group case studies appear. I think we can leverage that more. Design and usability are built into the corporate training that all new employees go through, into individual internal courses, and into corporate events. We had a Design Day a couple of months ago that a lot of managers attended (along with the design and usability communities). Several of us spoke, there were panels, and there were booths. We were able to play an educational role and network in ways that helped grow our impact. There are many opportunities to do the public relations that opens doors.

One of the results of the focus on personas within Microsoft is that the personas get turned into posters that are mounted on walls. They direct people's attention to the users and heighten awareness of the research behind the personas. Here in our organization we are talking about creating design walls and user experience walls to surround the project teams with information about the users and the emerging designs. It keeps them focused on the users and what we do, and it engages them in where we are going and how we are thinking about it. It invites their input. We always try to get people involved in lab testing. We have even been taking advantage of the ability to stream the video from the testing over the intranet so product teams can participate from their desks without having to travel to the lab. The goal is to get as many people on the teams as possible engaged in the user-centered design process.

It is hard to estimate the time required to evangelize. It is closer to a lifestyle than a specific task, but certainly there are presentations to prepare and meetings to organize. The concrete elements of the evangelization role probably add up to a half- or full-time position in a large organization. The manager of the usability team often assumes much of this responsibility.

Evangelists must have a certain charisma that expresses itself as a burning desire to share the knowledge of user-centered design. They must create excitement as they show how user experience design can directly transform the listener's life. The commitment of an evangelist is contagious—and it's very necessary: if the central group staff becomes complacent and bored, the whole effort is likely to flounder.

Training

During the initial phases of your institutionalization program, a series of training classes probably brought people up to speed and conveyed essential skills. While this training was imperative, training is never completely finished in a competitive organization. The internal user-centered design team should take charge of the ongoing training program. The team may not need to be responsible for all training, however—in most organizations, it doesn't make sense to maintain the more complex and infrequently used courseware, nor are there enough presentations of most training classes to keep trainers fully occupied or their memory of the course material fresh. Nonetheless, the central group must assume overall responsibility for the training program.

User experience design training should be a part of the orientation of new staff. If not, the user-centered perspective—and its benefits—may be slowly diluted by new staff members who have not received a solid UX orientation. In addition to the basic orientation, some new members need to learn specific skills to work on particular types of projects or particular user experience design activities. You may need someone to specialize in wireless devices, for example, or persuasion engineering or usability testing.

Over time, your ongoing skills training will probably need to cover the full range of user experience engineering capabilities as new staff members come on board. That includes initial orientation to the user-centered perspective—including skills training, training on standards, and training on aspects of user experience design engineering specific to the organization's domain—as well as training on new and special topics.

Existing staff members also need continuous training and professional development. Personnel in the central group may benefit from attending technical conventions, where they can learn about new research or methods and share problems and tips with colleagues in other industries. User experience design staff can also benefit from taking advanced courses. These courses may cover such topics as research updates and new usability methodologies (e.g., remote testing).

It is motivational for team members to see that the process is working. It also motivates them to have a growing set of credentials showing their competency. Many benefits accrue when staff members gain advanced degrees and certifications: coworkers in other groups develop more respect for the user experience design team; the field stays new and interesting to UX staff members and their skill sets increase. Credentials are also a confidence builder—even certificates of completion can build confidence.

Mentoring

User experience design staff members working on project teams have a "dotted line" relationship with the central group: the central group cares about them, advocating for them in political and policy matters and helping to handle problems. Most directly, however, the central group should be available to mentor usability staff on the project teams. Depending on the corporate culture, this could be either a very formal process or an informal one.

Mentoring is challenging because there is no single path to follow. Some staff members need insights into data gathering methods; some need to build confidence so they can run their first solo usability test; others need help interacting with developers.

Mentoring may be only one part of a person's job, and it generally requires a different perspective than a practitioner has while working on projects. The mentor should attend to the growth of the practitioner without worrying about meeting deadlines and ensuring the efficacy of design on a project at the same time.

Supporting Standards

In the Setup phase of UX design institutionalization, the organization created a set of methodological standards and interface design standards. Developing these standards required a big investment, but the standards will not endure or even be used unless they are supported.

Standards are living documents. New and improved procedures will be added to the methodology, and new page types and additional rules will be added to the design standards. The user experience design team must constantly monitor the design process and find opportunities for improvement. Innovations rarely come from theoretical analysis of existing standards; instead, they emerge from observations of the direct contact between the standards and the design work. Necessity spawns invention, and the user-centered design team must gather these inventions and add them to the standards.

The time required to collect new methods and add them to the standards varies based on the complexity of the design challenges involved, as well as the process required for getting consensus and approval for changes. At HFI, for example, we have four cycles of upgrades to our methods and templates each year. The GUI standards require fewer changes by now, but the browser standards are still growing. The time required to collect enhancements and facilitate the approval process might amount to a half-time job.

There is little value in having a methodology or a design standard if there is no one to go to with questions. No document is so thorough that issues will never crop up regarding the design decisions. Inevitably, special needs emerge based on users, taskflows, environments, technologies, and business strategies. Sometimes design teams need someone to talk to—someone with wider experience and the ability to provide definitive guidance on methods and design. Team members need a consultant—and they can talk to one on the central team.

Advocating Usability through a Strong Sense of Community

Feliça Selenko, Former Principal Technical Staff Member, AT&T

I think one of the most important ways to share an understanding of usability is to do it one person/one project at a time. Usability experts need to take the time to look for and take advantage of every opportunity to advocate usability, its bottom-line cost benefits, and the respective user performance research. They need to have their "soapbox" and a usability road show ready to go at all times, so as to support any and all requests for information about usability and its benefits. This creates a strong network of supporters and "prophets" to help spread the word.

Colleagues have said that my enthusiasm and consistent commitment throughout the years have kept the team going through any hard times experienced by the telecommunications industry. The words that come to mind that create a sense of community are enthusiasm, camaraderie, empathy, dedication, sincere support, responsiveness, optimism, and fun—really believing in the value of the usability discipline and treasuring the community we have. Logistically, we have a grassroots, committed, cross-organizational team that meets monthly on a two-hour conference call. We discuss everything: project dilemmas, rumors, industry articles/conferences, organizational issues, usability tools and standards, as well as personal changes and triumphs. Because we keep it practical, focused, and fun, we all look forward to maintaining our connection.

It is important to have consistent guidance from the central group regarding standards issues. This is not a call for rigidity—standards need to be interpreted in each context—but a recognition that there must be coherence to the answers that teams get from their standards consultants. Therefore, it is best to charge just one or two people with handling this task. If two people are assigned to fill this role, they should work closely together. For most organizations, however, a single person can answer standards questions, and in smaller organizations this might be half of one person's responsibilities.

In addition, tools need to be supported. This may include getting the best software and usability testing equipment to be used in the methodology, or working with systems staff to select content management systems and other productivity-enhancing applications to ensure that the user-centered design process is supported. This will be a half- to full-time job in most organizations.

Supporting the Community

Often, user experience design practitioners will quickly form a community of interest within their company. Even if they are not formally connected within the organization, they have traditionally banded together. In the past, the user experience design team typically consisted of a small group of people who were undervalued and often under attack. Developers saw UX practitioners as an annoyance, obsessed with a "soft," unimportant area, and tried to marginalize them. Generally, a persecuted minority clings together, and user-oriented staff members were no exception. That mutual support—often all that sustained the effort—provided a conduit of information and resources as well as a source of mutual emotional support. Alone, surrounded by people with a system-centered view, it was easy to start thinking you were crazy and to lose the will to keep working. That small circle of colleagues made all the difference in keeping the momentum going.

Fortunately, user experience engineering communities are seldom the same small, surrounded groups today. The user-centered focus is more likely to be accepted and routine. Even that cultural change poses its own challenges, however: we need to work to keep the UX community's identity, mission, and spirit lively.

The simple act of working together increases group cohesiveness, creates relationships, spurs on the institutionalization effort, and increases the transfer of information and support. For this reason, the central group should engineer shared projects that can bring practitioners together. These projects may include standards, tools, or collective presentations to management.

Another powerful method is the project-sharing presentation. Periodically, practitioners can share presentations with one another to recount the best insights and breakthroughs from their projects. These aren't long-winded process discussions or explanations of the whole project—each project team has only a short time, perhaps 15 minutes, to share major insights and innovations. Teams can even present skits or interactive demonstrations. Concrete before/after examples, preferably with metrics of success, are a quick, powerful way to share lessons learned among the community of practice.

Performing Usability Testing

Practitioners on project teams can certainly do all their own usability testing and other types of evaluations. There are two major reasons to have some of the testing done by the central group.

The first reason is the ability to economize. You can easily and practically maintain a small pool of usability testing staff members who are not experienced or trained in a complete range of user-centered design tasks but are knowledgeable about running usability tests. Running A:B tests, surveys, and other metrics is primarily a technical task (once those tests are set up).

The second reason to have the central group support assessments is objectivity. Some practitioners, while good designers, have trouble accepting the idea that users might find problems with their designs. Some will even argue with usability testing subjects to try to convince them that the design makes sense. Once, I watched a developer try to explain to a participant the difference between the OK and Apply buttons. With enough explanation, the participant seemed to agree that there was a difference (more likely, he was bored by the discussion and just wanted to move on). In such a case, it helps to have someone else run the test.

Focusing on Metrics

A common management principle advises, "If you can't measure it, you can't manage it." By measuring user experience, you can determine whether your investment is working. You can tell which areas need more work and can improve your process. The central team needs to create and maintain the usability metrics that make sense to your business.

One type of metric describes the process of user-centered design. For example, it is a good idea to track the number of staff hired and trained, the number of people working on user-centered issues, and the number of projects that do or do not apply the user-centered methodology. The main purpose of these metrics is to validate that user experience design work is actually being done, and to show the growth and stability of practice within the organization. Such metrics are basically means of cost accounting. Although you may be happy to see a solid investment in the UX design process, it does not really measure anything valuable from the perspective of the organization. With an indication of the costs in hand, there had better be a solid improvement in the business results to justify these expenditures.

Given this fact, it is helpful to have periodic, empirical demonstrations of the value of user-centered work. These focused studies generally look at a very specific before/after design scenario. For example, the site may have a point of high drop-off. If user-centered design work can reduce this drop-off, you may be able to attribute a significant improvement in sales to that change. If specific functions in an application can be improved, those improvements can be measured and reported.

Be wary of being satisfied simply by hearing that "the users liked it." This kind of anecdotal feedback is better than nothing—and certainly better than being told the users have created their own system on Excel as an alternative to your dysfunctional design. Nevertheless, it is far better to have specific data and surveys showing a specific movement in the rating for the site or application. Even more encouraging would be a 25% drop in the time needed to complete a checkout process. But the most compelling information is directly tied to the business needs—how much money the usability effort makes, how much money it saves, and how customers have responded (i.e., a specific, quantifiable increase in customer satisfaction).

If you do not know where you have been, it is hard to demonstrate progress. A summative usability test at the end of the design process reporting that applications for insurance are completed in 2.5 minutes is rather difficult to interpret. It seems like a reasonable time, but is it an improvement? This is the reason you need benchmark testing. In a benchmark test, participants complete a set of representative tasks, and usability testing staff measure time, error rate, and subjective ratings. A similar group of participants completes the same testing with the same tasks every 6 or 12 months. By examining these results periodically over time, you can see whether your changes have affected the user experience or performance. This practice also allows you to benchmark the time required for expert users to complete the representative tasks. Collectively, this combination of data gives a very good indication of progress.

Many metrics look at user performance and subjective reports from customers. These kinds of metrics are interesting, but can be misleading. Jared Spool, founding principal of User Interface Engineering, had the following insights on privacy and the Internet, demonstrating that you cannot rely only on what users say:

> In April of 2002, Princeton Survey Research Associates surveyed 1,000 adult Internet users about their concerns with privacy on the Internet. In the survey, only 18% said they never read privacy policies when shopping online; 57% said they check the privacy policy most of the time, or every time they shop.
>
> Yet, in our study of more than 1,000 shopping sessions, where we actually observed what users did while shopping, we

noticed that only two users ever checked the site's privacy policy. And for those two users, it had no effect on their shopping behavior. This is yet one more case of users doing something different from what they say they do.[1]

Different business models require different objectives to measure the metrics directly connected to the success of the site or application. It could be the sale of an application, conversion of site visitors, size and breadth of the shopping basket, cross-sell volume, average call-handling time, or qualified leads generated and resulting sales. There are potentially hundreds of useful metrics. In the end, however, they need to be tied firmly to business results. While it might be encouraging to learn that 92% of customers responding on a questionnaire say they would purchase something on a Web site, it is much more meaningful to see how many actually make a purchase.

Having Responsibility

The central group takes responsibility for user experience throughout the organization. This responsibility includes an attitude of involvement and concern, as well as a set of specific activities. The central group should watch for projects that need user-centered design help and areas of the company business that will benefit from such work. The central group needs to make sure that the projects get the attention they need. We must drive for routine inclusion of user-centered design methods in every design program.

Ensuring that there are user experience design practitioners working on every important project is the primary goal of the central team. After assigning a practitioner to a project, the organization must provide the necessary skills, methodology, standards, tools, and channels of communication to that project. In addition to a constantly review of the internal process, the central group must consider the lessons learned and opportunities uncovered.

It is challenging to quantify the time it takes to do this type of management work, but it should be noted that much of the work occurs

---

1. From a letter to Human Factors International, September 2003. Reproduced with permission.

in the context of other activities. For example, a central group consultant reviewing a voice response system might hear about issues on a new project or might find a new menu type such as "Skip and Scan" that applies to all voice systems throughout the organization. If this new menu reduces drop-through to a human operator by 5%, the modest savings seen from a single, small application can be vastly multiplied if applied throughout the organization. The central usability team is the only group likely to be a good conduit for such insights.

Reporting to Executives

Adopting a user-centered perspective is one of those challenging, yet valuable initiatives that does not happen on its own. In addition to ensuring that user experience design is taking place within the company, the central team must maintain a usability presence within the executive suite.

Such an initiative will include many different elements, and few you can afford to forget. You must address complex issues of change management and acceptance. Management will eventually understand that user experience metrics are as critical to the business as gross sales and support costs. The executive champion helps deliver this message, but the content of the message comes from the central group. The members should have examples that demonstrate how user experience design makes a difference and the metrics to prove it. This group must understand the champion's strategic perspective and move forward on that track, improving the process and ensuring its continuation.

Some of the central group's attention must always be focused on the executive champion and the other key executives in the organization. The amount of time required for that effort varies depending on the dispersion of the executive team. A closely knit team, all in one location, is easy to manage. Doing so takes only a few days of effort each month. Once key people are properly briefed, there is little more to do. By comparison, with a more complex executive team, it can be nearly a half-time job keeping everyone apprised of the progress, value, and needs of the user experience effort.

My Nine Principles to Keep Institutionalization Motivated

Colin Hynes, President, UX, Inc.
Former Director of Site Usability, Staples

1. *Go deep first and that will help you go wide later.* Get the solid gains first and don't try to sell yourself too thin. If you work on 10 different projects with three usability experts, you won't do any of them well. Then you'll just be perceived as a veneer on the process instead of having real impact. When we started this group, I knew we needed to get some solid wins in a very deep and effectual way. We did that, and then we went on to other projects that helped us spread our influence as we built the group.

2. *Quantify gains made from projects* that were led or deeply impacted by usability and translate that into ROI. We have held up the improvements that usability made to the Staples.com registration process as one of our hallmark projects. We improved the drop-off rate—the percentage of users leaving our site—in that area by 72%. As I speak about the usability group, I constantly reference that number and say, "Look what happens when you include usability and then tie that back to numbers." The business folks listen when they see these types of gains.

3. *Create a selling document* with video clips and numbers that resonates with budget owners. I spent a lot of time putting together a usability document a while back. One high-level goal of the document was just teaching people what usability is and why it's important. However, the document also gets into the deep details of how we use usability at Staples relative to our structure and how it has produced measurable gains. I structured the document so it could be discussed in about an hour, so that it could be scheduled more easily into the calendars of busy senior executives. Some video clips show folks struggling with applications. Whenever somebody says, "What is usability and how does it

work?" I use that document to educate them and get the point across.

4. *Speak the language of science, technology, and business.* I think that that's a really important one—it's that "chameleon" idea. You need to be able to go into these people's "dens" and say, "I understand what you're going through. I understand why we can't use JavaScript on this page, but think about the ROI from a business perspective." You really need to speak in a language they understand. You should not approach it as some Ph.D. scientist in an ivory tower saying, "We should do this because it's right for the user," without really thinking about why it's important to the business or considering it from a technology perspective.

5. *Create a differentiated team.* For example, all my permanent employees and consultants have a master's degree or above in human factors, cognitive psychology, or a related discipline. Many people with great talent in usability do not have these academic credentials. However, having staff with these backgrounds has helped me greatly in selling the usability competency as science throughout the company. Also, I started building the team with the hope that someday we'd move from our original Staples.com roots into other areas of the organization. So I hired folks with backgrounds in retail environments, back-end applications, marketing materials, and paper catalogs. They also had dot-com experience so that until we expanded past dot-com, they would be able to fill the immediate need. As we have grown to support the paper catalog, retail environment, AS-400, and so on, these key folks have been able to grow into other areas of the company.

6. *Tie the group's performance reviews to measurable business metrics.* In the annual performance reviews of my group, I ask them to meet certain measurable criteria. For example, how are we going to increase the conversion rate or decrease drop-off in Checkout or BizRate Ease of Order survey

(continues)

My Nine Principles to Keep Institutionalization Motivated (continued)

scores? By tying the group to these metrics, I'm making the statement, "I am a business owner." It helps socialize the idea of usability as a business group. In addition to keeping the usability group focused on business goals, it's a great supplement to having actual profit and loss responsibility.

7. *Work closely with PR to tell the story.* A lot of people may say, "Instead of spending time talking to the media, you should be doing project work." While I agree that spending too much time at conferences and in interviews takes you away from core responsibilities, press coverage has been extremely valuable for us for two reasons. First, it helps get out the positive customer message, which is core to Staples values. Second, publicity is extremely valuable in hiring—we have a great PR halo over the usability group. We do good work, but we also talk about the good work that we do. I hope that it helps the usability industry as a whole, but it certainly helps us in hiring. When people say, "Wow, there's a job opening at Staples. Those guys are so focused on usability—I would love to work there," it helps us build a great group.

    A couple years ago, I was fortunate enough to take a taxi back from a store to the airport with Tom Stenberg, who was our CEO at the time and is the founder of the office supply superstore concept and of Staples. He said to me, "I read something the other day about the good work your usability team is doing. It must be gratifying to see all the visibility that usability is getting in the press." So when people who are this high up in the organization read the stories, they internalize the ideas. It really helps the internal communication about usability and certainly the external communication about customer focus.

8. *Join professional groups and leverage free advice.* There's lots of free advice out there, from people going through the same

things we are, whether it's SIGCHI, or UPA, or HFES,[2] or other groups. There's a lot of good information you can get from picking those brains, and lots of value you can add in return by sharing your own experiences.

9. *Pick your spots.* Speak with passion when necessary—but know when something is good enough. That's a hard thing for a lot of people, especially usability perfectionists. But you need to embrace "good enough." You can't be someone who cries, "Wolf!" all the time. Not everything is the biggest issue to ever happen to the site or the product. You have to keep a sense of perspective. Is this a page that's going to be out there for two days and 10 people are going to see it? Or is it something that's going to live with us for years so that millions of people will see it? Pick your spots and don't be a "Chicken Little" whose sky is always falling. It's a basic engineering principle, too. "The perfect is the enemy of the good" [Rubinstein and Hersh 1984]—if you try to do everything, you can't get anything done. You have to be a pragmatist.

Summary

The level of effort and commitment displayed by the central user experience design team will pay off in the long term only if team members allow time for maintenance, reinforcement, demonstration, and integration. Together, the team must continue to focus on these goals to keep user-centered design a vital focus of the organization.

---

2. The Special Interest Group on Computer–Human Interfaces of the Association for Computing Machinery (SIGCHI), the Usability Professionals Association (UPA), and the Human Factors and Ergonomics Society (HFES).

Chapter 15

The Future

➤ The field is now mainstream, with ease-of-use being recognized as a basic business requirement.

➤ The new market differentiators will be UX strategy, systematic innovation, and persuasive design.

➤ The field will mature in process and capabilities.

➤ The field will mature in staffing.

➤ We will adapt to new technologies—which is not that difficult.

Today, if you want to be in business, you have to be able to make digital experiences easy and efficient. Usable digital channels and efficient, staff-facing systems are expected by the market. If you don't provide them, your competitors will.

No matter which industry or vertical market you are in, a substantial component of your digital business will have to be optimized. And basic usability is no longer enough—the future will require strategic work, innovation, and persuasion engineering.

Symptoms of Leaping the Chasm

In the past, early adopters applied usability work. Following the model of technology adoption created by Geoffrey Moore [1999], usability has clearly leapt the chasm and become a generally accepted approach: most organizations are engaging in some systematic usability efforts, and the laggards are at least interested in doing so. Even the most unintelligible applications are touted as "usable" and "easy." The reality may not always match the marketing, but the motivation is there.

At HFI, we have witnessed years of early adoption behavior. Aggressive and visionary managers have completed thousands of isolated user experience design projects, usually with good results. It is common to encounter organizations that are interested in how to make user-centered processes a part of their routine practices. Experimentation is typical for early UX adopters. But while experimentation has played an important role in the development of user-centered design, UX is transitioning to a mainstream practice now. It is becoming large scale, process driven, repeatable, and supported with a solid infrastructure.

In general, when a technology takes the jump to wide usage, it is met with a tornado of interest. The mass market suddenly wants the technology, and there is not enough of it to go around. A bit of frenzy occurs until the market supply ramps up to meet this demand. We saw this kind of tornado in the late 1990s. The bursting of the dot-com bubble put a damper on the excitement, yet in the years that followed we saw a "usability tornado"—a period during which both excellent and weak usability companies were overwhelmed with projects and requests. Unfortunately, the recession in recent years has again slowed progress. As of today, however, we can clearly see renewed focus on user-centered design. Interestingly, there is a shift toward stronger internal user experience design teams. The global best practice is no longer having a bunch of vendors doing the work; it is now widely understood that bringing in outside contractors for individual projects results in a hodgepodge of impressive but incoherent designs. In response to this realization, almost every organization is building an internal user experience design capability of some kind.

Usability Trends

Harley Manning, Research Director, Forrester Research

I haven't noticed that people in general are getting smarter. I think what we'll see is the continuation of the old story of the human race, which is that some people will get it and some people won't.

We do a lot of website reviews—heuristic evaluations—and we meticulously track both the scores per question and the total scores over time. This is one way to approximate an average "goodness" number for websites of major corporations. And the average score has not been going up. Now, this could be a statistical anomaly because even 1500 sites is a small sample. Part of the analysis, then, is looking at the sites and asking, "Does this look like an improvement to you?" For the most part, we are still seeing some incredibly basic errors—even at companies that claim to be putting a lot of effort into improving usability.

For example, text legibility is criminal on many sites, just awful. And yet it's so easy to understand what causes poor legibility, and it's so easy to fix it. It costs nothing; it doesn't require you to be a great designer. There's little debate—nobody would argue that it's a good idea to make your customers squint or make it hard to read some marketing communication that you've spent a fortune writing.

Clearly, no one would argue that poor legibility is a good thing, and very few people are stumped by the fact that the cure for poor legibility is increasing type size and increasing foreground/background contrast. But legibility problems don't get fixed, even when you point them out to people.

Some companies really do get it; they do take usability into account and make very serious efforts to improve it on an ongoing basis. So, while the average website is not getting better, there are leaders who really are ahead of the pack and pulling farther ahead.

Maturity

As user-centered design becomes even more mainstream, it is rapidly becoming mature.

The maturity of the software industry is something to envy. When coding began 40 years ago, the programming process was primarily an individual activity, completed by unique people who stayed up late and struggled to debug their creations. Their work was a function of flashes of insight and unique, elegant solutions. In a few decades, however, the industry has completely changed in character.

The Future of Usability within a Government Agency

**Sean Wheeler, Lead Usability Specialist,
Social Security Administration**

I think the recognition of and need for usability services will continue to grow. I believe that as we improve the business case for positive, powerful user experiences and then deliver that kind of experience, the public use of our website will increase. This is a critical part of the challenge for agencies like the Social Security Administration if we want more people to choose the information technology channel to contact us.

Quite simply, we must provide a Web experience that meets or exceeds the quality of the experiences that people get when they call our 800-number service or visit their local Social Security office. This was the challenge that our 800-number people faced when we first initiated that service. They had to answer those tough questions about how you communicate that sense of friendliness and provide service on the telephone when you can't see the public visitors face-to-face and share documents with them across a desk. We learned a lot from that channel shift, and we are just now learning what the shift to Web-based service delivery means.

Today, software companies have well-documented processes, defined skill sets and programs to teach their methods to new employees, and tools and reusable object code to make the process faster and more consistent. They know how to accurately estimate and track the development effort for a coding project. They can assure the quality of their projects, and they continuously improve their process.

User experience design is making a similar transformation. While it is fun to be unique, user-centered design has to be made more uniform and manageable to be part of the business solution. You cannot rely on having one of the superstars in the field at your disposal: user experience design must become institutionalized.

Your Organization's Maturity

There are many dimensions of maturity in user experience engineering, and organizations take many different pathways to reach them. However, over the years, we at HFI have discovered typical maturity levels for companies climbing the gradient to institutionalized proficiency. We developed a model that we use to help grow an organization's user-centrality and to certify the level of its user experience design practice (Figure 15-1).

We are happy to report that these objective criteria tell us that many organizations are steadily increasing their UX maturity. The future of the field, it seems, is to have a mature practice in which user experience design work is routinely applied to projects, with resources being made available to do everything that needs to be done.

Process, Capabilities, and Staffing

As user-centricity becomes routine, there will be a growth in the field's capabilities. We will see a shift to process-driven user experience design. In other words, the quality of design will no longer be dependent on the particular practitioner assigned to it. Certainly,

Usability Activity	Level 1 Beginning Usability	Level 2 Executive Champion	Managed Usability		
			Level 3 Essential Capabilities	Level 4 Full Capability	Level 5 Mature Practice
Strategy					
Written Strategy	○	●	●	●	●
Infrastructure					
User Centered Design Methodology	○	○	◐	●	●
User Interface Standards	○	○	◐	●	●
Repository of User Ecosystem Data	○	○	○	◐	●
Usability Test Laboratory	○	○	◐	◐	●
Metrics and Continuous Improvement	○	○	○	◐	●
Education and Training					
Regular Executive Briefings	○	○	◐	◐	●
Usability Introduction for Design Staff	○	○	○	◐	●
Professional Training for Usability Staff	○	○	◐	●	●
Advanced Training for Usability Staff	○	○	○	◐	●
Staffing					
Executive Champions	○	●	●	●	●
Managed Usability Organization	○	○	◐	●	●
Core of Certified Staff	○	○	◐	●	●
Sufficient Staff to Meet Demand	○	○	○	○	●
Organization Certificate Audit			III	IV	V

Usability Maturity Chart Version 2.0 — Human Factors International

Legend: ○ Not there   ◐ Some what present   ● Present

Figure 15-1: *HFI's Maturity Model*

there will always be elements of creativity and art in the field, but we will have a solid, repeatable process. This in itself is groundbreaking. Ad hoc user experience design, in contrast, will make it difficult for us to get better in creating user-centered processes.

Think of shoes. At one time, shoes were made by cobblers. Shoe repair shops could be found everywhere because the soles would inevitably come loose. Today, however, soles don't come loose—industrial operations have been refined to make sure of that. In the same way, the repeatability of industrial-strength user experience design will allow us to refine the process of UX. Thousands of small improvements will accumulate and result in a seriously improved operation.

The refinement of processes will drive the development of a more extensive UX design toolkit. We will improve our efficiency through reuse, remote operations, and investigative tools, and will find

A Vision of the Future of Usability

Aaron Marcus, President, Aaron Marcus and Associates

I believe that usability groups will try to grow their organization and undertake new initiatives through some of the umbrella developments happening in the corporate world. One of these is the growth of user experience design and user experience engineering. Another growth area is universal design and universal access. A third is cross-cultural usability and the globalization of usability. All of these new concepts lead to new attention and new energy. Whenever paradigms change, it's an appropriate time to move in quickly to obtain additional funding and human resources and to strengthen one's core concerns.

By the way, to clarify: *User experience design* refers to making products and services that are not only usable, but also useful and appealing. *Universal design* refers to developing products and services that also meet the needs of the disabled and the elderly. *Globalization* refers to developing products and services that take into account localized needs and desires of a more diverse set of users. Users from different cultures may have very different values for and concepts of power struggles, gender roles, individuality, ambiguity, long-term time orientation, and so on. All of these differences have an impact on what makes products and services usable.

many opportunities to repurpose devices from other applications, such as sports cameras for observational research.

There will also be a major shift in staffing. A class of executives will emerge whose profile makes them candidates for the CXO position. While they will not necessarily be practitioners with deep skills in applied psychology, they will be leaders, with leadership training, equipped to deal with the strategic issues around optimizing an internal user experience design practice. The growth of the field will also certainly be fueled by increasingly focused and effective educational programs.

The staffing of user experience design work will continue to rely on generalists who have master's degrees and certifications. In addition, the field will include a growing body of specialists, such as persuasion engineers, cross-cultural specialists, and domain/technology experts. For example, whole careers may become focused on optimization of the customer experience in call centers.

Strategy, Innovation, and Persuasion

Basic ease-of-use will most certainly not be enough for the user experience design practice of the future. Currently, most teams focus on usability: getting the detailed human–computer interface design right. They spend all their time on wording, layout, color, highlighting, and control selection—but they really don't look at the bigger picture. Are you designing a usable wrong thing? It is commonplace to find a siloed team working on a mobile application that does not fit with the rest of the channels the customer sees. For example, one bank offered customers "telephone banking," "cell phone banking," and "speech banking." Without a comprehensive, cross-channel design, the customer is presented with a confusing mess. It might be a usable mess, but it is a mess, nonetheless.

Designers need to avoid being tasked with the design of a wrong thing. In addition, practitioners should find new, innovative, correct things to design.

The pace of change has been accelerating exponentially in recent years. In turn, that means the old strategy of being a "fast follower" will no longer offer a path to business success. Failure to innovate can put the entire organization at risk.

In the arena of innovation, there are really three distinct approaches. First, there is the technology approach, in which new capabilities are developed in the hope that someone will want to buy them. Second, there is the business approach, in which we look at the business models that will be profitable. Third, there is the user experience design approach, in which we study the customer's ecosystem and invent what the customer needs. Ideally, all three methods should be functioning simultaneously, in a synergistic and systematic operation. This is very different from asking individuals to "be innovative." There is nothing wrong with that vague direction, of course, but a serious organization needs serious, industrial-strength innovation. The user experience design team gathers models of the customer and the customer ecosystem. This knowledge then defines the opportunity points that can be addressed with the innovation work. Finally, the user experience design team helps assess the value of each innovative concept based on the customer's needs (both task based and psychological).

Aside from strategy and innovation work, the user experience design team will often need to carry out persuasion engineering tasks. Team members will need to develop a persuasion architecture, defining the overall plan for how to motivate customers to convert and to return. They will need to apply persuasion tools to create the desired emotional response, trigger conversion, and develop habits. The importance of persuasion varies, depending on the type of organization that is being supported. In an extreme example, companies that make slot machines really deliver nothing more than customer experience; not surprisingly, slot machine companies invest heavily in user experience design [Schüll 2012]. In other cases, there is much less focus on persuasion—in a company that delivers bulk chemicals to business buyers, for example. However, even those buyers will be susceptible to methods of persuasion. Consequently, virtually all teams will eventually have to demonstrate some level of persuasion engineering capability.

New Technologies

As the information age progresses, the user-centered design field will encounter new challenges. There will be a wave of wearable information appliances, including those that are physically embedded in users (under the skin or in a tooth). Information technology will be applied to new domains and user populations. Each of these domains will present new and interesting challenges. While user experience design professionals will continue to use the same basic methods and insights, they will have to master some new challenges.

The user experience design field will also speed the progress of technology evolution. No longer will we create new offerings, only to have them rejected as impractical and awkward. User experience design work will soon smooth the introduction of new ideas.

Looking forward a decade or two, user-centered design will become so routine that it will no longer be a differentiator because all companies will apply a solid process. Today, users do not really clamor for software that performs calculations correctly. Instead, they expect software to work correctly the first time and every time— and if the software does not calculate correctly, they are furious. The same dynamic will occur with user experience design in the future. Users won't clamor for products that are usable because they will expect them to be usable. If products fall short of this expectation, customers will be furious. The interface quality today will draw derisive laughter from customers in the future. They will expect usability; it will just be one more requirement to stay in business.

The time for this transformation, this maturing of user-centered practice, is now. For-profit companies and nonprofit organizations alike are making the serious investment to build such a practice and integrate it into their very DNA.

Chapter 16

Design for Worldwide Applications

Apala Lahiri is the CEO of the Institute for Customer Experience (ICE) and an expert in cross-cultural design. With ICE, a not-for-profit initiative by HFI, Apala has been working with her team to investigate practical approaches for institutionalized user experience design practices to create sites and applications that will be used in countries around the world. It is a problem that many multinational organizations face, yet one of such complexity and scale that few have even attempted a solution.

Do International Markets Really Matter?

Is there a compelling reason for organizations that build facilities for domestic use to be concerned about usage in other countries—or around the world? If I had been asked this question 10 years ago, I would not have been able to give a definitive answer. In today's globalized market, however, the answer is a resounding *yes*.

The shift in focus to the new consuming class in emerging countries accompanies a transformation as significant as that brought about by the Industrial Revolution. According to McKinsey & Company, annual consumption in emerging markets is expected to reach

$30 trillion by 2025—"the biggest growth opportunity in the history of capitalism."

For organizations to survive and grow, they have no option except to make their products and services attractive and persuasive to users from the emerging markets. Emerging markets that might once have been concentrated in East Asia are now spread around the world. Concern about global usage is now an imperative.

McKinsey Quarterly's 2010 article, "Winning the $30 Trillion Decathlon: Going for Gold in Emerging Markets," observed that

> *CEOs at most large, multinational firms are well aware that multinational markets hold the key to success. Yet those same executives tell us they are vexed by the complexity of seizing this opportunity.*[1]

How Does Bad Cross-Cultural Design Happen to Good Organizations?

With English increasingly becoming the language of the Internet and China's heavy investment in having Chinese students and business people learn English, it might seem as if the efficient solution were for everyone to use the same site and applications. Alternatively, it might seem logical to translate the English-language sites directly, changing units such as currency denominations where necessary.

The essence of localization extends far beyond language and formats, however. Making local language content and formats available is a very good start, but much more needs to be done.

Marketing and consumer psychologists have shown that "culturally congruent" Web content leads to decreased cognitive effort for categorizing, processing, and interpreting information on the site, creating in turn a more positive attitude toward the website.[2] Culturally

1. https://www.mckinseyquarterly.com/Winning_the_30_trillion_decathlon_Going_for_gold_in_emerging_markets_3002.
2. Luna, D., L. A. Peracchio, and M. D. de Juan. 2002. "Cross-Cultural and Cognitive Aspects of Web Site Navigation." *Journal of the Academy of Marketing Science*, 30(4), 397–410.

congruent content/communication, built upon a foundation of cultural schemas shared by users, requires less cognitive processing and generates a feeling of "flow" and satisfaction in the user experience.

In *The Culturally Customized Web Site*, Arun Pereira and Nitish Singh describe cultural schemas as "simple elements or conceptual structures which serve as prototypes for underlying real world experiences. . . . The cultural schemas we develop are a result of adaptation to the environment we live in and the way we have been taught to see things in our culture."[3] Since cultural schemas consist of much more than language and formats, it is unlikely that a single solution would resonate with everyone in the world even if they were able to read it in their own language and interact with familiar currency and date formats.

Cultural schemas are likely to vary widely among users from, for example, a high-power-distance, collective, long-term-oriented culture that values restraint over indulgence and users from a very low-power-distance, highly individualistic, low-uncertainty-avoidance culture that values indulgence. How users from these two very different cultures interact with a banking site—what they expect to find on the site and their expectations of the bank itself—will differ significantly. Understanding this difference in underlying cultural schemas informs the design of local sites that users will adopt and use.

Internationalization, Localization, and the Challenges of Current Practice

Internationalization (I18n) and localization (L10n) have been cornerstones of cross-cultural UX concepts for over a decade, particularly in the software development world. Looking back at the experience HFI has had with large corporations delivering products and services around the world, it is clear that most corporations

---

3. See Casson 1983; D'Andrade 1992; Quinn and Holland 1987; and Singh 2004 for extended discussion of schemas and cultural models.

have adopted some aspects of internationalization practices. Most of them make it possible for the base product/website design to accommodate local language scripts, images, formats for currency and dates, and other factors. From the perspective of more than a decade of cross-cultural UX advocacy, however, there has been much progress beyond that—not in terms of organization structure or process, and certainly not in a consistent manner.

Microsoft, for example, strongly advocates product-centered groups (often based in Redmond, Washington) rather than global and local teams:

> *Putting together an efficient product team is a challenge that can make a significant difference to your bottom line— "throwing headcount" at your international editions is not an efficient use of resources. If your entire team, including developers, designers, testers, translators, marketers, and managers, is committed to all language editions of your product, and if management holds them responsible for all language editions, you won't have to hire a lot of extra people.*[4]

On the other hand, Infosys, one of India's largest systems integrators, emphasizes the major role of software productivity tools in its internationalization process:

> *Staffing for i18n/L10n projects is normally done by bringing in people who have prior experience of internationalization along with a team which is well versed in the technology underneath (Java, C++, etc.). In these cases, there is generally the overhead of training the team on i18n and L10n concepts. Unless the whole team fully understands the internationalization process, they will not be very productive. In the real world, it is almost impossible to get a perfect team which has good internationalization experience in addition to the required technical skills. Also, with tight deadlines looming over us, most of the time it is not possible to invest a lot of time in training the team on i18n/L10n concepts. So the best way to execute the project is to improve the productivity of the team by using software productivity tools and*

---

4. http://msdn.microsoft.com/en-us/library/cc194771.aspx.

*in turn enhance the productivity of the internationalization
process itself.[5]*

In addition, organizations such as Facebook, YouTube, and Google
are considered models for internationalization owing to the speed
of their crowdsourced language translation and local content.

Organizations in domains other than technology, such as retail, logistics, banking, health care, and appliances must grapple with the
same issues. They must balance the time and cost involved in providing the most culturally appropriate design/products/services to
local customers across the world.

Between the Idea and the Reality Falls the Shadow

While the intent is to provide localized solutions, in a majority of
cases the result is quite different. The outcome usually ends up
being a solution or a set of solutions that is created in the country
of origin and then internationalized in terms of its language and
unit measurements. The blame can be laid squarely on the absence
of a practical, cost-effective of a process that goes from understanding the local ecosystem through design and validations of
the application.

The amount of time and cost involved is really the "shadow" that
falls between the intent of providing localized solutions and the
reality of researching and understanding many local ecosystems
throughout the world.

The Criteria for Success

The test for globalized design is, of course, how much adoption and
usage of localized websites, products, and services occur. Nothing
succeeds like successful conversion.

---

5. http://www.infosys.com.

The challenge lies in balancing the optimal "fit" of a solution to the local ecosystem with the cost and time required to deliver it. Our group, ICE, has been giving this topic a great deal of thought as it explores different possibilities for global corporations to deliver local solutions in a realistic, cost-effective time frame.

A New Global Delivery Model for Local User Experience

To create a set of localized solutions that delivers the necessary level of quality for adoption without serious damage to the bottom line, ICE has a draft model in place based on two key concepts.

Foundational Ecosystem Model

We believe that the creation of a foundational ecosystem model of its customers is a key first step that a global organization needs to take in its journey to provide local UX solutions. This model will in many ways approximate the current internalization (I18n) template for software, but features placeholders for deeper cultural factors in addition to formats, colors, language, and images (Figure 16-1). This ecosystem model will typically be based on previous primary and secondary research, marketing data, and Big Data insights—and, in the future, on data gathered increasingly by the Internet of Things and crowdsourcing.

This foundational model can then be used for creating first an internationalized, and then a localized, set of ecosystem models—the "cultural" equivalent of the L10n process. The localized ecosystem models can be iteratively edited, enriched, and tested by local, in-country professionals.

These models can grow over time, in both the range of data they are built on and the depth of their understanding. They can also grow in the number of regions and countries that are separately included.

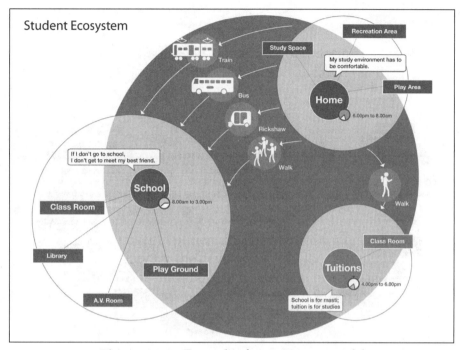

Figure 16-1: *Example of an ecosystem model*

"Cultural Factors" Training

Where would an organization embarking on its multicountry localization journey ideally find and hire large numbers of UX professionals in every country? Aside from the logistical challenges that this approach presents, the primary problem has been the dearth of UX professionals across the world.

We suggest a different approach to solve this problem, one that leverages remote training on "cultural factors"—a blend of human factors, cultural anthropology, and social psychology—as well as on how to conduct usability testing, to those who want to be certified in cultural factors and/or usability testing. Those taking the certification courses do not necessarily have to be UX professionals, but rather could be local staff of the organization or even local free-lancers.

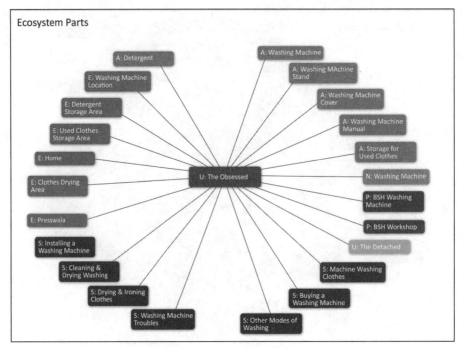

Figure 16-2: *Parts of the user's ecosystem: scenarios, artifacts, environment, needs, and opportunities*

Being able to access a large pool of certified professionals in cultural factors and usability testing across the world would enable multinational corporations to take a quantum leap in developing localized solutions in an accurate, efficient, and cost-effective manner.

Critical Tools

Even a good process will be useless if appropriate tools are not available to support the process. To build a foundational ecosystem model to support delivery of localized solutions, one that can be enriched over time in a cost-effective manner, it is essential to have a tool capable of breaking down the user data into components or objects (e.g., personas, scenarios, needs and opportunities, core values, artifacts) (Figure 16-2). This object paradigm will allow reuse of user data—adding, copying, and combining objects—rather than having to start from scratch as new user insights become available.

Figure 16-3: *Corporate memory of all user segments*

In addition, the tool should allow objects to be linked in a myriad of ways. With the progress of time, as additions are made to the foundational ecosystem model, new objects can be linked to older ones, and new insights/hypotheses can be inferred.

Finally, the tool should allow for seamless collaboration among everyone populating and adding to the foundational ecosystem model across the world.

This tool will serve as the corporate memory of an organization's global user segments (Figure 16-3).

Local Understanding, Global Success

For most organizations, this kind of object-oriented localization will represent a profound shift in approaching global markets. Can it produce designs that will compete with local companies, or succeed in diverse environments around the world?

I have always said, "Think globally; lose locally." There are very compelling reasons why paying attention to local needs can not only be very competitive, but also serve as a vital differentiator.

A look at India's smartphone usage landscape says it all. Goliaths such as Apple and Samsung are being overtaken by local Indian smartphone manufacturing Davids; local OEMs like Karbonn and MicroMax are on a roll.

A combination of low prices and "smart" features is fueling the local companies' rapid growth. *Businessweek*[6] notes that Karbonn, MicroMax, and other Indian hardware firms offer smart phones that are cheaper than the least expensive iPhones or even the Android models offered by U.S., Korean, and Taiwanese manufacturers. Considering that approximately 800 million people in India live on less than $2.00 per day, many of whom are hungry for new technology, this seems like a winning formula.

It is not just Apple and Samsung that have been affected by these local Davids. In the early 2000s, Nokia's early-mover advantage had allowed this firm to capture India's cellphone market. As Nokia stopped looking deeply at local needs, however, it ceded some of its dominance to new competitors, unheard-of local entrants in the Indian market.

What had seemed impossible had suddenly happened—a powerful multinational, considered a pioneer in the space, ousted by an unknown newcomer. That newcomer was MicroMax. Started by four friends in 2008, MicroMax used a "deep understanding of . . . consumer needs and the ability to swing their supply chain"[7] to become the largest mobile phone manufacturer in India by 2012.

---

6. Mehrotra, Kartikay. April 11, 2013. "iPhone Outpaced in Surging India by Less Costly Rivals." *Businessweek.*
7. http://micromaxcentral.com/micromax-company-profile/.

First published: February 2010

FUNCTIONALL | Captures the phenomenon of simple, small and/or cheap products and services designed for low(er)-income consumers in emerging markets, with cross-over appeal to consumers in mature consumer societies.

Figure 16-4: *Reversing the flow of products and services—from emerging markets to mature ones*[8]

The contextual innovation that comes from understanding local users can lead to success far beyond the local market, reversing the traditional flow of products and services from mature markets to emerging ones (Figure 16-4). Increasingly, designs created for emerging markets set a trend in mature markets (Figure 16-5).

The business case for investing in localization just got a whole lot stronger. When an organization creates localized products and services, the entire world becomes a potential market.

---

8. *Source:* Trendwatching.

Figure 16-5: *Emerging markets are the source, increasingly, of innovation*[9]

Are There Populations We Cannot Reach?

Businesses and designers, particularly those outside emerging markets, can be hesitant about designing for users of very limited means, particularly those in cultures that differ radically from their own. Yet poorer population segments constitute a significant proportion of the emerging markets. This approach to localization will actually make innovation for bottom-of-the-pyramid (BOP) segments around the world more likely, as well as more successful.

Ever since C. K. Prahalad's paradigm-shifting book *The Fortune at the Bottom of the Pyramid* was published, organizations have shown a considerable interest in servicing the BOP segment and "fighting poverty with profitability." Some major success stories have

---

9. *Source:* Trendwatching.

Figure 16-6: *A shop in Pondicherry, India, sells sachets of various products*

emerged as well. Consider the shampoo sachet (Figure 16-6; the forerunner of seemingly everything in sachets!), missed-call-based service models, and the distribution network (shakti ammas) created by Unilever in India and by MPesa in Kenya.

What made these ventures successful? The creators of these innovative bestsellers had their ears to the ground and made sure they understood the local ecosystem of the BOP population very well (Figure 16-7). Rather than simply "poorify" existing products and services, they started with a clean sheet of paper—and no assumptions. Intensive research yielded critical "cultural factors" such as the resonance of the "pay as you use" model—the preferred pattern of infrequent but regular consumption of a small quantity. And so came the shampoo sachet, one of the most successful innovations in recent times.

In short, a robust local ecosystem model helps an organization serve all its user segments, rich or poor, in an optimal manner.

Figure 16-7: *Apala Lahiri gathering ecosystem data in Africa*

Can We Look Forward to a Unified Globe?

There are those who say that the logical end of the information age is homogenization, a time in which there is enough commonality among people of the world that localization is unnecessary. I don't share that view—certainly not with the entire population of the world in mind. Of course, the miniscule 2–3% of the population that sits at the very top of the income pyramid in every country has always been rather homogenous across the world (Figure 16-8). With access to the abundance of global resources and exposure over several generations, this segment tends to speak of their motivations and needs in a common language.

The other 98% of the population—especially in the emerging countries—have not had shared in those resources or had the same access to information and global markets until very recently (Figure 16-9). This rising middle class tends to stick closer to its roots—it is open to using Western-style products and services but with a local flavor. For this segment, unlike earlier generations of consumers, foreign (read *Western*) products/services do

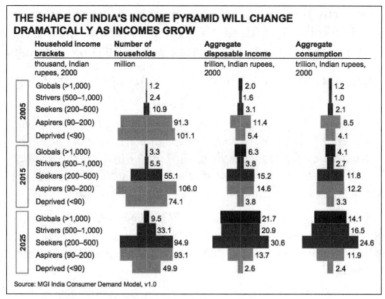

Figure 16-8: *Incomes and the growth period*[10]

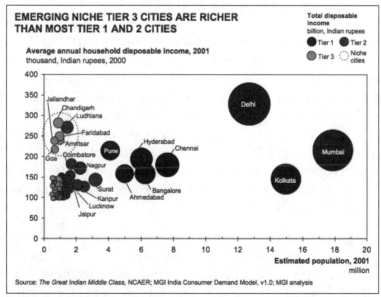

Figure 16-9: *The surprising wealth of emerging economies*[11]

10. *Source:* McKinsey Global Institute, "The Bird of Gold: The Rise of India's Consumer Market," May 2007.

11. *Source:* McKinsey Global Institute, "The Bird of Gold: The Rise of India's Consumer Market," May 2007.

not necessarily have an advantage over local ones. Given that this segment is likely to continue to grow throughout emerging economies, the demand for that "local flavor" will only increase.

According to leading market research consultant Rama Bijapurkar:

> It is interesting to note that between 1995–96 and 2005–06 the shape of income distribution in urban India changed from the traditional poor country shape of a triangle or pyramid (indicating far more people at the bottom than in the middle and even fewer at the top) to a diamond, with less people at the top and the bottom but many more in the middle.
>
> Projections are that the shape will change to that of a cylinder standing on a narrow base, with equal numbers in the top four income groups and very few at the lowest income group.[12]

Emergence of the "Third China"

The same trend is evident in China. Hitherto peripheral Chinese population segments are becoming significant consumers. Their emergence constitutes a significant new market segment in a country historically represented by a relatively elite sliver consuming goods like computers, washing machines, and cars, with the vast majority of the population lacking access to those goods. Now there are about 45 cities in China with a population of at least 1 million, and they are growing fast in terms of buying power (Figure 16-10). Yet the requirements of this "Third China" are also very much mediated by local preferences.

With the rise of new consuming classes in emerging countries, it cannot be assumed that those groups reaching certain income levels will have needs and preferences equivalent to those who have enjoyed the benefits of being at that income level for a much longer period.

---

12. Bijapurkar, Rama. 2008. *We Are Like That Only*. India: Penguin Books.

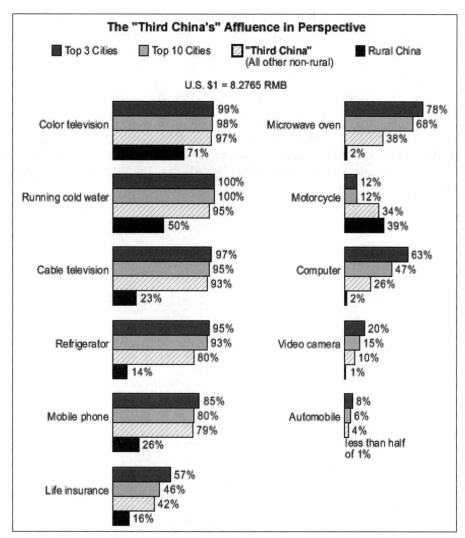

Figure 16-10: *Understanding affluence in the "Third China"*[13]

It is important to understand that simply looking at income levels may not always provide a real and clear picture of the consumer and his/her motivations and buying behavior. It is very common to find two people with the same income BUT with very different socio-economic environments behaving very differently as consumers.

---

13. *Source:* Gallup, "Still 'Two Chinas'—But a Third Is Being Born," February 8, 2005.

> *For example: Television buying is more income-driven, but the programs watched are socio-economic class driven. Several computing products fall in this category, where income is not the best predictor of consumer behavior.*[14]

The future, in sum, will present us with quite the opposite of a homogenous world. Likewise, the profile of the "typical" global consumer will very soon be very different from those of the past. Without a "template" of this emerging consumer, understanding this new consumer ecosystem at the local level becomes essential.

---

14. Bijapurkar, Rama. 2008. *We Are Like That Only*. India: Penguin Books.

References

Bernard, Michael. 2002. "Examining User Expectations for the Location of Common E-Commerce Web Objects." *Usability News 4.1.* Accessed November 2003 at psychology.wichita.edu/surl/usabilitynews/41/web_object-ecom.htm.

Bias, R. G., and D. J. Mayhew. 1994. *Cost-Justifying Usability.* San Diego, CA: Academic Press.

Bijapurkar, Rama. 2007. *We Are Like That Only.* New York: Penguin Books.

Brooks, Frederick P. 1995. *The Mythical Man-Month: Essays on Software Engineering, Anniversary Edition* (2nd ed.). Reading, MA: Addison-Wesley.

Card, Stuart K. 1982. "User Perceptual Mechanisms in the Search of Computer Command Menus." In *Proceedings of Human Factors in Computer Systems* (New York: Association for Computing Machinery), 190–196.

Casey, Steven. 1993. *Set Phasers on Stun: And Other True Tales of Design, Technology, and Human Error.* Santa Barbara, CA: Aegean.

Chavan, Apala L. 2002. *The Bollywood Technique.* Unpublished paper presented at User Needs Research Special Interest Group, CHI 2002: Conference on Human Factors in Computing Systems (April 20–25, Minneapolis, MN).

Cooper, Alan. 2004. *The Inmates Are Running the Asylum: Why High-Tech Products Drive Us Crazy and How to Restore the Sanity.* Indianapolis, IN: Sams Publishing.

Earthy, J. 1998. "Usability Maturity Model: Human Centredness Scale." Telematics Applications Project IE 2016, Report from the European Usability Support Centres, WP 5, Deliverable D5.1.4(s), Version 1.2. Accessed November 2003 at www.ipo.tue.nl/homepages/mrauterb/lecturenotes/USability-Maturity-Model%5B1%5D.PDF.

Ergonomics of Human–System Interaction: Specification for the Process Assessment of Human–System Issues. ISO/TS 18152. First published in 2010.

Goldberg, Jeff, Geoffrey Montgomery, and Maya Pines. 1995. *Seeing, Hearing and Smelling the World: New Findings Help Scientists Make Sense of Our Senses.* Chevy Chase, MD: Howard Hughes Medical Institute.

Gothelf, Jeff, and Josh Seiden. 2013. *Lean UX: Applying Lean Principles to Improve User Experience.* Sebastopol, CA: O'Reilly.

Kotelly, Blade. 2003. *The Art and Business of Speech Recognition: Creating the Noble Voice.* Boston, MA: Addison-Wesley, 2003.

Krug, Steve. 2000. *Don't Make Me Think: A Common Sense Approach to Web Usability.* Indianapolis, IN: Que Publishing.

Kruger, Justin, and David Dunning. 1999. "Unskilled and Unaware of It: How Difficulties in Recognizing One's Own Incompetence Lead to Inflated Self-Assessments." *Journal of Personality and Social Psychology,* 77(6), 1121–1134.

Lund, Arnie. 2011. *User Experience Management: Essential Skills for Leading Effective UX Teams.* San Francisco, CA: Morgan Kaufmann.

Mayhew, Deborah. 1999. *The Usability Engineering Lifecycle: The Practitioner's Handbook for User Interface Design.* San Francisco, CA: Morgan Kaufmann.

Miller, George A. 1956. "The Magical Number Seven, Plus or Minus Two: Some Limits on Our Capacity for Processing Information." *Psychological Review,* 63, 81–97.

Moore, Geoffrey. 1999. *Crossing the Chasm: Marketing and Selling High-Tech Products to Mainstream Customers* (rev. ed.). New York, NY: HarperBusiness.

Najjar, Lawrence J. 1990. *Using Color Effectively (or Peacocks Can't Fly)* (IBM TR52.0018). Atlanta, GA: IBM Corporation.

Nielsen, Jakob. 1994. *Usability Engineering.* San Francisco, CA: Morgan Kaufmann.

Nielsen, Jakob, and Shuli Gilutz. 2003. *Usability Return on Investment.* Fremont, CA: Nielsen Norman Group.

Nielsen, Jakob, and Marie Tahir. 2001. *Homepage Usability: 50 Websites Deconstructed.* Indianapolis, IN: New Riders Publishing.

Norman, Donald. 2002. "Emotion and Design: Attractive Things Work Better." *Interactions Magazine,* 9(4), 36–42.

Norman, Donald. 1988. *The Design of Everyday Things* (originally published as *The Psychology of Everyday Things*). New York, NY: Basic Books.

Paap, Kenneth R., and Renate J. Roske-Hofstrand. 1986. "The Optimal Number of Menu Options per Panel." *Journal of the Human Factors Society,* 28(4), 377–385.

Quinn, N., and Dorothy Holland, eds. 1987. *Cultural Models in Language and Thought.* London, UK: Cambridge University Press.

Rehder, Bob, Clayton Lewis, Bob Terwilliger, Peter Polson, and John Rieman. 1995. "A Model of Optimal Exploration and Decision Making in Novel Interfaces." In *Proceedings of CHI Annual Meeting.* Accessed November 2003 at www.acm.org/sigs/sigchi/chi95/Electronic/documnts/shortppr/br_bdy.htm.

Rubinstein, Richard, and Harry Hersh. 1984. *The Human Factor: Designing Computer Systems for People.* Burlington, MA: Digital Press.

Schaffer, Eric. 2001. *The Institutionalization of Usability* [white paper]. Fairfield, IA: Human Factors International.

Schaffer, Eric, John Sorfaten, Glenn Miracle, and Meena Venkateswaran. 1999. "Interactive Voice Response (IVR) Case Study: Testing Your Telephone-Based e-Commerce." *Journal of Electronic Commerce,* 12(2), 78–84. www.humanfactors.com/downloads/ivr.asp.

Schroeder, Will. September/October 1998. "Testing Web Sites with Eye-Tracking." *Eye for Design.* Accessed July 2003 at www.uie.com/eyetrack1.htm.

Schüll, Natasha Dow. 2012. *Addiction by Design: Machine Gambling in Las Vegas.* Princeton, NJ: Princeton University Press.

Singh, N. 2004. "From Cultural Models to Cultural Categories: A Framework for Cultural Analysis." *Journal of American Academy of Business,* 5(1–2), 95–102.

Singh, N., and Arun Pereira. 2005. *The Culturally Customised Website.* Oxford, UK: Routledge.

Tinker, Miles A. 1965. *Bases for Effective Reading*. Minneapolis, MN: University of Minnesota Press.

Tinker, Miles A. 1963. *Legibility of Print*. Ames, IA: Iowa State University Press.

Waite, R. 1982. "Making Information Easy to Use: A Summary of Research." In *Proceedings of International Technical Communication Conference* (Washington, DC: Society for Technical Communication), 120–123.

Ward, Toby. 2001. "Measured Intranet ROI Benefits." *TrendMarkers Newsletter*, 3(7). Accessed November 2003 at www.techmetrix.com/trendmarkers/publi.php?C=2IOFO.

Index

A

AAMI (Association for the Advancement of Medical Instrumentation), 10
Aaron Marcus and Associates, 279
A:B test engines, 131
Abbott Laboratories, 10
ACM SIGCHI (Special Interest Group on Computer-Human Interfaces), 221
Actors, in ecosystem models, 112
Adams, Scott, 6
A.G. Edwards & Sons, Inc., 5, 81
American Electric Power, 18, 245
"ANSI/AAMI HE 74:2001 Human Factors Design Process for Medical Devices," 10
Apple smartphones in India, 292
Assessing operational health
  certification, 182–184
  maturity model, 182–184
  metrics for, 181
  overview, 180–181
  tools for, 181–182
Assessing usability. *See* Usability testing.
Assessment methods, 76–77. *See also* Controlled experiments; Expert reviews; Usability testing.
Association for the Advancement of Medical Instrumentation (AAMI), 10
AT&T, 61, 261

B

Basic interface design standards, 94
Bijapurkar, Rama, 298–300
Board of Certification in Professional Ergonomics, 150, 226
Bollywood testing method, 136–137

Books and publications
  The Usability Engineering Lifecycle: The Practitioner's Handbook for User Interface Design (Mayhew), 35
  Cost-Justifying Usability (Bias and Mayhew), 36
  The Culturally Customized Web Site (Pereira, Singh), 285
  Emotional Design: Why We Love (or Hate) Everyday Things (Norman), 15–16
  "Ergonomics of Human-System Interaction . . . ," 36
  The Fortune at the Bottom of the Pyramid (Prahalad), 294–295
  Gould and Lewis (1985), usability methodology, 36
  Innovative Solutions: What Designers Need to Know for Today's Emerging Markets (Lapari), xl
  "The Institutionalization of Usability" (Schaffer), 5
  Institutionalization of Usability: A Step-by-Step Guide (Schaffer), xxxii
  Manter and Teorey (1988), usability methodology, 36
  Mayhew (1992), usability methodology, 36
  Nielsen (1992), usability methodology, 36
  Outside In: The Power of Putting Customers at the Center of Your Business (Manning, Bodine, Bernoff), 197–198
  Predictors of Successful Arcade Machines (Schaffer), 15
  "ROLTA India Accelerates on Receiving HFI Level V Certification," 6
  Schneiderman (1992), usability methodology, 36

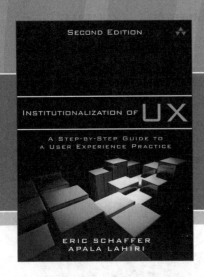

Safari
Books Online

FREE
Online Edition

Your purchase of **Institutionalization of UX, Second Edition,** includes access to a free online edition for 45 days through the **Safari Books Online** subscription service. Nearly every Addison-Wesley Professional book is available online through **Safari Books Online**, along with thousands of books and videos from publishers such as Cisco Press, Exam Cram, IBM Press, O'Reilly Media, Prentice Hall, Que, Sams, and VMware Press.

Safari Books Online is a digital library providing searchable, on-demand access to thousands of technology, digital media, and professional development books and videos from leading publishers. With one monthly or yearly subscription price, you get unlimited access to learning tools and information on topics including mobile app and software development, tips and tricks on using your favorite gadgets, networking, project management, graphic design, and much more.

Activate your FREE Online Edition at
informit.com/safarifree

STEP 1:   Enter the coupon code: ZRNMPEH.

STEP 2:   New Safari users, complete the brief registration form.
Safari subscribers, just log in.

If you have difficulty registering on Safari or accessing the online edition,
please e-mail customer-service@safaribooksonline.com